Neill F. Maclaine was born in 1963 in Highams Park in North East London.

Educated at The Plume School in Maldon, Essex and at the Chelmer Institute of Higher Education in Chelmsford, Essex, he went on to have a successful career in Construction Management and now holds the position of Director in a highly regarded Property Management company based in London. Since 2000 he has been a Freeman of The City of London and since 2004, a Member of the Chartered Institute of Building. He is a member of both the Clan Maclaine of Lochbuie and Clan Maclean Association.

Neill lives with his family in the village of Tiptree in Essex, famous for its strawberry jam making, where he devotes as much of his spare time as possible—usually late at night when everyone else has turned-in—to his genealogical researches and writings.

He is a direct descendant of Rev. Archibald Maclaine D.D. (1722–1804), James Maclaine's elder brother.

Author photograph by Michael Bryant Photography.

THE GENTLEMAN HIGHWAYMAN

The Life and Death of James Maclaine
(1724–1750)

Neill F. Maclaine

THE GENTLEMAN HIGHWAYMAN

The Life and Death of James Maclaine
(1724–1750)

Vanguard Press

VANGUARD PAPERBACK

© Copyright 2016
Neill F. Maclaine

The right of Neill F. Maclaine to be identified as author of
this work has been asserted by him in accordance with the
Copyright, Designs and Patents Act 1988.

All Rights Reserved

A CIP catalogue record for this title is
available from the British Library.

ISBN 978 1 84386 750 0

Every effort has been made to trace copyright holders and to obtain their
permission for the use of copyright material. The publisher apologises for
any errors or omissions in the above list and would be grateful if notified of
any corrections that should be incorporated in future reprints or editions of
this book.

*Vanguard Press is an imprint of
Pegasus Elliot MacKenzie Publishers Ltd.*
www.pegasuspublishers.com

First Published in 2016

Vanguard Press
Sheraton House Castle Park
Cambridge England

Printed & Bound in Great Britain by CMP (uk) Limited

For my children
James, Thomas, Ashlea and Heather

CONTENTS

ILLUSTRATIONS

(i)   Front cover; 'The Ladies Hero or the Unfortunate James McLeane [sic] Esq.' (1750) – George Cruikshank (1792–1878). © The British Museum

(ii)   Map of the Isle of Mull. (2011) – N.F.M.

(iii)   Photograph of Moy Castle at Lochbuie, Isle of Mull. Photographed by N.F.M. 22 June 1992

(iv)   Clan Map of the Inner Hebrides (2011) – N.F.M

(v)   Maclaine of Lochbuie Linage. (2006) – N.F.M.

(vi)   FAMILY TREE OF A HIGHWAYMAN. (2006) – N.F.M.

(vii)   'A Perspective View of the Grand Walk in Vauxhall Gardens and the Orchestra'. (c.1750) – Anonymous. © The British Museum

(viii)   'Horace Walpole, Youngest Son of Sir Robert Walpole Earl of Orford'. (1757) – James McArdell (1729–1765). © The British Museum

(ix)   'A View of the Canal, Chinese Building, Rotunda Etc., in Ranelagh Gardens, with the Masquerade'. (1750) – Giovanni Antonio Canaletto (1697–1768); engraved by Charles Grignion (1714–1810). © Government Art Collection

(x)   A small segment of 'John Rocque's Map of London 1746' (1746) – John Rocque. (1709–1762). © Motco Enterprises Limited

(xi)   'BY HIS MAJESTY'S COMMAND. The JUBILEE BALL after the Venetian manner, Or MASQUERADE at Ranelagh Gardens April the 26th, 1749.' (1749) – Anonymous. © Peter Jackson Collection

(xii) 'An Exact Representation of MACLAINE the Highwayman Robbing LORD EGLINTON on Hounslow Heath on the 26ᵗʰ June 1750'. (13ᵗʰ August 1750) – Charles Mosley (fl. 1737–1765). © The British Museum

(xiii) 'James Macleane [sic], the Gentleman Highwayman at the Bar'. (29ᵗʰ September 1750) – Anonymous. © The British Museum

(xiv) 'Engraving of Newgate Prison frontage circa. 1750'. (1750) – Unknown. © The Guildhall Library

(xv) 'JAMES MACLEANE [sic] EXECUTED OCT 3ᴿᴰ 1750 AGED 26 YEARS'. (September 1750) – Louis Philippe Boitard (fl. 1734–1760). © The British Library

(xvi) 'Newgate's Lamentation or the Ladies' Last Farewell of Maclean [sic]'. (1750) – Anonymous. © The British Museum

(xvii) Photograph of Tyburn Tree plaque; Edgware Road, London. Photographed by N.F.M. 22 September 2011

(xviii) 'Industry and Idleness, Plate II: The IDLE 'PRENTICE Executed at Tyburn'. (30ᵗʰ September 1747) – William Hogarth (1697–1764). ©The British Museum

(xix) 'THE REWARD OF CRUELTY' [Plate IV of IV from series 'The Four Stages of Cruelty']. (1ˢᵗ February 1751) – William Hogarth (1697–1764). © The British Museum

(xx) Family Tree of Another Highwayman. (2011) – N.F.M.

Acknowledgments

I owe a sincere debt of gratitude to those who have over the years encouraged me in this project. These include:

David Newstead and the Team at Pegasus Elliot Mackenzie Publishers Limited; in particular Robert Judkins for his patience and tenacity in dealing with the many copyright issues and Jasmine Molton for her sheer hard work on the indexing and finishing touches.

Dr A Harmens (1925 – 2015) of Bowden, Cheshire, who provided some of my main reference materials; Archibald Maclaine Pont (1925–2012) of Ke Bussum, The Netherlands; Lorne Maclaine of Lochbuie, who encouraged me from his home in Natal, South Africa; my parents, my wife and my children.

William Fergus Maclaine of South Woodford, London, who contributed some of the sources.

Dr. Gale Newton Maclaine of Galashiels, Scotland; for his introduction to The London Burkers.

Lucy Moore, the historical consultant to the film 'Plunkett & Macleane' [sic] and author of books of the same genre, who kindly gave me a steer in the right direction towards further sources of information. If ever I had won the Lotto I would have commissioned her without hesitation to write this book.

The staff of The Bishopsgate Institute Library, The London Metropolitan Archives, The Guildhall Library and The British Library, in London, who were always courteous and professional.

The staff behind the bar at 'The Railway Tavern' in Kelvedon, Essex, who kept me fed and watered and where much of this book was drafted.

My various permanent and temporary secretaries at work, who helped with the trickier typing e.g. updating of the family trees in their lunch hours, including Anita Munro, Anita Engleman, Katharine Austin, Serena Zucchi, Andrea Rothbart, Jacinta Dunn and, most of all, Shahanaj (a.k.a. 'Kat') Runa.

Claire Webster for taking the time and trouble with proof-reading and providing suggestions for improvements.

Last but not least my good friend, Jegathkumar Kandasamy, who provided the original encouragement and gave me the determination to make this dream a reality.

God bless you all.

Neill F. Maclaine
November 2016

FOREWORD

The dealer's eyes narrowed shrewdly as he poked the grimy stem of his clay pipe at the richly-worked jacket on the counter. A few feet away, a sturdy young man with sandy hair regarded him casually while maintaining a perceptibly nervous grip of a gold-capped cane.

"Mmm, it's a fine coat," muttered the dealer disinterestedly. "Why you selling it?" The question followed suddenly in a puff of foul tobacco smoke. The young man's eyes twinkled, "Well, to tell you the truth, the police are after me and I have to get rid of it," he replied gravely in a deep Irish brogue. The dealer, returning a quick glance at the coat, cackled in uncertain appreciation of the joke. Mumbling an excuse about keeping money in another room, he backed through a curtain door and two minutes later re-entered the shop at the front. A burly law officer with him promptly arrested the young Irishman. [1]

As a young boy these were the first words I ever read about James Maclaine, 'The Gentleman Highwayman'; it is fair to say they were enough to get me hooked for life.

Of all the many hundreds of highwaymen who took to the roads of England in the 17th and 18th Centuries, James Maclaine would undoubtedly feature in any historian's "All-time Top Ten". In terms of his notoriety and fame at the time of his death, Maclaine would rightly rank alongside (in chronological order of their deaths and hence the era of their exploits):

(i)	Captain James Hind (1616–1652)
(ii)	John Cottington (1614–1655)
(iii)	Claude Duval (1643–1670)
(iv)	William Nevison (1639–1684)
(v)	William Davis (1627–1690)
(vi)	John Sheppard (1702–1724)
(vii)	Richard Turpin (1705–1739)
(viii)	William Page (1730–1758)
(ix)	John Rann (1750–1774), and
(x)	Lewis Avershaw (1773–1795)

Brief details of their lives and exploits are contained in Chapter 3.

All of the above highwaymen, and including James Maclaine, who was a contemporary of William Page, had at least one thing in common…they all met their maker at the end of a rope! If they had not been caught and had their "lives" written up at the time of their trials and executions, then there is little doubt in my mind that they would all probably have been lost to history. Maclaine's motives were much the same as any of the others; he wanted "easy money" to live the life of a gentleman, in grand splendour, never needing to work. Like the others he was able to flourish for a while to enjoy the "high life" as far as his conscience would allow, until his capture and comeuppance. What set Maclaine apart, however, was that he was a prolific letter writer and some of his correspondence, having been early committed to print about the time of his death, survives for us to this day. With the inclusion of some of it here, the Reader has an opportunity to get inside the mind of a real highwayman from the heyday of the phenomenon.

It has long been a "pipe dream" of mine to sit down and write this story. I have been researching the life and death of James Maclaine since about 1988 when the passing away of my grandmother sparked an interest in Maclaine genealogy that I had hitherto only paid scant attention. Sure, I had previous knowledge of the existence of a highwayman in our family tree and was always interested, but I could never have imagined the voyage of discovery that was awaiting me.

Much of my research over the years has been through snatched lunchtime visits to The Bishopsgate Institute Library, The Guildhall Library and The British Library. I recall on occasions feeling elated at uncovering another piece of Maclaine's jigsaw, such as the time, some fifteen years ago, that I came across the notes of his trial at The Old Bailey hidden on a microfilm spool at The Guildhall Library, that was difficult to find, awkward to print and almost impossible to read. Nowadays things are very different, particularly with the advent of the Internet. With such websites as the remarkable 'The Proceedings of The Old Bailey 1674 to 1834', everything is available, indexed and linked, and laid on a plate. Anyone researching a criminal ancestor today has a huge head-start there.

In a sense this is exactly why I have chosen to write the book now and not leave it to a retirement project, or for my son James to pick up the reins on, when I am gone. I simply did not want to be beaten to it as I am convinced Maclaine's story is one well worth re-counting, and if not I, then someone else will pretty soon be re-telling his tale. When I first read, at the end of 1997, that a film was going into production called 'Plunkett & Macleane' [sic]; to be directed by Jake (son of Ridley) Scott and starring Robert Carlyle as Plunkett [sic] and Jonny Lee Miller as

Macleane [sic] ['Begbie' and 'Sick Boy' from Danny Boyle's international film success 'Trainspotting' (1996)] and Liv Tyler as Macleane's [sic] "love interest", I was on the one hand "chuffed to pieces" and on the other "crushed" with the prospect that there would inevitably be a book to accompany the film, destroying my dream! Inexplicably this turned out not to be the case and left the path clear for me, but at that stage in my own personal life and career development I had not the time to devote to the project; nor were my researches then quite complete.

According to the promotional material for 'Plunkett & Macleane' [sic], the film is based on real-life characters but their names were changed to protect the innocent. As we shall see as we go through their true stories, there was not too much innocence about the real Plunket and Maclaine.

Other films that have told the story of a James ('Jim') MacLaine are 'That'll Be The Day' (1973); directed by Claude Whatham (1927–2008) and starring David Essex, Ringo Starr, Billy Fury (1940–1983), Keith Moon (1946–1978) and Robert Lindsay; together with its sequel 'Stardust' (1974); directed by Michael Apted; with David Essex and Adam Faith (1940–2003). These two told the story of the rise and fall of a rock'n'roll star. Also the political thriller, 'Big Jim McLain' (1952), directed by Edward Irving Ludwig (1899–1982), starring John Wayne (1907–1979) [real name Marion Mitchell Morrison] and James Arness (1923–2011). These films however clearly had nothing to do with any historical highwayman.

The sheer range of material on Maclaine, and now as it transpires, Plunket, that is becoming available on the Internet, such as their joint letter to Horace Walpole (see Chapter 4) has made me realise this project, if it is to have my name on the front cover, cannot be put off a moment longer. Even the free on-line encyclopaedia called 'Wikipedia' has picked up on Maclaine with its first entry on him on 25 November 2005; now that particular web page is being regularly updated. I do hope to see my pipe dream become reality. Who else would know so much about Maclaine's ancestry other than a descendent of his (or to be exact of his elder brother) and one whose pastime for over twenty years has been researching Maclaine genealogy?

The Reader may consider I have gone too far indulging my own passion for Maclaine ancestral research by taking you back to the earliest history of the Macleans / Maclaines in Chapter 1, but I feel this is justified in that James Maclaine was fiercely proud of his ancestry and would have known much of it himself. As Robert Louis [Balfour] Stevenson (1850–1894), the famous Scottish novelist, poet and travel writer, whose most famous works were 'Treasure Island' (1883), 'Strange Case of Dr. Jekyll and Mr. Hyde' (1886) and 'Kidnapped' (1886); once wrote: *"The mark of a Scot of all classes is that he stands in an attitude to the past unthinkable in Englishmen, and remembers and cherishes the memory of his forebears, good or bad; and there burns alive in him a sense of identity with the dead even to the twentieth generation."* This was included with his unfinished novel: 'Weir of Hermiston: an unfinished romance'. Chapter 1 also goes a long way to explaining why there are so many variations of the spelling of Maclaine's surname found scattered throughout the literature.

I am by no means the first to attempt to write a complete history of James Maclaine, however the last to do so had their work published over two hundred and sixty years ago, and the time they spent on their research was weeks, not years, like mine. Their only goal was to get his story printed as quickly as possible so that it could be sold at the scaffold on the day of his hanging, or shortly after whilst the memory of his antics and scandalous affairs were still ripe in the mind of the London public of the time. At the height of Maclaine's notoriety, at the time of his trial and execution, there were several publications on him, many concentrating on different aspects, which have helped me no end, as it has been a straightforward job to pull the most plausible and reliable information together from all of them to help tell his tale for a modern audience. All the "more modern" publications that have devoted whole Chapters to Maclaine, such as 'Half Hours with the Highwaymen' by Charles George Harper (1863–1943) [1908; Chapman and Hall, London], 'Lives of Twelve Bad Men' by Thomas Seccombe (1866–1923) [1912; Brentano, New York] and 'Discovering Highwaymen' by Russell Ash (1946–2010) [1999; Shire Publications Limited, Oxford]; or the odd page or reference here and there, such as 'The English Highwayman; A Legend Unmasked' by Peter Haining (1940–2007) [1991; Robert Hale, London], 'Highwaymen and Outlaws' by Michael Billett [1997; Arms & Armour Press, London] and the reverse titled, 'Outlaws and Highwaymen' by Gillian Spraggs [2001; Pimlico, London] have all tended to follow what went before and, through no fault of the authors involved, have brought little new to bear. I feel I have at least brought something more comprehensive to the telling of his story. I hope I have done it justice in my capacity as an amateur genealogist as opposed to a trained historian. I have been careful not to embellish his tale and push the boundaries of what is definitely known of this remarkable fellow or his sidekick, William Plunket.

This work has turned out very much as I anticipated it would. I wanted to use the letters that Maclaine either wrote or received, or that were written about him, to form the backbone; telling his story in as close to "in his own words" as possible. It was always my intention to leave the original spellings untouched [the only change I have consciously made is to do away with the "long 'S's" for ease of reading] and write, almost in the style of an Editor, stringing the letters together and adding the "flesh to the bones". I may have included one or two too many quotations from the original sources, however I wanted to fully rejoice in the richness of the language used in the mid-18th Century. What has come as a complete surprise to me has been my absolute compulsion to include wherever possible a brief biographical remark or two, including dates of birth and death where I could find them, concerning each of the various other persons [often themselves becoming "recurring characters"] e.g. Horace Mann (1706–1784), see Chapter 5; or an additional note about the contemporary events e.g. the London Earthquake of 1750 (see Chapter 6), that were made reference to within the letters themselves. Therefore I feel I may have unwittingly produced a miniature 'Who's Who' and Chronology of mid-18th Century London. I hope that the Reader will forgive this very enjoyable self-indulgence on behalf of the Writer, and at the same time appreciate the corresponding increased overall value of this book. I hope you enjoy reading it as much as I have enjoyed both researching and writing it.

Foreward – References

---

[1] *James Maclaine – Gentleman Highwayman*, Anonymous (Undated, unpublished three-page article), p. 1

CHAPTER 1

MACLEANE / MACLAINE

Whenever I attempt to explain to anyone who knows me that I have an ancestor who was in his time a famous highwayman, who lived in 18th Century London; and when I go on to explain that a movie was made about him in 1999 called 'Plunkett and Macleane' [sic], the first question coming back from those who know of it is always: "How come his surname is not spelt the same as yours?" I only wish there were a simple answer to that, but regrettably there is not. Anyone who bears the surname Maclaine will have suffered throughout his or her lifetime with a myriad of alternate spellings; in fact there may be as many as two hundred ways to spell the name Maclean / Macleane / Maclaine. It is simply something that we just have to learn to get along with.

Sometimes when I am asked to spell my surname I will say: "Maclaine; spelt like Shirley MacLaine, the actress, but without capitalising the 'L'." This will usually result in the desired effect, but even then cannot be guaranteed. I have never dared go on to explain that actually Shirley MacLaine, sister of actor Warren Beatty, is not really a MacLaine at all; her mother's maiden name was MacLean (often spelt MacLane) and she herself just liked the alternative spelling! This simple truth begins to explain the problem, but the fact is the real answer, as I will soon demonstrate, is steeped in Scottish history. For those readers not remotely interested in the latter, your best bet is to fast-forward to Chapter 2 after reading the next and the final paragraphs of this Chapter; but please be warned: you will be missing out!

When James Maclaine lived and died, a little over 265 years ago, the situation was just the same. If he announced his name in public then those who heard it would automatically have a pre-conceived idea of how to spell it. The most common miss-spellings I have come across in the historical literature about him, either with or without the capitalised 'L', include: Maclean, Maclane, Macleane, Mclean, Macklaine and M'lean; not bad for starters! The name Maclean was certainly very well-known in London in the late 1740s as the Macleans were one of the Scottish highland clans (see Illustration (iv) – Clan Map of the Inner Hebrides) that had risen as Jacobite supporters of "Bonnie" Prince Charles [Silvester Severino] Stuart (1720–1788), a.k.a. "The Young Pretender", whose rebellion in 1745 got as far South as Derby, in the East Midlands of England, putting London into panic, before he and his advisors got "cold feet" and turned-tail, heading back for the safety of Scotland. They were eventually annihilated on 16 April 1746 at the Battle of Culloden which turned out to be the last major battle on British soil. Many of the captured Jacobite sympathisers were executed in London shortly thereafter.

We know that Maclaine was fiercely proud of his ancestry and obsessed with, in his mind, his gentlemanly status. As we will discover later, shortly before his execution, Maclaine tore a page from his Bible, presumably to pass on to his young daughter, which no doubt, considering the Scottish tradition of recording family pedigrees in the front leaves of family Bibles, would have been too precious to for him to lose with all his other remaining possessions to the Hangman. Maclaine and his immediate Irish / Scottish ancestors (see Chapter 2) were descended from the Clan Maclaine of Lochbuie (see Illustration (v) – Maclaine of Lochbuie Linage). Lochbuie is a beautiful sea loch below the mountain of Ben Buie on the Southern coast of the Isle of Mull, within the Inner Hebridean Islands, just off the Western coast of mainland Scotland. Lochbuie, which means 'Yellow Lake', did not escape having its own range of spellings over the centuries including: Lochbui, Lochbuy, Lochbuye, Lochbuidhe, Lochbowie, Lochbowy, Lochboy and Lochboyg, to name but a few, but Lochbuie best represents the phonetic pronunciation and is certainly the name in most common use since about James Maclaine's time. The Lochbuies had been spelling their surname Maclaine or MacLaine for at least 100 years before his birth in 1724. Before that his more distant ancestors had been more than happy to call themselves Maclean and had not felt the need to distinguish themselves from their fellow kin in the overall Clan Maclean, or Clan Gillean to give it its proper name, by any other means than by reference to the place names from where their various branches hailed.

Ben Buie is classified as a 'Graham' under the standardisation system introduced in 1891 by Sir Hugh Munro (1856–1919), 4th Baronet of Lindertis, the famous Scottish mountaineer. The Isle of Mull boasts only one of the highest classification, the 'Munros', naturally, and that is Ben More which stands at 3,169 feet or 966 metres above sea level. The Munro Society has members who have climbed all 282 such peaks. Ben More is ranked 189th in the list by height.

All Macleans / Maclaines, no matter what their chosen spelling, descend from one man. He was said to have been a fierce warrior who is generally recognised to have been be born about 1210, by the name of Gillean na Tuaighe, or "Gillean of the Battleaxe"; hence all his descendants being considered of the Clan Gillean. By now it should be no surprise to learn that the history books also have a range of spellings for this man's name such as Gilleathain, Gilleoin, and Gilleain, to consider the most popular. The name Gillean translates as "the Servant of John". The old Scottish family historians or "seannachies" recorded him a long ancestry as *"the son of MacRath, son of Maolsruthain, son of Neill, son of Cuduilig, Abbott of Lismore, son of Raingee, son of Old Dougall of Scone."* [1] Perhaps one day this will all be confirmed and taken for certain rather than conjecture or as a work of pure fiction in the minds of the other old Scottish highland clans with more certain roots.

The most popular story of Gillean is that he was once caught out by dense fog whilst stag hunting on Beinn an t-Seilg, "the Hunting Hill", which has been interpreted, most probably incorrectly, as Beinn Tulàidh, a tall mountain on the Isle of Mull. After wandering around for some time he became exhausted so planted the shaft of his battleaxe in the ground beside a cranberry bush and fell asleep beneath it. Eventually the fog cleared and Gillean's hunting companions first caught sight of the head of his battleaxe and then found him and were fortunate to be able to restore him back to full health. So it transpires it was for this reason and not his valour in battle, wielding said weapon, which got this warrior his nickname.

Gillean, who died after 1300, is said to have had three sons, Malise, Gillebride and Bristi. Malise, the eldest son, born about 1235, whose name was styled Maolisa mac Ghilleathain (or "Malise the son of Gillean") in Gaelic; pronounced Mac'illane or

Maclean in English, was effectively the first Maclean and progenitor of all those who bear the name in whatever form. His name fully translates as "the Servant of Jesus, Son of the Servant of John". He is said to have lived at Castle Gillean (now Gylen), on the small island of Kerrera in Oban Bay in the Firth of Lorne, which is also known to be the death place of King Alexander II (1198–1249) of Scotland, and in Mull. He is believed to have fought, alongside his father and brothers, under King Alexander III (1241–1286) at the Battle of Largs on 2 October 1263 where Håkon Håkonarson (1204–1263), King Håkon IV of Norway, led 20,000 Vikings in 160 warships to crush the Scots. The Vikings lost the battle due to a combination of stormy weather and apparently a thistle that one of their men stood on, losing the element of surprise as he cried out in pain whilst they were attempting to creep up on the Scottish camp under cover of darkness. Hence the thistle became the national emblem of Scotland.

Nothing other than their attendance with him at Largs is known of Malise's brothers, but he himself went on to have two sons, Malcolm and Milmore (or Gilmore). Their names were styled Maolcaluim mac Ghilleathain, "the Servant of Columba", and Gille-Mhoire mac Ghilleathain, "the Servant of Mary", respectively. Both signed the 'Ragman Roll' which were a series of parchments, signed on 28 August 1296, by over 2,000 Scottish landowners, church leaders and burgesses, making an oath of loyalty to King Edward I (1239–1307) of England. The Ragman Roll could have received its name due to the number of ribbons attached to its many wax seals, but more likely in reference to the earlier Papal Taxation records prepared by a man called Ragimunde, whose name was corrupted to Ragman. Malcolm

Maclean fought under Robert the Bruce (1274–1329), formerly the Earl of Carrick, at the Battle of Bannockburn, near Stirling, on 24 June 1314. This was a battle in which the Scots, who amounted to barely 13,000 men, overwhelmingly beat the 40,000 strong army of King Edward II (1284–1327) [known as Edward of Caernarfon; son of King Edward I (1239–1307) a.k.a. "Edward Longshanks" and "The Hammer of the Scots" who captured the infamous William Wallace (1272–1305), 'The Guardian of Scotland', and had him hanged, drawn and quartered after his capture some time after the latter's defeat at the Battle of Falkirk in 1298] of England and proclaimed Scotland free of English rule. After the battle Bruce is said to have given Maclean lands that had belonged to the MacDougalls of Lorne.

Malcolm was born about 1270 and lived on the Isle of Kintyre, a large mainland peninsula on the West coast of Scotland, and married Rioghnach, daughter of Gamail, Lord of Carrick. They had three sons: John, Donald and Neil, who remained in much favour with Robert the Bruce and in 1325, when the latter made a trip to the Western Isles, Donald Maclean sent a ship in the King's service around the Mull of Kintyre to West Tarbert and both John and Neil Maclean sent some of their men to watch over it whilst it remained there. Not long after this Bruce appointed Neil Maclean, constable of the Royal Fortress of Cairnburg on the Treshnish Isles, about two miles off the West coast of the Isle of Mull (see Illustration (ii) – Map of the Isle of Mull).

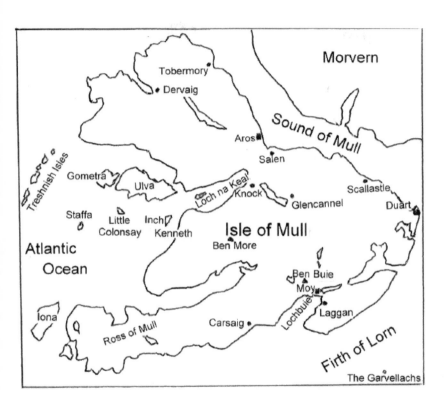

Illustration (ii) — Map of the Isle of Mull

Both Donald and Neil Maclean went on to have sons of their own, but the future of the leadership of the Clan Maclean naturally rested with their elder brother John, whose name was styled Iain Dubh, or "Black John" in English. He lived at Seil Castle which is located to the South of Oban on the Western coast of mainland Scotland. After 1330 he is known to have lived on the Isle of Mull and is said to have married a daughter of John Comyn (1277–1302) of Lochaber. He could also, and more probably, have been married to a daughter of Eachann (Hector) MacDonald, grandson of Alexander MacDonald, as this would help explain his unusual choice of Christian names for his two elder sons and the fact that one of them at least went on to have need of Papal Dispensation to marry, due to the closeness of their relationship, his intended MacDonald bride. He may also have had a third (natural) son, John, but little if anything is known of him. Black John's first son, Hector, styled Eachainn Reaganach or "Hector the Stubborn / Stern", was to become progenitor of the Clan Maclean of Lochbuie (or the Siol Eachainn; the Race of Hector) and the second, Lachlan (c.1330–1405), styled Lachlainn Lùbanach or "Lachlan the Crafty / Wily", became the progenitor of the Clan Maclean of Duart (or the Siol Lachlainn; the Race of Lachlan). These were the two most prominent branches of the overall Clan Maclean and all those sub-branches that came along later either stemmed from or fell under the wing of one or other of Lochbuie or Duart. The vexed question as to which of these two was, or should have been, the senior branch, has been subject of much rigorous debate over the centuries and as it is not of any particular relevance to the story of James Maclaine, shall not be dwelled upon here. James was, however, very firmly, of the former.

Hector and Lachlan Maclean appear to have been close brothers who profited together as they amassed their lands and power, sometimes by acting in the most audacious manner. Traditional Maclean Clan histories inform us that these two, in or about 1354, killed their arch rival Lauchlan Mackinnon of Strathordil (or Strathardle / Strathbairdle; a small town on the Isle of Skye), who at the time was said to be plotting to have them assassinated, and who was himself the Master of the Household to John MacDonald (1340–1386), a.k.a. Good John of Islay, 1st Lord of the Isles. John MacDonald was the most powerful man in the whole of the Hebridean islands at the time, sitting at the head of a great confederacy of Scottish Clans, whose chiefs had sworn allegiance to him and in return had received charters of their lands. The Lords of the Isles were for many years the greatest landowners and most powerful Lords in the British Isles, behind the Kings of England and Scotland. Fearing a reprisal the Maclean brothers took the bold step of capturing John MacDonald and taking him to their original patron, Sir John 'Bacach' (meaning "The Lame") MacDougall (c.1257–1317) of Lorne who was known as "the Admiral of the Seas" under King Edward II. On route they got word that whilst John Bacach was delighted with their boldness in slaying MacKinnon on this occasion, that *"he would through time bridle their forwardness and insolence."* [2] Not liking the sound of that too much the brothers decided that perhaps a better bet for them in the long term would be to switch their allegiance. They therefore took MacDonald away from MacDougall's Dunstaffnage Castle which was later famous for being a temporary prison for Flora MacDonald (1722–1790) who aided and abetted "Bonnie Prince Charlie" in his escape after Culloden (see earlier), where they had been heading, to the small island of Garbh Eileach, itself the largest of the uninhabited isles known as 'The Garvellachs' that lie in the Firth of Lorne, between Mull and the mainland. There, in turn for his freedom and their future loyalty, they made MacDonald swear solemn promises to them to forgive them for killing Mackinnon and taking himself captive; to give them lands and as it appears, at least for Lachlan, the hand of one of his daughters (Mary) in marriage, together with a handsome dowry and a high ranking place in the Lord's service.

It is possible that Margaret, an elder daughter of John of the Isles's, was similarly betrothed to Hector Maclean, but eminent Maclean historians have hotly contested this in recent years. Due to his close blood relationship with Mary MacDonald, who was also a granddaughter on her mother's side of King Robert II (1316–1390) [known as 'The Steward' from which the name 'The House of Stewart' was derived], Lachlan Maclean needed Papal Dispensation to marry her. It was Pope Urban V, Guillaume Grimoard (1310–1370), who granted this on 13 May 1367. No similar record can be found to back up the claim that Margaret MacDonald was allowed to marry Hector Maclean. A certain genealogist did suggest that there exists a Dispensation dated 14 April 1356, but this has not been proven. Current studies indicate that Hector Regannach Maclean of Lochbuie was in fact married twice; firstly to Christina, daughter of Murdoch MacLeod of Harris (one of the larger islands of the Outer Hebrides), and secondly to Mor, or Marion in English, daughter of Godfrey O'Balhan of the children of Fergus mac Róich, one of the Kings of Ulster.

From Garbh Eileach the Maclean brothers took their captive to the Isle of Iona which is famous for being first settled by (the eventual Saint) Columba (521–597) , the Gaelic missionary monk who restored Christianity to Scotland during The Dark Ages, and the resting place of the early Scottish Kings such as Mac Bethad mac Findláich, a.k.a. MacBeth (c.1005–1057). There they made him swear, on certain sacred Black Stones, to abide by all his promises to them and to live in perpetual friendship with them. John of the Isles went on to make Lachlan his Lieutenant General and assigned to the Macleans the privilege of being on the right wing of his army in battle. He also made Lachlan the Chamberlain of his Household which was the highest ranking position in the feudal hierarchy, a designation that was to stay in Lachlan's family for at least one hundred years. John MacDonald and his heirs went on to bestow on Lachlan Maclean charters for the custody and constableship of Duart, a.k.a. Dowart, Doward and Duvayrd, Castle on the East coast of the Isle of Mull and many other lands on the isle and the other islands of the Inner Hebrides. Duart Castle was chosen as a location for the 1999 film 'Entrapment' directed by Jon Amiel and starring Sean Connery and Catherine Zeta-Jones. When King James IV (1473–1513) of Scotland finally forced the forfeiture of John II MacDonald (1434–1503) of Yle, Earl of Ross and the 4th and last Lord of the Isles, in 1493, it was natural that all those who had held lands under the old dynasty should now become direct vassals of the Crown. So it was that King James IV, on 13 July 1495, confirmed on Lachlan Og (1432–1498), meaning "Lauchlan The Younger", Maclean, 4th of Duart, all the lands that he controlled at the time.

Hector Reaganach was granted by "Good John MacDonald" eighty merks [Scottish money worth approximately 1/12 of its equivalent in sterling; 1 merk was worth 13 shillings and 4 pence] of land at Lochbuie on the southern coast of Mull. As this was a direct charter his family were therefore feudally independent of Duart. *"It is related that when Hector went to Lochbuie he found the lands possessed by the Chief of MacFadyean, and obtained permission to build a fortalice or keep at the head of Lochbuie. When it was completed Hector ascended to the top, and, taking a bow and arrow, took aim at a bone MacFadyean was then eating from, and pierced it with the arrow. MacFadyean simply remarked, "It is time I was leaving;" took his departure, and gave Hector no trouble."* [3]

The fortalice Hector built became known as Caisteal Magh or Moy Castle, meaning "Castle of Threatening". It first appeared on record in a Royal Charter of March 1494. It was built on solid rock from local materials such as Schitose slabs, quarried from nearby Laggan; harled stone and beach boulders; all laid in lime mortar. The quoins or corner stones were all fine-grained sandstone, quarried at Carsaig on the Ross of Mull, which is the south-western peninsula of the Isle of Mull. Moy Castle was built in 'Tower House' style, with walls up to 7 feet thick. The lower floors had vaulted stone ceilings and the upper floors were timber with spiral stone staircases between. The castle had a well, in which the water level remained somewhat mysteriously constant, a pit-prison and a funeral chamber. The Maclaine of Lochbuie Chief's family finally moved out of the old castle in 1752 in favour of the smaller Lochbuie House. A larger Georgian style Lochbuie House was built in 1790 and the castle at that point was allowed to fall into ruin. Moy Castle featured in the very popular 1945 film 'I Know where I'm Going' which was written, directed and produced by the prolific film-making duo of Michael Latham Powell (1905–1990) and Emeric Pressburger (1902–1988). It is said to remain in the possession of the Maclaine family and the

Clan Maclaine of Lochbuie Association continually raises funds for its restoration.

There is a very detailed technical description of Moy Castle contained in the painstaking produced 'Royal Commission on the Ancient and Historical Monuments of Scotland; Argyll, Volume III; Mull, Tiree, Coll and Northern Argyll' [1980; HMSO], however there can be no better, fuller, non-technical description than that provided to us by J.P. Maclean in his 'A History of the Clan MacLean' [1889; Robert Clarke & Co] which is as follows:

> *It is now one of the best-preserved castles in the Hebrides, and until within the last few years* [the mid-1880s] *its roof was kept entire. It is located on a low rock nearly midway across the head of the bay, and at high tide its base is washed by the sea. For the most part it is built of flat stones, thoroughly cemented together, being broadest at the base. The gate or door-way faces the north, and was formerly protected by a fosse [a ditch or moat]. The gateway is protected by a wooden door, which swings inward; and in turn is guarded by an iron grating on hinges, which again is secured by a wooden beam built into the wall, which may be moved at will, but can not be taken out of the wall. In the wall, to the west, is a recess, where the gateman was constantly stationed. The floor of the interior of the first story is a solid rock, in the center of which is a basin four feet in depth, which is always full of water, but never overflows. Where the water comes from is unknown. In the east wall is a passage-way*

leading to the stairs, which passes through the east wall to the south-east corner of the second story. From that point upward the stairway is spiral, all of the steps composed of stone. Over the first passage-way, and in the wall, is the vault which held the dead during the funeral obsequies. The second and third floors are formed of solid stone arches. The second story was the judgment hall, and just off from it, and within the east wall, is the chapel, which is reached by a door-way from the spiral stairs. In the south-west corner is the dungeon, which extends from the second floor down to the level of the ground floor. It does not admit of a ray of light, and so constructed as to contain water, and on the floor is placed a single stone, upon which the prisoner must stand, or else drown. Where the water comes from is unknown. There is an escape to prevent an overflow. The third floor was the banqueting hall. The fourth and fifth stories had their floors composed of wood. Here chimneys, fireplaces, and windows may be seen. On the summit, at the north side, is a parapet, where a watchman was constantly on duty. The height of the castle is fifty-five feet, and on the north and the south sides the walls, on the exterior, are thirty-two feet; on the east and west sides, thirty-seven feet. At all places the walls are seven feet in thickness. [4]

Illustration (iii) — Photograph of Moy Castle at Lochbuie,
Isle of Mull. Photographed by N.F.M. 22 June 1992

Like his brother, Lachlan Lùbanach, Hector Reaganach and his Clan continued to flourish under the confederacy of the Lord of the Isles. With his first wife, Christina, he had six sons: Charles, Murdoch, Donald, Ewen, Thomas and Malcolm; with his second, Mor, a further two: Ferchar and Neil. The eldest son Charles, styled Tearlach mac Eachainn, was made Constable of Urquhart Castle at Loch Ness in 1394. Having resigned his claim to the Chiefship of Lochbuie to his next youngest brother, Murdoch, Charles went on to possess lands at Balmacaan (or Baile-mac-Eachainn) in Glenurquhart, and at Carna, Kilmalieu, Kingairloch, and Ardmarnock (or Ard-Mhearnaig; now Glensanda), in Morvern. He thus became the progenitor of the feudal baronial families of the Macleans of The North, the Macleans of Dochgarroch, the Macleans of Glenurquhart, the Macleans of Kingairloch and the Macleans of Glenachad; all part of the Clan Tearlach o'Buie or "the Family of Charles of Lochbuie".

With Charles very busy elsewhere, Hector's second son, Murdoch, styled Murchadh Ruaidh or "Red Murdoch", took over from his father as 2nd Chief of Clan Maclean of Lochbuie. He married Margaret, daughter of Roderick Macleod (1426–1496), 4th of Lewis, and had two sons and two daughters. His son John, 3rd of Lochbuie, in October 1461 received twenty-one more lands in Lochiel, Duror and Glencoe and other places, from John II MacDonald. He married Elizabeth Mackay, daughter of Angus Mackay (1414–1486), 2nd Chief of the Mackays of Strathnaver, and had both a son and a daughter. The son, Hector Maclean, 4th of Lochbuie, married either a Margaret Campbell or a Marian, daughter of Alastair Crottach, meaning "The Humpbacked", Macleod (1455–1554), 8th of Harris; or both. He died in 1478 and was succeeded by his son John Og, styled Iain Og or in later life, John Beàrnach, "Iain the Toothless", 5th of Lochbuie.

These were particularly turbulent times for the Isle of Mull. Rather unwisely as it turned out, John II MacDonald, had entered into a secret treaty in 1462 with King Edward IV (1442–1483) of England, to make himself sole ruler of the Hebrides and Western Highlands, completely independent of the King of Scots. In 1475 King James III (1452–1488) discovered the pact, which became known as the 'Treaty of Westminster / Ardtornish' and became determined to bring the Lordship to heel. Ardtornish was a stronghold of MacDonald, a mile southeast of Lochaline in Morvern on the Scottish mainland coast, just on the other side of the Sound of Mull. King James immediately forfeited MacDonald's lands, only leaving him some on which to live on the promise of future good conduct by the MacDonald Clan. This was something John MacDonald could not deliver as his own (natural) son Angus Óg (c.1450–1490) went to war with him and defeated him in 1481 at the Battle of Badh na Fola (or "Bloody Bay") near the port of Tobermory (meaning "Well of Mary"), just off the northern coast of Mull. In addition MacDonald's nephew, Sir Alexander MacDonald (1476–1497) of Lochalsh, led a further rebellion in 1493, culminating in the Battle of Drumchatt in Ross-shire in 1497; causing King James IV (1473–1513) to rescind all previous agreements and take back all the Clan MacDonald's lands.

Little is known of the 2nd, 3rd and 4th Chiefs of Lochbuie; however John Og and his sons more than make up for that as they were quite literally the stuff of legends. Their busy lives were not only recorded factually through various written records such as the Charters and Decrees of the Privy Council of Scotland, but also through some entertaining mythical, legendary stories. John Og, or "Young John", was born in 1470 and appears to have been a favourite of King James IV. Certainly when that monarch forced the final forfeiture of the Lord of the Isles in 1493, John Maclean of Lochbuie was one of the first, if not the very first, of the island clan chiefs to make his submission to the King, claiming his land rights. At Edinburgh on 22 March 1494, the *"King confirmed a Charter to his esquire, John Makgilleon of Lochboye* [sic]*, of all the lands that had been previously granted to his family and of the lands of Gronding, Culchelle, Kelbeg, Rengoun and some other lands in Invernesshire."*[5] These were clearly in addition to the office of bailliary of the south half of the island of Tiree, that had been subject of one of the Lord of the Isles's last ever Charters on 1 August 1492, at Oransay, which is another island in the Outer Hebrides.

In 1499 John Og joined Lauchlan Cattanach, meaning "Lachlan The Hairy", (1465–1523) Maclean, 7th of Duart, who was famous for marooning his wife Elizabeth Campbell on "The Lady's Rock" [a rock entirely covered each high tide] in the Sound of Mull, and John Maclean of Coll in an invasion of Cameron of Lochiel's lands. He supported the rising of Donald Dubh MacDonald (1503–1545) of the Isles in 1504 when the latter attempted to reinstate the Lordship. In 1506 he quarrelled with Lachlan Maclean of Duart over the ownership of lands in Morvern and Tiree and a year later the King stepped in to keep the peace between them. He fought against Duart in 1514 but received remission for his past offences in March 1517. He sold his lands in Lochiel, Duror and his Baillieship of South Tiree in June 1522 to Sir John Campbell of Cawdor (1490–1546). In 1526 he found his family and tenants under invasion by the wayward, natural, son of Lachlan Cattanach Maclean of Duart. This was Allan, styled Ailein-nan-Sop or "Allan of the Straws", Maclean (c.1500–1555) of Gigha; a small island between Islay and Kintyre. In 1529 John Og joined Maclean of Duart in ravaging Roseneath, Craignish and other Campbell lands. By 1530 he had possession of lands in Lochbuie, Molorish (now Killean), Scallastle and Glenforsa in Mull, and lands in the isles of Scarba, Jura, and Tiree.

From a "hand-fast marriage" (possibly to Helen Campbell, daughter of Sir Colin Campbell (1406–1475), 1st of Glenorchy) which was a marriage performed without the presence of a member of the Clergy, where a couple would live together for a year and a day and if the woman fell pregnant within that timeframe then the marriage would be considered good in law; John Og had two natural sons, Murdoch and Charles. From a marriage to a daughter of Alexander MacDougall (1452–1493), 12th of Dunollie, he had two further sons, John (killed in the invasion of Allan of the Straws in 1526) and Ewen. Two separate Clan legends revolve around Ewen and Murdoch. Ewen, styled Eòghan-a-Chinn-bhig or "Ewen of the Little Head", was a distinguished warrior in his time. He married one of MacDougall of Lorn's daughters (whose later conduct in precipitating his downfall earned her the name "The Black Heron"). John Og of Lochbuie had given his son and daughter-in-law as a wedding present, an island home (or 'crannog') on Loch Sguabain (or Sgnibhain) in Glen More, just to the north of Lochbuie. Ewen's bride apparently mocked her husband on the size of his estate and urged him to confront his father and demand more land. A quarrel then ensued that ultimately led to a great battle between

Ewen with his supporters and John Og who was supported by Hector Mor Maclean (1490–1568), 8th of Duart.

Illustration (iv) — Clan Map of the Inner Hebrides

On the eve of the fight, Ewen is said to have gone out alone to survey the proposed battlefield at Glen Cannir near the modern day village of Craig, due North of Lochbuie. There he heard a girl's voice, singing, down by a stream below. As he approached he realised it was not a girl at all, but an old Loireag (or Luideag), a Gaelic 'faery washerwoman', who was pummelling bloody shirts on the rocks of the stream. Ewen is said to have asked her, "Can you tell me who will win the day tomorrow?"

The Luideag simply responded, "If butter is given to you with your breakfast in the morning without you having to demand it, then you will win the Battle".

The next morning Ewen could not get out of his mind the fact that there had indeed been no butter at all on his breakfast table; still, against overwhelming numbers, he led his men into the battle. According to the most popular version of this legend, in the thick of the fight, Ewen's little head was struck clean from his shoulders and his horse promptly bolted from the scene, galloping at least five miles before finally dropping its gruesome, headless load at Lussa Falls. Ewen Maclean was initially buried on the spot where his body landed on the ground but was later exhumed and reinterred on the sacred Isle of Iona where his table tombstone can still be seen within the Abbey there. His headless ghost is still said to be sighted, riding a "ghostly dun horse" through Glen More, whenever a member of the Maclaine of Lochbuie family is about to die.

At some point, according to another legend, Hector Mor Maclean of Duart apparently took John Og of Lochbuie prisoner on the fortress island of Cairnburg Mor, within the Treshnish Isles. His intention was that John Og would remain captive and would be unable to produce any further heirs to Lochbuie, thus making it easier for Duart to claim Lochbuie's lands for himself when the latter died. Foolishly he allowed John Og the comfort of an ugly old maid servant on the island, who was put to good use by his captive as he immediately succeeded in making her pregnant. When Duart heard about the maid servant he had her removed from the island and taken to Torloisk, which is a village in the northwest of Mull, where the Mull doctor, Ollamh Muileach of Pennyghael (a village to the North of The Ross of Mull) was told to keep a close eye on her. If she produced a boy, he would need to be smothered; a daughter would be allowed to survive. One version of this tale goes on to describe the birth of twins, a boy and a girl, with the nursemaid smuggling the boy to Glencannel, a village South of Salen and North of Lochbuie, where a family from the Clan Gillivray raised him.

This boy grew up to become the 6th Chief of Lochbuie, styled Murchad Gearr, or "Short / Little Murdoch". As Murdoch Maclean was supposedly born in 1496 the foregoing, fanciful, story is likely to be just that. It is much more probable that after the death of "Ewen of the Little Head", John Og found himself without legitimate heir and therefore arranged to have the birth of his natural sons legitimised in order to ensure a legally recognised heir to his estates. He achieved this on 13 September 1538 when he also transferred lands to Murdoch in Morvern, including Achlennan and Drimmin, but seems to have himself died shortly thereafter.

At this point John Og's younger brother, Murdoch Maclean of Scallastle, which is an area just south of the town of Salen in central Mull, tried to seize the Lochbuie lands for himself, believing he was the only true heir to his brother's estate. Charles was killed and Murdoch Gearr fled to Antrim in Ireland where he lived under the protection of Somerled, styled Somhuirle Buidhe, or 'Sorley Boy' (meaning "Sorley of the Yellow Hair") MacDonnell (1505–1590), a.k.a. MacDonald of Dunnyveg. In 1540 MacDonnell gave Murdoch Gearr thirteen men and a small ship in order to provide him an opportunity to regain his legacy. Murdoch sailed from Derry to the Isle of Jura and from there to Craignure on the Southeast coast of Mull. He and his small force of men reached Moy Castle under cover of darkness and were assisted by Murdoch Gearr's old nursemaid who helped them devise a strategy for taking back the castle. She told them she would let the calves out of their enclosure and that when the supporters of Murdoch of Scallastle came out to catch them, they could be despatched. Knowing the nursemaid's own husband was the Gatekeeper, Murdoch Gearr asked her how his men could recognise her spouse so as to spare his life, to which she is supposed to have replied, "Leig an tearbull leis a chraicionn" or "Let the tail go with the hide!" The plan was completely successful and that night Murdoch Gearr and his men retook the castle. The chief swordsman in Murdoch's band was one MacCormick and to show his gratitude Maclean arranged to have the words 'Biadh is deoch do MacCormaig' or 'Food and drink to MacCormick' carved into the lintel above the door to the castle; MacCormick's would be forevermore welcome there.

Next Murdoch Gearr prepared his supporters, who were the MacGillivrays and the Macleans of the Ross of Mull, for battle against Murdoch of Scallastle, the latter being supported by the Stewarts of Appin, which is an estate to the southwest of Lochaber, on the mainland. The first skirmish between the two forces took place at Grulin, between Salen and Knock, on the

East bank of Loch na Keal, on Mull. From there Scallastle marched his forces to the glen to the east of Ben Buie known as Glen More, almost in sight of Moy Castle, and made camp in readiness to make an assault. That night "Little Murdoch" stole into the camp where he fastened the couples of an old kiln to his uncle's tent and twisted his dirk through Scallastle's hair, skewering it to the ground. When the latter awoke he recognised the dirk and kiln and realised that his nephew had just shown him the greatest mercy. He immediately disbanded his men, went back to his own estates, and gave Murdoch no further trouble.

In June 1542 Murdoch Gearr Maclean, 6th of Lochbuie, received a Charter from the King of all the lands that had belonged to his father and was 'erected into the Barony of Moy'. King James V (1512–1543) died within a year and was succeeded by his infant daughter Mary I (1542–1587), Queen of Scots. About this time Donald Dubh MacDonald (1503–1545) managed to escape from his prison cell in Edinburgh and once more re-asserted his claim to the Lordship of the Isles. Murdoch Gearr joined the other highland Chiefs behind Donald Dubh and the Macleans of Lochbuie were part of the overall force of 1800 men that invaded the Earl of Argyll's lands and killed a great many people, making off with immense booty.

Scotland at this time was again in a period of great upheaval throughout. Whilst Protestants and Catholics were quarrelling, King Henry VIII (1491–1547) of England was trying to secure a marriage between his son, Prince Edward (1537–1553), and the infant Mary of Scotland. Henry VIII claimed to be "Overlord of Scotland" and ordered a series of invasions, led by Matthew Stewart (1516–1571), 4th Earl of Lennox. Donald Dubh MacDonald held a Clan Conference on the Isle of Eigg, which is a small island to the South of Skye, held at that time by the MacDonalds, and agreed to recognise Lennox as King's Regent for Scotland. Donald Dubh and Lennox travelled to Ireland to meet with Henry VIII and enter into dialogue concerning a plan to conquer the whole of Scotland. While they negotiated with one another, their combined army, totalling about 8,000 men, who were already dissatisfied with their conditions and wages, dissipated. Effectively the fourth attempt to resurrect the Lordship of the Isles collapsed and Donald Dubh in fact died shortly thereafter. His son, Donald Gorm, meaning "Blue-eyed Donald", MacDonald, again attempted to get the backing for himself to become Lord of the Isles but by this time the Clansmen were fed up of championing lost causes and refused to support him. The title 'Lord of The Isles' apparently currently now rests with Prince Charles [Philip Arthur George], Prince of Wales, as the eldest son of the reigning monarch of the British Isles.

Murdoch Gearr Maclean married Anne, a daughter of Somerled MacDonnell. She was also a sister of Randal MacDonnell, who became 1st Earl of Antrim, and between them Murdoch and Anne had sons named John, Allan, Ewen and (the eventual Reverend) Lauchlan, together with a daughter, Anne. He also married a daughter of Tormod (Norman, in English) Macleod (1509–1584), 12th of Dunnvegan. The eldest son John, styled Iain Mór, went on to become 7th Chief of Lochbuie, but not until after he had fallen out with his father. In January 1576 Murdoch Gearr complained to the Privy Council of Scotland of the bad treatment he had received from his son John, and in 1578 the said John sued his father for casting him in chains. Despite his deteriorating relationship with his father, John seems to have been a favourite of King James VI (1566–1625) of Scotland [I of England]. He was an accomplished swordsman and once accepted a challenge thrown out by a famous Italian master swordsman who was touring Scotland and who had boasted he could beat any man in the King's army. On stage in Edinburgh, in front of the King and Court, John Maclean fought and killed the Italian, much to the pleasure of his fellow Scots.

John married a daughter of MacDonald of Islay and had three sons: Hector, Murdoch and John. In June 1581, with his eldest son, he attacked and wounded the Burgess of Glasgow, a goldsmith by the name of Peter Lymeburner, who was travelling through Mull at the time. They took 3,000 merks from their victim and were immediately condemned for their act by the Privy Council of Scotland, but were never actually punished in any way. In March 1588 John Mór was forced to appear before the Privy Council as a rebel and to explain himself in imprisoning, seemingly for no reason, his own clansman John Roy Maclean, since April 1586. He was ordered to release him forthwith.

It was Hector Maclean, 8th of Lochbuie, who was generally credited with changing of the spelling of the clan surname from Maclean to the phonetic pronunciation of Maclaine. Certainly his descendants and those of his brothers are universally recorded as Maclaine after him. Hector Maclaine had every good reason to want to disassociate and distance himself from the Macleans of Duart, not least for their treatment of him after he found himself on the losing side in the last of many battles between the Macleans and the MacDonalds of Islay. Since 1564 the two great Clans had fought over the Stewardship of The Rinns which represented the entire western peninsula of the Isle of Islay. In 1564 the MacDonalds had invaded Mull, Tiree and Coll, plundering and killing. Hector Og Maclean (1490–1573), 9th of Duart, retaliated in 1566 by laying waste to the MacDonalds' island of Gigha. In 1567 Mary Queen of Scots commissioned Archibald Campbell (1532–1573), 5th Earl of Argyll, to stop the feud but the depth of hatred between the two Clans was too deep rooted and trouble flared up time and again.

In October 1588 Lachlan Mor Maclean (1558–1598), 10th of Duart, took advantage of a Spanish Galleon (either 'The Florencia' or more likely, according to modern research, the 'San Juan de Sicilia') from the famous Armada of King Phillip II (1527–1598) of Spain, that was attempting to return home by sailing anti-clockwise around the coast of Britain, having been beaten in the English Channel by the fleet of Sir Francis Drake (1540–1596). When the ship limped into Tobermory Bay for repairs and supplies, Sir Lachlan struck a deal with the Captain. In return for safe anchorage and provisions the Captain was to loan the Macleans 100 foot soldiers to help fight the MacDonalds. Maclean immediately attacked the islands of Canna, Rum, Eigg and Muck and laid siege to the castle of the MacIans of Ardnamurchan, a sept i.e. a family that is absorbed into or closely affiliated with an overall clan for mutual benefit, of the Clan Donald, at Mingary; he already had their Chief, John MacIan, held as a captive at Duart Castle. Eventually the Spaniards completed the repairs to their ship and the Captain recalled his troops in readiness to leave. Lachlan Mor was furious and saw the Captain's actions as breaking their agreement. He bade one of his cousins, Donald Glas Maclean a.k.a. "The Grey Donald of Morvern", to stow away in the galleon's powder magazine, and as the vessel pulled out into the Sound of Mull, he blew it to pieces. The ship apparently lies there to this day complete with its supposed £300,000 worth of gold bullion. The story of the sunken Spanish Galleon quickly became a legend and later inspired Robert Louis Stevenson (mentioned in the Foreword) to write a short story called 'The Merry Men…etc' (1887) in which he described gigantic breaking waves *"that roar a hundred feet high around the rocks and are called "the Merry Gentlemen" due to the vast noise they make, like shrieking laughter."*[6]

In 1598 the feud kicked-off again and Lachlan Mor was killed at the Battle of Traigh Gruinnart on the northern coast of the Isle of Islay by his own nephew, the MacDonald Chief, Sir James MacDonald (bef.1616–1626). Hector Og or "Young Hector" Maclean (1578–1623), 11th of Duart, then, before the year was out, avenged the death of his father by completely crushing the MacDonalds of Islay at the Battle of Benvigory (a.k.a. Beinn Bhegier), which is a hill on the East side of Islay. Unfortunately for Hector Maclaine, 8th of Lochbuie, he was fighting alongside the MacDonalds at the time, in support of his mother's family. He was taken prisoner by Duart's ally, Allan Cameron (1568–1647), 16th of Lochiel, and kept in chains for six months. He did however get his own back on the latter to some extent when he some time after found himself in a position to buy Lochiel's lands for a small sum. He sold them in 1609 to Archibald Campbell (1576–1638), 7th Earl of Argyll, for 700 merks.

King James VI became increasingly disgusted by the lawlessness and constant feuding of the clans of the Inner Hebrides (see Illustration (iv) – Clan Map of the Inner Hebrides) and was determined to find a solution. In 1608 he sent a fleet of warships to Mull and orders to all the island chiefs, including Hector Maclaine, 8th of Lochbuie, to attend his representative Andrew Knox (1585–1632), Bishop of the Isles, at Aros Castle near the port of Salen on the northern coast of the Isle. At the meeting the chiefs were enticed to leave behind their various followers and were tricked into boarding the Bishop's ship, the HMS Moon, by themselves for private discussions. The moment they set foot on board they were immediately taken as prisoners and the fleet sailed away, after scuttling the many galley-ships of the clansmen. From Mull the Chiefs were confined in prisons across the mainland including Edinburgh, Stirling and Dumbarton. A year later they were released and taken to Iona and made to swear several promises that became known as 'The Statues of Iona' (or 'The Statutes of Icomkill' as the island was also known), upon the sacred Black Stones (the same ones that Good John of Islay had sworn upon in 1354). These Statutes were carefully designed to suppress the Gaelic language and customs of the highlanders and effectively anglicise them. They banned the carrying of arms and the sale of strong drink; they banished bards, whose poetry was renowned for recalling past feuds and seen as instrumental in inciting further violence. They further demanded restoration of the churches and notably, particularly in relation to James Maclaine's immediate ancestors, they insisted that the eldest son of any moderately wealthy family should receive an education in the Lowlands where they would learn to speak English.

Hector Maclaine became the first of the Maclaines of Lochbuie to be a Protestant. He was married to Margaret, eldest daughter of Archibald Campbell (1530–1594), 2nd of Lochnell, and had four sons and two daughters. It was his grandsons, through his second son, Charles, who went to Edinburgh to be educated for the ministry, and who were the immediate ancestors (see Chapter 2) of James Maclaine, "The Gentleman

Highwayman". In Hector Maclaine's case he not only tried to repair the churches on his lands, but also aimed to make provision to ensure that there would be Maclaine ministers available to preach in them.

Hector Odhar, or "Swarthy Hector", Maclaine (1575–1628) became the 9th Chief of Lochbuie and it was his descendants that led the Clan through the trials and tribulations of their history from then until the present day. They certainly had their highs and lows over the centuries. Some of the more memorable highs included Murdoch Maclaine (1605–1662), styled Murdoch Mor, 10th of Lochbuie, fighting under James Graham (1612–1658), 5th Earl of Montrose, when the latter raised an army in support of King Charles I (1600–1649), against those who were taking the Covenanting idealism to extremes. The Covenanters were part of a Presbyterian movement in Scotland that wanted to stay loyal to King Charles I at the same time as steadfastly refusing to accept his proposed reforms to their religion and his new English version of The Bible; they sought to overthrow the King for their own gain. Over 700 Maclaines / Macleans were present at the Battle of Kilsyth on 15 August 1645.

Another memorable high included the appointment on 21 March 1689, by the exiled King James VII (1633–1701) [II of England], of Hector Maclaine (1649–1706), 12th of Lochbuie, as Lieutenant Colonel of the Argyllshire Regiment. Under John Graham of Claverhouse (1648–1689), who was better known as Viscount "Bonnie Dundee", a.k.a. "Bluidy Clavers" by the "Williamites" i.e. the English (mainly lowland Scots) army of King William III (1650–1702), Maclaine lead the Jacobites in their opening campaign in June 1689 by defeating a cavalry unit under the command of Lt. Gen. Sir Thomas Livingstone (1651–

1711), Viscount Teviott, at Knockbreck in Badenoch. He went on to lead 300 Maclaines into the successful (although "Bonnie Dundee" was killed) Battle of Killiecrankie on 27 July 1689. Having lost so many of their followers in the disastrous Jacobite rebellion of 1715, and on the strength of some friendly advice, the Maclaines of Lochbuie did not turn out en masse in support of "Bonnie Prince Charlie" in 1745. Considering the Macleans of Duart lost all but 37 men out of a force of 500 that they took to the Battle of Culloden on 16 April 1746, it proved very wise advice indeed! In the aftermath of Culloden the Macleans were stripped of their lands whilst the Maclaines were able to keep theirs', at least for the time being. James Maclaine, in the heart of London in 1746, would not have been slow to remind his English friends and acquaintances of his connections to the side of the Clan that stayed loyal to King George [Augustus of Hanover] II (1683–1760).

Another proud moment came when John Maclaine (1700–1778), 17th Laird of Lochbuie, was the incumbent Chief of his Clan and played host to the writers Dr. Samuel Johnson (1709–1784), one of England's finest critics, poets, essayists and biographers. It was Dr. Johnson who produced the first English Dictionary in 1754 and he who is currently subject of the successful West End play, 'A Dish of Tea with Dr Johnson' and James Boswell (1740–1795), the eminent English diarist and writer; as they toured the Hebrides together in 1773, of which they each published their accounts in 1775 and 1786 respectively. They reached Lochbuie on Thursday 21 October 1773 and left the next day having stayed the night in Lochbuie House and having toured the inside of Moy Castle. Apparently Johnson politely refused Lady [Isabel Maclean of Brolas] Lochbuie's offer of cold sheep's head for breakfast! Boswell said of Maclaine, *"We had heard much of Lochbuy's* [sic] *being a great, roaring braggadocio, a kind of Sir John Falstaff* [a recurring fictional Shakespearian character (sometimes a highwayman)], *both in size and manners, but we found that they had swelled him up to a fictitious size, and clothed him in imaginary qualities... The truth, is that Lochbuy* [sic] *proved to be a bluff, comely, noisy old gentleman, proud of his hereditary consequence, and a very hearty and hospitable Landlord."[7]* Whilst on the tour Dr Johnson met Flora MacDonald (see earlier) and described her as *"a woman of middle stature, soft features, elegant manners and gentle presence."[8]* John Maclaine placed a plaque above the door of Lochbuie House to commemorate the visit.

A further high point came when Donald Maclaine (1816–1863), 22nd Chief of Lochbuie, amassed a fortune as a merchant in Batavia, working for the firm Maclaine Watson and Partners, and was able to pay off the debts that had built up on the Lochbuie estates whilst his immediate ancestors had pursued their military careers, fighting in the Scottish Regiments in the American and European wars; regrettably he was too late to stop many of the clearances of the mid 19th Century. Major Kenneth Douglas Lorne Maclaine (1880–1935), 24th of Lochbuie, took to the stage as a singer in an effort to raise funds to keep the estates in Maclaine hands, but he ultimately lost them in 1920 in a lawsuit with one Sir Stephen Herbert Gatty (1849–1922), one time Chief Justice of Gibraltar. The Chiefly line of Maclaine of Lochbuie continues to this day with the present Chief, Lorne Gillean Iain Maclaine, 26th of Lochbuie, who lives in Natal, South Africa. He has a daughter, Robyn Vanessa, and son, Angus Gillean Matthew, and two Maclaine grandsons, Cameron

Gillean Hilton and Gregor Gillean Allistair, together with one Maclaine granddaughter, Natalie Allison. Angus and his family presently reside near London. We wish them all well.

James Maclaine, during his life in London, would have enjoyed the ambiguity over the spelling of his surname, no doubt turning it to his advantage when he needed to. Certainly when he was in danger of being caught as a deserter from the army (see Chapter 2), even before he had officially started his military career, it would have suited him to be James Maclean [sic]. Once arrested (see Chapter 5), he would have had little opportunity to influence or correct what was being written of him. To be bringing shame on the name Maclean or any other variant spelling, as opposed to Maclaine, would have at least offered some protection to his family. When he was able to exert influence however, for example when he commissioned a Presbyterian Minister to write an account of his behaviour behind bars whilst under sentence of death (see Chapter 6), he did ensure his name was correctly recorded.

Maclaine of Lochbuie Linage

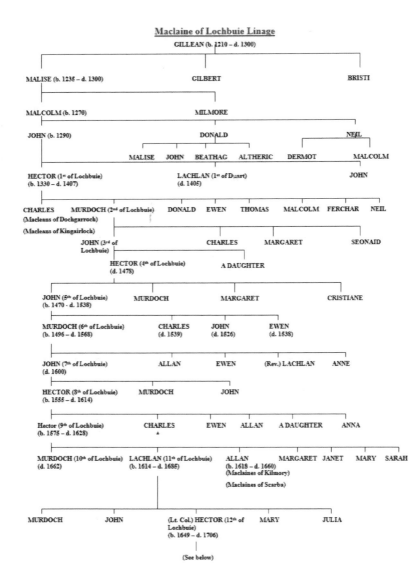

GILLEAN (b. 1210 – d. 1300)

MALISE (b. 1235 – d. 1300)   GILBERT   BRISTI

MALCOLM (b. 1270)   MILMORE

JOHN (b. 1290)   DONALD   NEIL

MALISE JOHN BEATHAG ALTHERIC DERMOT MALCOLM

HECTOR (1st of Lochbuie)   LACHLAN (1st of Duart)   JOHN
(b. 1330 – d. 1407)   (d. 1405)

CHARLES   MURDOCH (2nd of Lochbuie) DONALD EWEN THOMAS MALCOLM FERCHAR NEIL
(Macleans of Dochgarroch)

(Macleans of Kingairloch)

JOHN (3rd of   CHARLES   MARGARET   SEONAID
Lochbuie)

HECTOR (4th of Lochbuie)   A DAUGHTER
(d. 1478)

JOHN (5th of Lochbuie) MURDOCH   MARGARET   CRISTIANE
(b. 1470 - d. 1538)

MURDOCH (6th of Lochbuie) CHARLES JOHN EWEN
(b. 1496 – d. 1568) (d. 1539) (d. 1526) (d. 1538)

JOHN (7th of Lochbuie) ALLAN EWEN (Rev.) LACHLAN ANNE
(d. 1600)

HECTOR (8th of Lochbuie) MURDOCH JOHN
(b. 1555 – d. 1614)

Hector (9th of Lochbuie) CHARLES EWEN ALLAN A DAUGHTER ANNA
(b. 1575 – d. 1628) *

MURDOCH (10th of Lochbuie) LACHLAN (11th of Lochbuie) ALLAN MARGARET JANET MARY SARAH
(d. 1662) (b. 1614 – d. 1685) (b. 1618 – d. 1660)
      (Maclaines of Kilmory)

      (Maclaines of Scarba)

MURDOCH   JOHN   (Lt. Col.) HECTOR (12th of MARY   JULIA
      Lochbuie)
      (b. 1649 – d. 1706)

(See below)

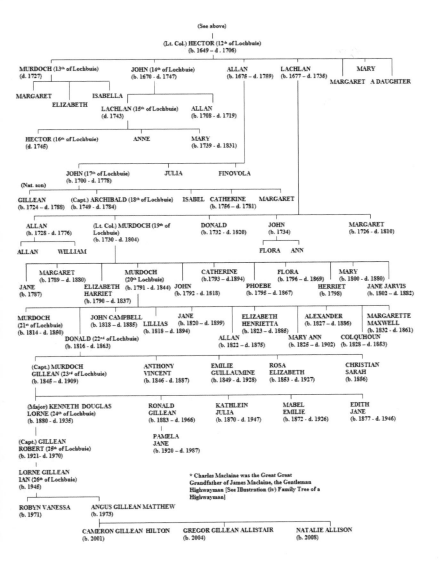

Illustration (v) – Maclaine of Lochbuie Linage. (2006) –
N.F.M.

Chapter 1 – References

[1] *Celtic Scotland: a History of Ancient Alban Volume III*, Skene, William Forbes D.C.L., LL.D (David Douglas, Edinburgh, 1890), p. 480

[2] *The Clan Gillean, Sinclair, Alexander Maclean* (Haszard and Moore, Charlottetown, Prince Edward Island, 1899), p. 46

[3] *A History of the Clan MacLean from its first settlement of Duard castle in the Isle of Mull, to the present period including a genealogical account of some of the principal families together with their heraldry, legends, superstitions, etc*, MacLean, J[ohn]. P[atterson] (Robert Clarke & Co., Cincinnati, 1889), p. 235

[4] *Ibid*, pp. 235–6

[5] *Burkes Landed Gentry*, 18th Edition (1972)

[6] *The Merry Men and other Tales and Fables*, Stevenson, Robert Louis (Charles Scribner's Sons, New York, 1887)

[7] *Journal of a Tour to the Hebrides with Samuel Johnson LL. D. 1773, Boswell*, James (1785)

[8] *A Journey to the Western Isles of Scotland*, Johnson, Samuel (1775)

Chapter 1 – Suggested Further Reading

In addition to the above:

Renaissance of the Clan MacLean. Comprising also a History of DUBHAIRD CAISTEAL and the Great Gathering on August 24, 1912, MacLean, J[ohn]. P[atterson] (The F. J. Heer Printing Co., Columbus, Ohio, 1913)

Road to the Isles: Travellers in the Hebrides 1770–1914, Cooper, Derek (Routledge & Kegan Paul Limited, Glasgow, 1979)

Royal Commission on the Ancient and Historical Monuments of Scotland; Argyll, Volume III; Mull, Tiree, Coll and Northern Argyll, (HMSO, 1980)

The Story of Mull and Iona. A Pictorial History Written and Illustrated by Nick Hesketh, Hesketh, Nick (James Thin, The Meercat Press, Edinburgh, 1988)

Scottish Battles, Archibald, Malcolm (W&R Chambers Limited, Edinburgh, 1990)

The Clan Almanac. The Definitive List, Maclean, Charles (Lochar Publishing, Moffat, Scotland, 1990)

Warriors and Priests. The History of The Clan Maclean 1300–1570, Maclean-Bristol, Nicholas (Tuckwell Press Limited, East Lothian, 1995)

Murder Under Trust: The Crimes and Death of Lachlan Mor Maclean of Duart, Maclean-Bristol, Nicholas (Tuckwell Press Limited, East Lothian, 1999)

Mull: The Island & Its People, Currie, Jo (Birlinn Limited, Edinburgh, 2000)

Macleans: A Biographical Dictionary of Mull People mainly in the 18th and 19th Centuries, Currie, Jo (Brown & Whittaker, Tobermory, 2002)

To the Hebrides. Samuel Johnson's journey to the Western Isles of Scotland and James Boswell's Journal of a Tour to the Hebrides, Black, Ronald (2007: Birlinn Limited, Edinburgh)

From Clan to regiment. Six Hundred Years in The Hebrides, Maclean-Bristol, Nicholas (Pen and Sword Aviation, South Yorkshire, 2007)

Death or Victory. Tales of the Clan Maclean, Maclean, Fiona (White & Maclean Publishing, Belgium, 2011)

CHAPTER 2

ANCESTRY / YOUTH / EARLY YEARS IN LONDON

Not a great deal is widely known about James Maclaine's immediate ancestry. Modern historians, when they choose to mention him, either by inclusion within a few paragraphs of their own work on another famous highwayman or on the subject of highway robbery in general, tend to use the same sources. These would include The Dictionary of National Biography which itself, at least until the entry on James Maclaine was substantially revised in 2004 by Andrea McKenzie, took as its main references the so called 'genuine accounts' and 'complete histories' that were written about him at the time of his death.

The problem with these mini-histories is that they were written by Fleet Street hack-writers of the mid-18th Century, who were more concerned with speed of publication than factual accuracy. They needed to sell copies of their stories before 'The Gentleman Highwayman' became no longer the scandal of the day. It is certain that few of them ever met Maclaine otherwise they would not have so often mis-spelled his surname nor got the detail of his father's Christian name so completely wrong. Sure they all knew enough to quote that James's father was descended from a reputable family from the North of Scotland and that he was a well loved Presbyterian Minister who settled in Monaghan, but their knowledge was quite flawed and certainly did not seem to go much deeper. Where it did they would record his father as being Lauchlan Maclean [sic], whereas we know for certain, thanks to such sources as the Fasti of the Ecclesiastical Church of both Scotland and Ireland, that his father was one Rev. Thomas Maclaine (1685–1740).

This mistake may not have been due to complete idleness or error on the part of the researchers as there had been a noted and generally considered odious character by the name of Lauchlan Macleane (1727–1778), an East India Company speculator, M.P. and one time (1766) Governor of the island of St. Vincent; one of the largest of the Grenadine Islands in the Caribbean, alive at the same time. Dr. James Noël MacKenzie Maclean (1900–1978) recorded this gentleman's history in his book 'Reward is Secondary' [1963; Hodder & Stoughton, London], speculating that he may have been the man behind the mystery political writer, 'Junius'. It is possible that James Maclaine's biographers were happy to link one odious character to another. Dr J N M Maclean never got to the bottom of this before the time of publishing his work so when it came to making reference to James Maclaine's father in his book, he hedged his bets and referred to him as Lauchlan Thomas Maclaine!

James Maclaine's great grandfather was the Rev. Alexander Maclaine (c.1625–1680). He was the second son of Charles Maclaine, who himself was the second son of Hector Maclaine, 8th of Lochbuie, the Chief of the Clan who we met in Chapter 1 and who changed the spelling of the surname to "Maclaine". Rev. Alexander Maclaine had an elder brother, Rev. Archibald Maclaine (c.1618–1690). As young men these two were liberally trained for The Church and both attended Edinburgh University, receiving Master of Arts qualifications in 1646 and 1639 respectively. The elder brother Archibald had the honour of being presented with his award by none other than King Charles I on 18 January 1645.

Rev. Alexander Maclaine became the Minister of Kilmory after 10 April 1651 and transferred to Kilbride on the Isle of Arran on 11 January 1652, before moving again on 19 May 1652 to Kilmaglass (nowadays known as Strachur). The word Presbyter means 'elder' and the Presbyterian Church was and still is very much based on the leadership and guidance of Elders. Presbyterianism is a form of Protestant Christianity practiced particularly in Reformed Churches that traces its roots back to the teachings of John Calvin (born Jean Chavin) (1509–1564), an important French Christian theologian during the Protestant Reformation. It was John Knox (1505–1572), a Scot who had spent time studying under Calvin in Geneva, who returned to Scotland and led the Scottish Parliament to reform the Church following Presbyterian principles. As with all Presbyterian Ministers of the time Rev. Alexander Maclaine would continue to be sent from one posting to another by the Synod, the governing council/assembly of the Presbyterian Church. He was also required by the Synod to get involved in the enormous task of translating the Metrical Psalms, which task he undertook from 1655 to 1659. When the Synod proposed translating the Scriptures in Gaelic in 1660 he was apportioned the Book of Joshua. He was moved to the Ministry of Kingarth on the Isle of Bute, in the Firth of Clyde, on 25 April 1660 but this was the start of unsettled times for him as just two months later he suffered the indignity of being deprived of his living for adhering to Episcopal Doctrines by an Act of Parliament of 11 June 1660, which was reinforced by the Privy Council of Scotland on 1 October 1662. Fortunately he was eventually reinstated by the Privy Council on 3 September 1672 as Minister of Kilchattan, also on the Isle of Bute.

Rev. Alexander Maclaine brought up four boys, two of whom followed in their father's wake and became Presbyterian Ministers. The eldest son, the Rev. Archibald Maclaine (1660–1734) [James Maclaine's grandfather] was born in 1660 when his father was first unable to work. At a young age Archibald was enrolled in Glasgow University where he is known to have achieved a Master of Arts Degree. His first assignment after leaving University was, following in his father's exact footsteps, to the Ministry of Kilmaglass from 1680 to 1682 and then onto Kingarth from 1682. He passed trials before the Presbytery of Dunoon and following a testimonial on 5 November 1684, ordained in the Parish of Dunoon and Kilmun, on the north shore of Holy Loch, before 4 February 1685.

Rev. Archibald Maclaine was transferred to the Parish of Lochgoilhead and Kilmorich after 5 May 1686. In 1690 he married Jane Kennedy (1669–1753), daughter of Rev. Thomas Kennedy (1624–1714), Minister of Carland, County Tyrone, Ireland. He was received into the Communion of the Synod on 16 December 1691 and was admitted on 7 July 1692 to the Ministry of Kilbride, on the Isle of Arran, the largest island in the Firth of Clyde. After five years in this charge, and before 23 October 1697, he was called to Markethill in the county of Armagh, Ireland, by the Presbytery of Omagh, and was declared transportable, in readiness, on 26 October 1698.

Initially, on arrival in Monaghan, Rev. Archibald Maclaine only administered in Markethill before assuming the full Ministry on 16 January 1700. He had the unfortunate distinction of becoming the first Presbyterian Minister in the whole of Ireland to be prosecuted by the Bishop's Court for celebrating marriage in the Presbyterian form. However on a more positive note, in his day, he was considered one of the finest masters of the Irish language. His greatest achievement was in 1711when he became the Moderator of the Synod of Ulster, the highest Presbyterian rank.

Whilst it is certain that the Rev. Archibald Maclaine would have known all his grandchildren, he regrettably died on 20 July 1734, when James was just 10 years old. He would have been delighted however to see all three of his own sons grow up and become Presbyterian Ministers in Ireland, married to the daughters of his friends, and fellow Presbyterian Ministers, and his own two daughters, married to Presbyterian clergymen who were themselves sons of Presbyterian clergymen. In other words the generation before James Maclaine (see Illustration (vi) – FAMILY TREE OF A HIGHWAYMAN) was as pious as could possibly be.

The first son of Rev. Archibald Maclaine was the (eventual Rev.) Thomas Maclaine who was born in c.1685. Like his father and so many other Irish Presbyterians before him he followed the well-trodden path to Glasgow University and graduated with his Master of Arts Degree in Divinity in 1711. Having lived much of his youth in Ireland with his family it was natural that he would attempt to find a posting in that country rather than return to the Scottish mainland or Isles. In 1717, in passing the first steps to ordination, he was licensed by the Presbytery of Armagh and from 19 March 1718 he ordained in Monaghan. He married Elizabeth Milling (–1742), daughter of Rev. James Milling and sister of Rev. Robert Milling (1679–1749), Pastor to the English Church at The Hague in Holland. Thomas and Elizabeth started a family in 1722 with the birth of their first son, the (eventual Rev.) Archibald Maclaine (1722–1804). He was quickly followed by their next born, a daughter, Anne Jane (1723–   ) who was followed a year later by a second son James Maclaine (1724–1750), the eventual 'Gentleman Highwayman'.

Rev. Thomas Maclaine remained the Minister of Monaghan from his arrival in 1718 until his death on 17 November 1740. He was well respected and held in high esteem by his congregation. He was a Member of the Belfast Society which was a meeting of Presbyterian Ministers and laymen started by Thomas's younger brother's father-in-law, Rev. John Abernethy (1680–1740) in 1705, with the aim of fostering theological disputation to challenge the accepted religious notions of their day. The Members of the Society would gather to discuss the Bible and evolve theological wisdom. They would pool their resources to purchase books to review and to publish pamphlets containing their own interpretations and comments on the work of others as well as their own generated works.

The second son of Rev. Archibald Maclaine was another (eventual Rev.) Archibald Maclaine (1695–1739) who was born on the Isle of Arran whilst his father was Minister there. This Archibald Maclaine became a Reverend after achieving a Master of Arts Degree at Glasgow University. He was licensed to preach by the Presbytery, Rev. James Johnson of Armagh, on 17 September 1719 and ordained at First Bainbridge, County Down, from 26 April 1720 until his death on 22 February 1739.

Like his elder brother he was a Moderate Subscriber and Member of the Belfast Society.

With his wife, Katherine Malcolm (1693–1766), daughter of the Rev. John Malcolm of Dunmurry, and widow of William Brown, this Archibald raised a family of three boys and two girls, just like his father before him. Only one of these boys grew up to be a Presbyterian Minister: the Rev. John Maclaine (1730–1761) of whom we know very little, other than he may have emigrated to America. Archibald's eldest son, yet another Archibald Maclaine (1728–1790), did emigrate to Philadelphia on 24 April 1750, just a few months ahead of the shocking news of his cousin's antics in London hitting the headlines, and settled in Wilmington, New Hanover County, North Carolina. He married Elizabeth Rowan (1731–1806), daughter of Jerome Rowan and Elizabeth Lyon of Dublin. He went on to have a very long and distinguished career in the legal profession and amongst other notable achievements, was the author of 'The Court System of North Carolina'. When he died on 20 December 1790 he was buried the next day at 'Maclaine's Bluff', just outside Wilmington. Many of this Archibald's children failed to live beyond infancy, including two sons, both named Archibald in the hope of keeping that name going on in the family to the next generation, one born on 29 June 1758, and the other on 21 March 1764. His eldest son, Jerome Maclaine (1753–1777) did survive to adulthood, only to be killed in action in the Civil War on 10 June 1777, a year after becoming Captain of the 4th Regiment. His eldest daughter, Catherine Maclaine (1755–1810) married one George Hooper who was a brother of William Hooper (1742–1790), a signatory to the Declaration of Independence on 4 July 1776.

The third son of Rev. Archibald Maclaine was another (eventual Rev.) Alexander Maclaine (–1759). Again, he was educated at Glasgow University and was awarded his Master of Arts Degree, like his father and brothers. He was licensed by the Presbytery of Monaghan in 1731 and ordained in First Ballynahinch in County Down, Ireland, by invitation of the Presbytery of Killyleagh on 1 August 1735. In 1742 he moved to Antrim and joined the Non-subscribing (or Unitarian) Party, started by his father-in-law, the Rev. John Abernethy (1680–1740) (see earlier), who was known as 'The Father of Non-subscription' and who led many Presbyterian Ministers (including his in-laws) and congregations out of the Synod of Ulster into a separate liberal-minded denomination, known today as the Non-subscribing Presbyterian Church of Ireland. It was this Rev. Alexander Maclaine who preached the National Fast Sermon at Antrim on 18 December 1745 that was published a year later in Dublin.

Of the two daughters of Rev. Archibald Maclaine we only have very scant detail. The elder of the two, Ann Maclaine, married the Rev. John Milling, Minister of Leiden in Holland from 1696 to 1702 (and later of Dublin); he was the second son of Rev. James Milling and thus an uncle to the eventual highwayman twice over, once as a maternal uncle, being brother to James's mother Elizabeth, and secondly as husband to his aunt, Ann. The younger daughter, for whom we do not even know a Christian name, married one Rev. John Menogh of Magheralin, County Down, the son of another Rev. Menogh.

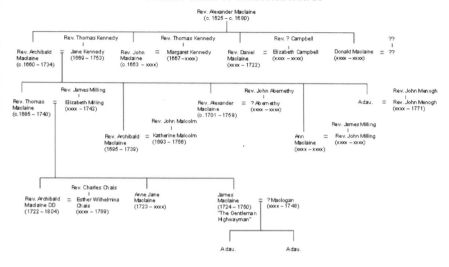

FAMILY TREE OF A HIGHWAYMAN

Rev. Alexander Maclaine
(c. 1625 – c. 1680)

Rev. Thomas Kennedy | Rev. Thomas Kennedy | Rev. ? Campbell | ??

Rev. Archibald Maclaine (c.1660 – 1734) = Jane Kennedy (1669 – 1753) | Rev. John Maclaine (c.1663 – xxxx) = Margaret Kennedy (1667 – xxxx) | Rev. Daniel Maclaine (xxxx – 1722) = Elizabeth Campbell (xxxx – xxxx) | Donald Maclaine (xxxx – xxxx) = ??

Rev. James Milling

Rev. Thomas Maclaine (c.1685 – 1740) = Elizabeth Milling (xxxx – 1742) | Rev. John Abernethy | Rev. John Menogh

Rev. Alexander Maclaine (c.1701 – 1759) = ? Abernethy (xxxx – xxxx) | A dau. = Rev. John Menogh (xxxx – 1771)

Rev. John Malcolm

Rev. Archibald Maclaine (1695 – 1739) = Katherine Malcolm (1693 – 1766)

Rev. James Milling

Ann Maclaine (xxxx – xxxx) = Rev. John Milling (xxxx – xxxx)

Rev. Charles Chais

Rev. Archibald Maclaine DD (1722 – 1804) = Esther Wilhelmina Chais (xxxx – 1789) | Anne Jane Maclaine (1723 – xxxx) | James Maclaine (1724 – 1750) "The Gentleman Highwayman" = ? Maclogan (xxxx – 1748)

A dau. | A dau.

Illustration (vi) — FAMILY TREE OF A HIGHWAYMAN.
(2006) — N.F.M.

All the foregoing has taught us that we do know a great deal more about James Maclaine's immediate ancestry than all previous biographers. We know that we can do considerably better than the fairly representative: *"Born at Monaghan in 1724, he was the second son of Lauchlin Maclaine, a Presbyterian minister, who, although settled in Ireland, was a Scotsman of unmixed Scottish blood, and of undoubted Scottish sympathies."* [1]. We can actually state that his immediate ancestors, over the previous three generations, included at least seventeen [count them!] Presbyterian clergymen, with his father's generation providing a "full house" of the most pious in the land. It was from this "whiter than white" background that an eventual highwayman emerged. It is hard to imagine a blacker, "Black Sheep" in any family; the term could have been invented for him! So where did it all go wrong?

In answer to this question and as we go on with James Maclaine's story we will see that it was not really one thing alone that had an overwhelming influence on his downfall; it was more a combination of factors. Times of course were, as they always are, changing. The big cities were becoming bigger with increased urbanisation as people moved off the land to find work at what was the beginning of the Industrial Revolution. British people were beginning to work across Europe and as far away as both the East and the West Indies. It was no longer the clergy who were being sent to work far and wide; other professions such as lawyers and accountants were becoming much more transportable. Increased urbanisation and increased transport also meant increased opportunity for crime. Whilst the immediately preceding generations of Maclaine's family had been born and bred to the Ministry it is notable that of James's four first cousins only one was to go on to become a clergyman. We will also see that the keeping of some bad company and as well as faults within the strength of Maclaine's own personal character played their part.

James Maclaine was by no means the only clergyman's son to go "off the rails" and turn to highway robbery. Sons of clergymen were constantly exposed to the wealthy families of the congregations of their fathers' and despite their class and financial backgrounds could not help themselves but aspire to becoming gentlemen. A few other noted examples were:

• Nicholas Horner (1687–1719) – of Honiton in Devonshire, who was captured after his first robbery and sent to

Winchester Jail. He was saved by his father's pleading to Queen Anne (1665–1714) who granted him a pardon, *"upon condition of his being transported out of her Majesty's dominions, or any other potentate's in Europe, for the term of seven years."²*. Having served his time away he returned to Devon and spent the £500 his, by then, deceased parents had bequeathed him and took up highway robbery. He was soon apprehended and hanged in Exeter on 3 April 1719.

• William (a.k.a. Thomas) Barkwith (1708–1739) – from the Isle of Ely in Cambridgeshire, who was a talented scholar, proficient in Greek, Latin, French and Italian. His extravagance in courting a particular young lady led him into debt and he stole money from his Master and then turned to highway robbery. Having stolen only 12 shillings from his one and only victim on Hounslow Heath (see Chapter 3) he was relentlessly pursued by witnesses, until he was spotted off his horse, relieving his bladder. When finally cornered he tried to shoot himself but his pistols failed and he was taken. He was hanged at Tyburn (see Chapter 6) on 21 December 1739.

• Paul Lewis (1740–1763) – born at Hurstmonceaux in Sussex, who ran away to sea at a young age and rose to the rank of Lieutenant in the Royal Navy. He stole from his shipmates and on later turning to highway robbery was captured at least twice and escaping justice before eventually being tried at the Old Bailey (see Chapter 5). *"Such was the baseness and unfeeling profligacy of this wretch that when his almost heart-broken father visited him for the last time, in Newgate* [see Chapter 6], *and put twelve guineas into his hands, to defray his expenses, he slipped one of the pieces of gold into the cuff of his sleeve, by a dexterous sleight, and then opening his hand showed the venerable and reverend old man that there was but eleven, upon which he took from his pocket another and gave it him, to make up the number he intended.*"[3]. He was hanged at Tyburn on 4 May 1763.

Rev. Thomas Maclaine did quite deliberately break from the family tradition that would have otherwise impelled him to ensure that both his sons were trained for the Church. For his first son, the (eventual Rev.) Archibald Maclaine (1722–1804), he did put all his efforts into the traditional course. Indeed Archibald did go to Glasgow University in 1739 and passed his Master of Arts Degree in 1746. He was tutored by Francis Hutcheson (1694–1746), a renowned moral philosopher of the time, and was a contemporary of Adam Smith (1723–1790), who went on to become an acclaimed philosopher and economist, who wrote his most famous work 'An Inquiry into the Nature and Causes of the Wealth of Nations' in 1776 and appears on the back of the current Bank of England £20 note. By the time Archibald finished his studies his parents had been dead for some years so he was sent straight to the English Church at The Hague in Holland to assist his maternal uncle the Rev. Robert Milling in his post. The latter had been Pastor there for over thirty years, but his health was ailing and he needed to slow down. When his uncle died in 1749, Rev. Archibald Maclaine took over and stayed in that place for almost fifty years and went on to live a full and illustrious life, mixing with the great and the good, including both Dutch and British royalty, great composers such as [George Frideric] Handel (1685–1759), and famous writers such as James Boswell who we met in The Hebrides in Chapter 1 and who visited Archibald Maclaine in The Hague in late 1763 and early 1764, recording their conversations in his diary. Rev. Archibald Maclaine was for a long time Preceptor [a teacher] to the family of Willem [Batavus] V (1748–1806), Prince of Orange-Nassau, the last Stadhouder [or "Steward"] of the Dutch Republic. Willem V was married to [Frederika Sophia] Wilhelmina (1751–1820) of Prussia with whom Rev. Archibald Maclaine shared much lengthy correspondence. The couple's eldest surviving son William (1772–1843) went on to become William I, King of the Netherlands.

Rev. Archibald Maclaine went on to have many of his own works published and was respected in many countries for his great learning; he was particularly famous for his 1764 annotated translation from Latin of John Lawrence Mosheim's [or Johann Lorenz von Mosheim (1693–1755) to be more precise] 'An Ecclesiastical History Ancient and Modern from the Birth of Christ to the Beginning of the Eighteenth Century' that went on to be republished many times, such was the demand. When he finally left The Hague in 1796 it was due to a combination of ill health, having suffered from apoplexy [a burst blood vessel in the brain], and the French occupation of Holland. He retired to Bath in Somerset where he met again and was able to spend time with his sister, Anne Jane, whom he had not seen in over fifty years. She had come to England in 1798 as a consequence of the United Irish Rebellion, a revolutionary rebellion along similar lines as had been seen in France and America that lasted from 24 May to 23 September 1798. Soon after he died on Sunday 25 November 1804 he was buried within the crypt of Bath Abbey. In the wall of the western portal giving access to the Abbey is a commemorative stone tablet with a Latin inscription in his honour.

For his younger son, James, the Rev. Thomas Maclaine considered it would be appropriate for him to follow an alternative career. Having carefully ensured his second son was well grounded in religious education and able to both read and write in Latin, he paid for James to become a *"perfect Master of Writing and Accompts."*[4]. Rev. Thomas had secured the promise of a Scottish merchant who would employ James in his Compting House in Rotterdam. Regrettably the good man died before he could see his designed intention come to fruition. Unlike the information contained in other biographies, James and his siblings were not orphaned at this time; their mother Elizabeth out-lived her husband by a further two years. It was only upon her death that each child received their portion of their father's inheritance. Archibald was already deep into his University life; Ann Jane was taken into the care of her Aunt, whilst James was pretty much left to his own devices.

We do not know anything of the quality of the relationship between James Maclaine and his father. Whilst inside his condemned cell in Newgate Prison (see Chapter 6), James wrote a letter which made reference to his father, describing him as *"that Old Gripe,"*[5] On the one hand this would indicate he despised his father, but we must recall these words would have been written at a time of extreme stress and whether they were chosen as a demonstration of outward bravado, as opposed to a sense of genuine malice, we are unlikely to ever establish.

In the immediate aftermath of the loss of his mother James Maclaine was said to abandon all designs of becoming an accountant despite his brother earnestly urging him to progress it. Being tall and forward for his age he thought himself above taking advice from his family and friends. Having received his inheritance he was not slow in supplementing it with the sale of his father's library of books. He equipped himself in the finest clothes that part of the country could offer, bought himself a fine gelding and *"gallanted all the Farmers['] Daughters within ten miles of him."*[6] He would visit all the local fairs and public places where he would seek to be the centre of attention, which would cost him dear as he attempted to prove he was a *"Man of Worth."*[7]

No doubt his aunts and uncles will have made some attempts to put him in mind that his inheritance would not last long at his current rate of spend. He appears to have turned a deaf ear to all of them as he changed *"the Scene of his Extravagance,"*[8] by leaving for Dublin without telling a soul. Once there *"he dress'd in tawdry Gaiety, with little Taste, and to as little Effect, for he was several Months in Dublin, without any Acquaintance, but Lacquies, Ostlers and some raw Boys at the University."*[9] It was from this company that James first conceived the idea of making his fortune through marriage, a notion that stayed with him throughout the remainder of his life. The "Lacquies" were unable to help him in this regard but were better equipped to help him part with his cash, which was finally exhausted within about ten or eleven months. Surprise, surprise, when the money ran out so did their friendship, and James found himself alone and penniless. It was with a heavy heart that he sold his treasured sword to raise the charges to get him, by foot, back to Monaghan. He predicted a frosty welcome judging by the responses he had received to his several letters asking for further funds whilst in Dublin; he was not to be disappointed on that score.

Unlike the happy ending for the Prodigal Son of the Scriptures who left behind his husks and harlots to be welcomed back into the bosom of his family, in James Maclaine's case there was no forgiving father, no home (he had already sold that!) and no fatted calf awaiting him. His aunts and uncles had been so disappointed in him that they point-blank refused to give him any audience. His former friends in Monaghan shunned him and *"render'd him the May Game of the Town."*[10] Only Ann Jane, by stealth, managed to see him and pass on her pocket money but that was nowhere near sufficient to support him.

When he was on the point of reaching rock bottom and had been refused credit for dinner at the inn where he was staying and was staring starvation in the face an unexpected opportunity presented itself. A Mr Howard, a gentleman travelling to England, that night put up at the same house whereupon one of his servants fell sick and died. When he heard of James Maclaine's plight, Mr Howard felt compassion towards him and offered him the role of the deceased servant. Maclaine swallowed his pride and accepted the position of footman and *"set out for England in no better Quality than that of a Livery Servant."*[11]

Needless to say the job did not last long. Maclaine found himself unable to adapt to a role so below his own view of his gentlemanly status. He was impudent and down-right rude to his master as well as being patronising to his fellow servants. After a final quarrel with Mr Howard he found himself discharged after just a few months and once again dependent on the small remittances from his sister. In the meantime Ann Jane had become engaged to be married to a man of some considerable wealth and James wasted no time in tapping this fellow up to see if he would be willing to fit him out for the West Indies or one of the British colonies of America where he might put to use his qualification as an accountant. Being encouraged by the prospect James left for Ireland but by the time he arrived he found the engagement broke off and his sister in no position to offer any further help. Worse still his other relations, who felt he had scandalised them and dishonoured the memory of his father by taking the position of a footman in the first instance, now refused to have anything whatever to do with him.

To spare him from living on the streets his brother Archibald would send him some money when he could, even though he had to see to his own subsistence at Glasgow University. Each such remittance came accompanied by a stern letter imploring James to get his life back in order and urging him to follow their father's original intended plans for his future. James soon realised that he had little choice but to seek some form of menial employment if he was to have any hope in regaining the stature he once enjoyed and that he felt he had a right to.

Through the recommendation of a friend of his father, with a military background, James finally found work as a butler to a Colonel Richard Tonson of Spanish Island and Dunkettle, near Cork. Once again the position did not last too long. The trouble was *"he took such excessive care of his Master's property he was unable to distinguish from his own."[12]* Caught stealing he was promptly dismissed in disgrace. When the Colonel refused him a character reference to another family James began to realise that he had little hope of ever procuring another place in that part of the kingdom.

Next we understand that he conceived the notion of joining the Irish Brigade i.e. the famous 'Wild Geese' or Catholic soldiers, loyal to King James II (1633–1701, who had left Ireland after their defeat at the Battle of The Boyne (a river near Drogheda, County Louth, Ireland) on 1 July 1690, in the service of France. In sharing his intentions with a gentleman of his acquaintance, he was dissuaded from the idea on the basis that he could have no prospect of promotion to Officer *"in such Popish surroundings."[13]* unless he was prepared to change his religion; a circumstance he was not inclined to consent to. As a second thought towards a military career he applied to a Major Johnson of the Life Guards, who had his leg shot off at the Battle of Dettingen in Bavaria on 27 June 1743, to help him join Lord Albemarle's Troop of Horseguards. Dettingen was a battle from the Wars of the Austrian Succession, only renowned for being the last time a reigning British monarch, King George [Augutus] II (1683–1760), took to the battlefield in person. Lord Albemarle was Willem Anne van Keppel (1702–1754), 2nd Earl of Albemarle; he was Colonel of the Coldstream Guards between 1744 and 1754. Still *"being prepossessed with the perfection of his person,"[14]* Maclaine could envision himself *"seated on a prancing steed,"[15]* and *"dress'd in something with plenty of blue or scarlet and gold in it, taking part in ceremonial processions and escorts."[16]* As he could not afford the ten guineas to join the Army as a Private Man he applied as a Supernumerary Man instead.

Maclaine then approached his old master for the 10 guineas required for this resolution and more for his passage to London where the Troop were enlisting, *"Accordingly he applied again to Colonel Tonson, who at first absolutely refused to lend it to him; but on his Tears and Intreaties, he at last consented to pay the Money for him into the Hands of the Major; and the Letters and Passes were wrote for his setting out in a few Days for the Troop which was then abroad."[17]* By the time Maclaine arrived in the metropolis, with his credentials accepted and his enlistment confirmed, he was horrified to find the Troop was already proceeding to Flanders on active service. With images of his imminent destruction in battle filling his mind, he quickly went absent without leave! Indeed the Troop was involved in the disastrous Battle of Fontenoy in April

1745 so Maclaine was clearly switched on to his self-preservation instincts at that moment. Unlike many less fortunate Scotsmen he also avoided being deployed against his own clansmen at the next battle where Lord Albemarle was in charge of the English front line: Culloden (see Chapter 1). London at the time had a population of about half a million people; probably a tenth of the overall population of England, and was growing quite rapidly; hence there were plenty of places to hide.

At this time Maclaine recalled his days in Dublin and his notion of making his fortune by marriage. He had also *"heard from an Acquaintance of his at Cork, that it was no uncommon Thing for such handsome young Fellows as he was, to make their Fortune in London."[18]* With this in mind he was delighted to be taken in by an unnamed Irish lady who offered to help him establish himself in the City. As one of his biographers noted he found himself *"depending for Support on the famous Miss_____ his Country-woman, then in high Vogue, and at that Time in Keeping by a nobel Peer of that Kingdom."[19]* She allowed him pretty handsomely and he made for a while *"a Flaming Beau,"[20]* at last enjoying the high life he had always craved. But all good things must come to an end and one day *"the Peer popping into his Mistress's Quarters, when Mr Maclean* [sic] *was making some warm Returns of Gratitude,"[21]* gave Maclaine a damn good trashing and he *"narrowly escaped being run through the body."[22]* *"The Lady was turned upon the Town,"[23]* and blaming Maclaine for her ruin, she accused him of behaving in a cowardly manner in the foregoing foray and wanted to have no more to do with him.

Maclaine's grandeur suffered an eclipse for a month or two, but just as his last suit was being *"laid in Lavender,"[24]* a *"noted Lady of Quality, likewise of his Nation,"[25]* spotted our man by accident and *"sent her Footman to dog him to his Lodgings, where he next Morning he received the following Billet:"[26]*

Sir,

By your Appearance you would seem willing to Serve a Friend in a Case of Honour. If I am not deceived in my Opinion, I beg the Favour of you to meet me this Evening precisely at ten o'Clock, at the bagnio in Long-Acre, ask for Number four, where you will hear further Particulars from

Your unknown
Humble Servant [27]

As well as keeping this brief epistle for one of his biographers to later find and publish, Maclaine appears to also have recognised the handwriting of being that of a lady and gone along to the appointment. This assignation led to a further stint for Maclaine as a *"petticoat pensioner,"[28]* i.e. a "kept man" or *"a Gallant maintained for secret service,"[29]* [a sort of 18th Century gigolo], to use the expression of the time. Francis Grose (1731–1791) defined the words in his 'Classical Dictionary of the Vulgar Tongue' [1785; Printed for S. Hooper, London] in 1785 along with many other canting slang words of the times; many of us today will still catch ourselves saying: "That's grose". Whilst Maclaine enjoyed his allowance, the fine clothes and the company of those in high society he *"scorned the Drudgery of Serving a Female Keeper,"[30]* and still hankered for a fortune of his own. He had many schemes for this purpose, but none so much as he relied upon as the one to snare the hand of his new benefactress's daughter, who was very rich in her own right. He used the mother's money *"to corrupt the young Lady's Waiting-Maid,"[31]* into his designs, offering her a considerable share of the spoil if she would help him ingratiate himself so deep into the girl's affections that it achieved the securing of a marriage. Showing uncommon loyalty for the time, the Waiting-Maid betrayed him to her overall mistress who wasted no time in dismissing Maclaine from her service. Wishing to see the back of him as soon as possible, so as to further protect her daughter, she arranged with two of her friends: a Lady _____C_____s of Putney and a Mr N _____t [most probably one Thomas Nugent (1714–1792), 6th Earl of Westmeath; an Irish remittancer], to fund Maclaine to the tune of £50 with a view to sending him to Jamaica in the West Indies to follow his fortune there.

Of course, no sooner had Maclaine come into possession of the money than his mind turned straight back to his favourite scheme of fortune hunting and, after dropping all thoughts of travelling, he moved to another part of Town to avoid bumping into his latest financiers. After some further disappointments he at last achieved his ambition and successfully *"made Suit to the Daughter of a considerable Inn-keeper, and Dealer in Horses."[32]* As yet we have been unable to establish the Christian name of his bride having searched the likely parish records and Boyd's Marriage Index, but we do know her maiden name was either MacLogan (or MacLegno) and her father was the Inn Keeper of 'The Golden Fleece' in Oxford Road; the Oxford Street of today. The marriage took place either in late 1745 or early 1746 when Maclaine was 21 years of age.

By all accounts Maclaine seems to have lived honestly and tried to make a success of his marriage. He wisely invested the £500 dowry that came with his bride into a shop *"in the Grocery and Chandlery Way,*[33] in Welbeck Street, near Cavendish Square. After the later discovery of Maclaine's identity as the infamous 'Gentleman Highwayman', his neighbours and customers from the Cavendish Square area recalled him to have been *"a careful and industrious honest Man."*[34] Whilst he was outwardly *"content to confine his energies to the dispersing of sand and small coal,"*[35] it became apparent, after his wife's early death, that may have been after only less than three years, that his continued extravagances had encroached upon their capital to such an extent that when he declared his intention to sell his business, his furniture and stock in trade amounted to scarcely £85. Maclaine's wife most probably died from Smallpox or possibly she died in childbirth. The life expectancy for anyone living in 1748 was only between 36 and 37 years of age, roughly half of what it is today, and for a woman the possibility of dying in childbirth was extremely high.

Published histories of Maclaine leave us somewhat confused over the child(ren) from his marriage. The majority agree that there were two daughters who were taken into the care of their grandmother, MacLogan, when their mother passed away. Again their Christian names are not known and it is likely that the younger girl died in infancy; certainly in 1748 infant mortality rates were 50% and death amongst children was often expected and so sadly accepted. When the Presbyterian Minister commissioned by Maclaine to write an account of his behaviour under sentence, see Chapter 6, spent time with Maclaine during his later incarceration, he asked him if he ever had a child to which Maclaine replied that *"he had a Girl of Five Years old,"*[36] without going on to mention the existence of another, then deceased, or any other details.

There was for a long time a family tradition within the Maclaine Pont family of Holland, descended from Rev. Archibald Maclaine (1722–1804) (see earlier), that James Maclaine's daughter was passed into the care of his brother, Archibald, who by then was established in his post at The Hague. This girl, Anna Maria Maclaine, grew into a young lady of outstanding beauty and made two good marriages; the second to the very wealthy Lieutenant General Johannes Galenus (1767–1839), Baron Van Sytzama. Current thinking considers this to be little more than a myth, the likelihood being that Anna Maria was the daughter of James's and Archibald's cousin, Henry Maclaine (c.1726–1790) who was an Ensign in the Gordon's Regiment of the Scots Brigade, Dutch Army, during the period 1763–1771. Henry being a son of Alexander Maclaine (–1759); but this is yet to be conclusively proven.

As we will learn in Chapter 4, Maclaine may have also sired an illegitimate child; but for now we need to move on to the next stage of his story...

Chapter 2 – References

1 Harper, Charles George (1863–1943). *'HALF-HOURS WITH THE HIGHWAYMEN,* Picturesque Biographies and traditions of the "Knights of the Road"'. [1908; Chapman & Hall Limited, London]. Page 271

2 Smith, Captain Alexander and Hayward, Arthur Lawrence. *'A Complete History of the Lives and Robberies of the most notorious Highwaymen, Footpads, Shoplifts and Cheats of Both Sexes'* [1926; George Routledge & Sons, London]. Pages 447 and 448

3 Knapp, Andrew and Baldwin, William Lee. *'THE NEWGATE CALENDAR; COMPRISING INTERESTING MEMOIRS OF NOTORIOUS CHARACTERS, Who have been convicted of Outrage on THE LAWS OF ENGLAND, SINCE THE BEGINNING OF THE EIGHTEENTH CENTURY'*. Volume II. [1825; J. Robins and Co., London]. Page 336

4 Anonymous. *'A COMPLETE HISTORY of James Maclean [sic], THE GENTLEMAN HIGHWAYMAN, who was executed at TYBURN on Wednesday, October 3, 1750, for a Robbery on the Highway'*. [1750; Printed for Charles Corbett, London]. Page 5

5 Beattie, J. M. *'Crime and the Courts in England, 1660–1800'*. [1986; Clarendon Press, Oxford]. Pages 152 and 153

6 Anonymous. *'A COMPLETE HISTORY of James Maclean [sic], THE GENTLEMAN HIGHWAYMAN, who was executed at TYBURN on Wednesday, October 3, 1750, for a Robbery on the Highway'*. [1750; Printed for Charles Corbett, London]. Page 6

7 Ibid. Page 7

8 Ibid. Page 7

9 Ibid. Page 7

[10] Ibid. Page 7

[11] Ibid. Page 7

[12] Seccombe, Thomas (1866—1923). '*LIVES OF TWELVE BAD MEN*; Original Studies of Eminent Scoundrels by Various Hands' [1894; T. Fisher Unwin, London]. Page 248

[13] Harper, Charles George (1863–1943). '*HALF-HOURS WITH THE HIGHWAYMEN*, Picturesque Biographies and traditions of the "Knights of the Road"'. [1908; Chapman & Hall Limited, London]. Page 276

[14] Ibid. Page 279

[15] Ibid. Page 279

[16] Ibid. Page 279

[17] Anonymous. '*A Genuine Account of the Life and Actions of James Maclean [sic], Highwayman, to the time of his trial and receiving sentence at The Old Bailey, containing his Robberies, Gallantry at Public Places, with other remarkable transactions; together with some account of Plunket his companion*'. [1750; Printed for W. Falstaff, London]. Page 7

[18] Anonymous. '*A COMPLETE HISTORY of James Maclean [sic], THE GENTLEMAN HIGHWAYMAN, who was executed at TYBURN on Wednesday, October 3, 1750, for a Robbery on the Highway*'. [1750; Printed for Charles Corbett, London]. Page 10

[19] Ibid. Page 10

[20] Ibid. Page 15

[21] Anonymous. '*A COMPLETE HISTORY of James Maclean [sic], THE GENTLEMAN HIGHWAYMAN, who was executed at TYBURN on Wednesday, October 3, 1750, for a Robbery on the Highway*'. [1750; Printed for Charles Corbett, London]. Page 10

[22] Ibid. Page 10

[23] Ibid. Page 10

[24] Anonymous. *'A COMPLETE HISTORY of James Maclean [sic], THE GENTLEMAN HIGHWAYMAN, who was executed at TYBURN on Wednesday, October 3, 1750, for a Robbery on the Highway'*. [1750; Printed for Charles Corbett, London]. Page 11

[25] Ibid. Page 11

[26] Ibid. Page 11

[27] Ibid. Page 11

[28] Seccombe, Thomas (1866—1923). *'LIVES OF TWELVE BAD MEN; Original Studies of Eminent Scoundrels by Various Hands'* [1894; T. Fisher Unwin, London]. Page 250

[29] Bailey, Nathan (—1742). *'Dictionary of Canting and Thieving Slang'* [1721; Printed for Thomas Cox, London].

[30] Anonymous. *'A COMPLETE HISTORY of James Maclean [sic], THE GENTLEMAN HIGHWAYMAN, who was executed at TYBURN on Wednesday, October 3, 1750, for a Robbery on the Highway'*. [1750; Printed for Charles Corbett, London]. Page 11

[31] Ibid. Page 12

[32] Ibid. Page 12

[33] Ibid. Page 13

[34] Ibid. Page 13

[35] Seccombe, Thomas (1866—1923). *'LIVES OF TWELVE BAD MEN; Original Studies of Eminent Scoundrels by Various Hands'* [1894; T. Fisher Unwin, London]. Page 246

[36] Allen, Rev. Fifield (1700-1764). 'AN ACCOUNT of the BEHAVIOUR of Mr. James Maclaine, From the TIME of his CONDEMNATION To the DAY of his EXECUTION, OCTOBER 3. 1750. By the REVEREND Dr. ALLEN, Who attended him all that time, to assist him in his PREPARATIONS for ETERNITY. Drawn up and published at the earnest Desire of Mr. MACLAINE himself. The

THIRD EDITION, With the Addition of a LETTER written by Mr. Maclaine to a Friend, the Morning of his Execution. Which did not come to hand time enough to be inserted before' [1750; Printed for J. NOON, in Cheapside: and A. MILLAR in the Strand, LONDON] [Price 6d]. Page 19

Chapter 2 – Suggested Further Reading

In addition to the above:

London Life in the Eighteenth Century George, Mary Dorothy (Routledge/ Thoemmes Press, London, 1925)

A Short History of the Presbyterian Church in Ireland, Barkley, Rev. Professor John M. (The Publications Board, Presbyterian Church in Ireland, Belfast, 1939)

Presbyterians; Their History and Beliefs Lingle, Walter Lee (John Knox Press, Atlanta, 1944)

Reward is Secondary: the life of a political adventurer and an inquiry into the mystery of 'Junius', Maclean, Dr. James Noël MacKenzie (Hodder and Stoughton, London, 1963)

Mid-Georgian London: A Topographical and Social Survey of Central and Western London about 1750, Phillips, Hugh (Collins, London, 1964)

English Society in the Eighteenth Century, Porter, Roy (Allen Lane, London, 1982)

London: The Biography, Ackroyd, Peter (Vintage, London, 2001)

1700: Scenes from London Life, Waller, Maureen (Hodder & Stoughton, London, 2001)

Hanovarian London, 1714–1808, Rudé, George F.E. (Sutton Publishing, Gloucestershire, 2003)

The Life of Rev. Archibald Maclaine DD., Harmens, Dr. A. (Bowdon, Cheshire. Unpublished, April 2004)

CHAPTER 3

"HIGH LIFE" / HIGHWAY ROBBERY

Before we get too deeply engrossed in James Maclaine's escapades in highway robbery it is important to describe the background and expand upon our knowledge of the social scene of mid-18th Century London. In this way we can perceive better the high life to which he aspired and therefore appreciate more what drove him to take up highway robbery against all his better principles. When he stepped out into the world of a Gentleman of Town in 1748 Maclaine found a whole myriad of entertainments and distractions awaiting him; *"bewitching Pleasures,"*[1] he called them. As a gentleman he could spend his days meeting friends in **Coffee Houses** and flirting with ladies as they strolled through **Pleasure Gardens**. The latter might also offer entertainment extending into the evening but, failing that, there would always be **Masquerade Balls** and **Gentlemen's Clubs** at which to party and gamble. Maclaine would go on to use the intelligence he gathered from his Coffee House and Gentlemen's Club conversations to learn who was worth stealing from and what their intended forthcoming travel arrangements might be. He would spend his ill-gotten gains attending Pleasure Gardens and Masquerade Balls vainly attempting to impress a rich heiress sufficiently enough to take a reciprocal interest in his advances.

So what exactly were these cornerstones of Maclaine's "high life" existence? As I describe them here in a little more detail here I should first apologise for the introduction of what must, at first sight, seem like a number of otherwise disconnected characters. The significance of many of them will however become apparent as they re-appear in Maclaine's story later.

Coffee Houses

Pasqua Rosee, a native of the port of Smyrna in Western Turkey, opened the first Coffee House in London at St Michael's Alley off Cornhill in 1652. By 1700 they numbered over 2,000 and had well and truly established themselves as an institution in the social, cultural, commercial and political life of the City. They were a gathering place where, for a penny entry fee, any reasonably dressed man could drink coffee, read the newspapers and enter into conversation with any other patron, provided he obeyed the House Rules. The Rules would be a little different in each establishment, but generally based upon the following, rather clunky, rhyme:

> *Enter Sirs Freely, But first if you please,*
> *Peruse our Civil-Orders, which are these.*
> *First, Gentry, Tradesmen, all are welcome hither,*
> *And may without Affront sit down Together:*
> *Pre-eminence of Place, none here should Mind,*
> *But take the next fit Seat that he can find:*
> *Nor need any, if Finer Persons come,*
> *Rise up for to assigne to them his Room;*
> *To limit Mens Expense, we think not fair,*
> *But let him forfeit Twelve-pence that shall Swear:*

He that shall any Quarrel begin,
Shall give each Man a Dish t'Atone the Sin;
And so shall He, whose Complements extend
So far to drink in COFFEE to his Friend;
Let Noise of loud Disputes be quite forborn,
No Maudlin Lovers here in Corners Mourn,
But all be Brisk, and Talk, but not too much
On Sacred things, Let none presume to touch,
Nor Profane Scripture, or sawcily wrong
Affairs of State with an Irreverent Tongue:
Let Mirth be Innocent, an each Man see,
That all his Jests without Reflection be;
To keep the House more Quiet, and from Blame,
We Banish hence Cards, Dice, and every Game:
Nor can allow of Wagers, that Exceed
Five shillings, which oft-times much Trouble Breed;
Let all that's lost, or forfeited be spent
In such Good Liquor as the House doth Vent,
And Customers endeavor to their Powers,
For to observe still seasonable Howers.
Lastly, let each Man what he calls for Pay,
And so you're welcome to come every Day. [2]

Writing home to his family in Lausanne, Switzerland, the eminent Swiss traveller, César [-François] de Saussure (1705–1783), left us the following comments on the English Coffee House culture of the time:

What attracts enormously in these coffee-houses are the gazettes and other public papers. All Englishmen are great newsmongers.

Workmen habitually begin the day by going to coffee-rooms in order to read the latest news.

A lady will offer five guineas reward for a little lost dog worth five pence. A husband will warn the public not to lend or sell his wife anything on credit. Another husband on the contrary, will be crazy enough to advertise for his beloved better half, who has abandoned him in order to follow her sweetheart, promising a reward to whoever will bring her home... A quack will advertise that he will cure all ailments. A person who has been robbed promises a reward for whoever will help him recover his stolen property. [This becomes important later... see Chapter 5] *Entertainment and spectacles are advertised; also offers of houses, furniture, carriages, horses for sale or on hire, books, pamphlets, etc, and by reading these papers you know of all the gossip and of everything that has been said and done in this big town.* [3]

Each Coffee House would become well-known for the specific interests of its clientele. It is not difficult to spot the present day institutions that sprung up from them:

Coffee House	Location	Specialism	Patrons
Will's	Russell Street, Covent Garden	Poetry, Literacy	Prose writers, playwrights
The St. James's	64 St. James's Street	Foreign and domestic news	Politicians
Lloyd's	16 Lombard Street	Business, maritime trade	Businessmen, insurance underwriters
The Grecian	Devereux Court, The Strand	Learning, sciences etc	Antiquarians
Jonathan's	Exchange Alley	Business, stock trading	Stock-brokers, traders

Apparently the Jockey Club began in 1750 in the Star and Garter Coffee House in Pall Mall before moving to Newmarket.

Pleasure Gardens

The New Spring Gardens at Vauxhall were one of the 18th Century London's most fashionable locations. Situated on the South side of The Thames, not far from Lambeth Palace, the Gardens could only be reached by a sixpenny boat ride [until Westminster Bridge was completed at the close of 1750] from Whitehall or the 'Westminster Stairs'. The Gardens had been transformed and were re-launched on Wednesday 7 June 1732 by Jonathan Tyers (1702–1767); one of London's greatest 18th Century entrepreneurs. Working alongside William Hogarth (1697–1764); the great 18th Century artist, painter, engraver, political satirist and editorial cartoonist; famous for his unique combination of horror and humour; and much loved critic of public moralism (see Chapters 6 and 7), Tyers had completely remodelled the original gardens on the site by adding assembly rooms, music rooms, supper-boxes, ruins, arches, statues, a Chinese Pavilion and over a thousand oil-fired lamp lights. To add to the growing popularity of the venue, he commissioned a sculpture in 1738 of the composer Handel by the famous French sculptor Louise Francois Roubiliac (1702–1762). The well-known English artist Francis Hayman (1708–1776), working alongside Hogarth, painted the supper-boxes and many other scenes on the various walls with the assembly / music rooms. For a shilling entry fee one could mix on an equal standing with royal dukes, aristocrats and wealthy landowners. Frederick Lewis (1707–1751), Prince of Wales and Duke of Cornwall / Lord of the Manor of Kennington in which the gardens stood, son of George II and father of George [William Frederick] III (1738–1820), was an enthusiastic patron and regular visitor.

A Perspective View of the Grand Walk in Vauxhall Gardens and the Orchestra.

Illustration (vii) 'A Perspective View of the Grand Walk in Vauxhall Gardens and the Orchestra' (c.1750) — Anonymous

Vauxhall Gardens was famous for its orchestral music, popular singing performers, lights, masquerades and firework displays. The Gentleman's Magazine for Friday 21 April 1749 carried the following report on the first and last aspects:

Was performed at Vauxhall Gardens the rehearsal of the music for the fireworks [Handel's 'Music for the Royal Fireworks' to be performed later in the year at St. James's Park, complete with fireworks], *by a band of 100 musicians, to an audience above 12,000 persons (tickets 2s 6d). So great a resort occasioned such a stoppage on London Bridge* [then the only bridge over The

Thames below Kingston], *that no carriage could pass for three hours. The footmen were so numerous as to obstruct the passage, so that a scuffle happened, in which some gentlemen were wounded.*

The Gentleman's Magazine, 21 April 1749 [4]

Maclaine would no doubt have attended the above event if he had not been in Holland, lying low, at the time (see Chapter 4). The Gentleman's Magazine was founded by printer, Edward Cave (1691–1754), in January 1731 and ran on a monthly basis, uninterrupted until 1922. The magazine provided Dr Samuel Johnson, whom we met in The Hebrides in Chapter 1, with his first employment as a writer.

The following record of a visit to Vauxhall Gardens gives us an excellent description of an evening spent there with friends. It is written by Horatio (Horace) Walpole, (eventual) 4th Earl of Orford, (1717–1797), youngest son of the man who was regarded as Britain's first and longest-serving Prime Minister, Robert Walpole (1676–1745). Horace Walpole, see Illustration (viii), was a very famous and well connected English letter writer, antiquarian and gossip. His *'Memoirs of the reign of George II'* and his vast correspondence provide us with a vivid and witty commentary on 18th Century living. Born in London, he was educated at both Eton and Cambridge. On completion of his education he took a "Grand Tour" of the Continent with the English poet, Thomas Gray (1716–1771), with whom he is suspected to have had a homosexual affair, before entering parliament in 1741. In 1747 he bought a house near Twickenham which over the course of the remainder of his life he transformed into a neo-Gothic "castle" called 'Strawberry Hill' (which featured in the BBC's 'Restoration' television series in 2004). Here he had a collection of art and a private printing press where he published the works of Gray, amongst others. He is probably best known for writing the first Gothic novel: 'The Castle of Otranto' in 1764. On the trip to Vauxhall, Walpole was in the company of *"the* [2nd] *Duke of Kingston* [upon-Hull; Evelyn Pierreport (1711–1773)], *Lord March* [William Douglas (1725–1810), 3rd Earl March, 4th Duke of Queensbury], *Mr. Whitehead* [William Whitehead (1715–1785), who went on to become the Poet Laureate to his Majesty the King in 1757 after Thomas Gray refused the honour], *a pretty Miss Beauclerc, and a very foolish Miss Sparre."* [5]

Lady Caroline [Petersham] *and the little Ashe*, or the Pollard Ashe as they call her; they had just finished their last layer of red, and looked as handsome as crimson could make them.. We marched our barge, with a boat of French horns attending and little Ashe singing. We paraded some time up the river, and at last debarked at Vauxhall... Here we picked up Lord Granby* [John Manners (1721–1770), Marquess of Granby], *arrived very drunk from Jenny's Whim* [a tavern and tea garden at Ebury Bridge, Chelsea]. *At last we assembled in our booth, Lady Caroline in the front, with the vizor of her hat erect, and looking gloriously jolly and handsome. She had fetched my brother Orford* [Robert Walpole (1701–1751), 2nd Earl of Orford] *from the next booth, where he was enjoying himself with his petite partie, to help us mince chickens. We minced seven chickens into a China dish, which Lady Caroline stewed over a lamp with three pats of butter and a flagon of water, stirring and rattling and laughing, and we every minute expecting the dish to fly about our ears. She had bought Betty*

[Elizabeth Neale (−1797), a well-known fruitier with a shop in St. James's Street] *the fruit girl, with hampers of strawberries and cherries from Roger's and made her wait upon us, and then made her sup by us at a little table.. In short, the whole air of our party was sufficient, as you will easily imagine, to take up the whole attention of the Garden; so much so, that from 11 o'clock till half an hour after one we had the whole concourse round our booth; at least, they came into the little gardens of each booth on the sides of ours, till Harry Vane* [Henry Vane (1726–1792), 1ˢᵗ Earl of Darlington] *took up a bumper and drank their healths, and was proceeding to treat them with still greater freedom. It was 3 o'clock before we got home.*

    Horace Walpole, 23 June 1750 [6]

    *little Ashe was Miss Elizabeth Ashe (1731–   ). It was an "open secret" that she was the illegitimate daughter of Princess Amelia Sophia (1711–1786); second daughter of King George II.

Illustration (viii) — 'Horace Walpole, Youngest Son of Sir Robert Walpole
Earl of Orford'. (1757) — James McArdell (1729–1765)

Ranelagh Gardens in Chelsea were so called as they occupied the site of a house built by the Richard Jones (1641–1712), 1st Earl of Ranelagh. They were opened in 1742 having been purchased and re-modelled by a syndicate led by Sir Thomas Robinson (1703–1777) M.P. and the proprietors of the Theatre Royal in Drury Lane. They built a stunning centrepiece, a 120 foot diameter rotunda, designed by William Jones (–1757), a surveyor to the East India Company. The central support of the rotunda incorporated a huge chimney and fireplaces. The young Wolfgang Amadeus Mozart (1756–1791), the child protégé and most enduringly popular of all the great composers, who was actually baptised as Joannes Chrysostomus Wolfgangus Theophiles Mozart, performed there in 1765. They also added an ornamental lake, a canal with gondolas, as well as a central bandstand. The entrance fee to the Gardens was set at 2 shillings and 6 pence, over twice as much as at Vauxhall; however Horace Walpole was still mightily impressed, as can be seen from his comments in the following letter to his friend Henry Seymour Conway (1721–1795), a distinguished politician, diplomat and soldier who became a Field Marshall in 1759:

Every night constantly I go to Ranelagh; which has totally beat Vauxhall. Nobody goes anywhere else – everybody goes there. My Lord Chesterfield [Philip Dormer Stanhope (1694–1773), 4th Earl of Chesterfield] *is so fond of it that he says he has ordered all his letters to be directed thither. If you had never seen it, I would make you a most pompous description of it, and tell you how the floor is all of beaten princes--- that you can't set your foot without treading on a Prince, or Duke of Cumberland.*
Horace Walpole, 29 June 1744 [7]

The Duke of Cumberland who frequented Ranelagh Gardens was William Augustus (1721–1765), third son of King George II. Having been on the losing side at Fontenoy (see Chapter 2) in 1745, he returned to England to lead the defence of his father's kingdom against the Jacobite uprising of 1745. After his victory at the Battle of Culloden (see Chapter 1), when asked for his orders in relation to dealing with the fleeing / surviving Scots, he apparently wrote "No Quarter" on the back of a playing card (the nine of Diamonds; still known as 'The Curse of Scotland'). He soon became known as 'The Butcher' for his merciless treatment of the defeated Scots. Whilst the English were happy to name a flower 'Sweet William' to mark his victory, the Scottish Nation would quickly re-Christen it 'Stinking Billy'.

Illustration (ix) — A view of the canal, Chinese Building, Rotunda etc., in Ranelagh Gardens, with the Masquerade' (1750) — Giovanni Antonio Canaletto (1697–1968); engraved by Charles Grignion (1714 – 1810)

Masquerade Balls

Masquerade Balls were the 18th Century equivalent of a fancy dress party / night club event. Johann Jacob Heidegger (1688–1749), a Swiss Count who came to London in 1708, is generally credited for having introduced the Venetian fashion of holding masquerades to England. In 1710 he held the first at Haymarket Opera House. By the late 1740s masquerades were very popular up and down the country, especially in London at such venues as Vauxhall and Ranelagh Pleasure Gardens (see above). From behind their masks, those attending such a ball would enjoy drinking, dancing and gambling and particularly mixing with everyone else from different class backgrounds, only revealing their true identities at the end of the night. Apart from observing a few formalities governing the preliminaries for engaging fellow revellers in conversation, it appears that pretty much "anything would go" at a masquerade. This would include some of the most outrageous behaviour that could never be dreamt of getting away with in everyday life. Attendees would hire their costumes for the night, the most popular of which was a plain, hooded garment called a 'domino'. The more flamboyant might hire a typical fancy dress item such as a Harlequin Clown or dress as a mythological figure such as a Greek or Roman god or goddess. Along with attending the theatre and listening to concerts or parading at Pleasure Gardens, masquerades were one of the most popular forms of 18th Century entertainment.

Gentlemen's Clubs

Maclaine attended White's Gentlemen's Club. Francis White's started its existence as a Chocolate House in 1698 at 4 Chesterfield Street; the owner was an Italian immigrant by the original name of Francesco Bianco. It became the first private Gentlemen's Club in London in 1736, hence from its members had to be elected. By 1745 it had become very popular, with so many gentlemen clamouring to obtain membership that it decided to split into two clubs (the 'Old' and the 'Young') under the same roof at 37–38 St. James's Street. James Maclaine would have undoubtedly joined the latter. As well as being excellent places to relax, socialise and supper, the 18th Century Gentlemen's Clubs, such as White's (1736; 37–38 St. James's Street), Boodle's (1762; 28 St. James's Street), Almack's (1764; Pall Mall) and Brooke's (1778; 60 St. James's Street) were all very much Gaming Clubs where the clientele would play games such as Hazard, Faro and Whist; sometimes for very large sums of money. White's Club had a very poor reputation for gambling and many young gentlemen managed to lose their entire family fortunes in a single evening. Lord George Lyttelton (1709–1773), 1st Baron Lyttelton; a British politician, statesman and patron of the arts, writing to Dr Philip Doddridge (1702–1751), a noted theologian and English Nonconformist leader in 1750, made the following remark:

> *The Dryads* [tree dwelling nymphs bringing good fortune] *of *Hogley are at present pretty secure, but I tremble to think that the rattling dice-box at White's may one day or other (if my son should be a member of that academy) shake down our fine oaks. It is dreadful to see, not only there, but almost in every house in the town, what devastations are made by* [that] *destructive fury, the spirit of play.* [8]

*Now better known as Hagley Hall; a new mansion was created by Lord Lyttleton in Hagley, Worcestershire, between 1754 and 1760.

Having had access to study the betting book at White's, Horace Walpole wrote several passages on the subject in his letters. One such passage is as follows:

At White's they betted on every possible thing, as shown by the betting-book of the establishment – on births, deaths and marriages; the length of life; the duration of a ministry, a placeman's [one who has a political appointment in the government] *prospect of a coronet; the last scandal at Ranelagh or Madame Cornely's*; or the shock of an earthquake. A man dropped down at the door of White's; he was carried into the house. Was he dead or not? The odds were immediately given and taken for and against. It was proposed to bleed him. Those who had taken the odds that the man was dead protested that the use of the lancet would affect the fairness of the bet.* [9]

*Walpole must have made this note much later as Madame Cornely was Teresa Cornely (1723–1797), a German or Venetian born opera singer who is generally credited with opening the first Night Club in London in 1763 at Carlisle House, Soho Square, where she regularly held masquerade balls.

Picking up from where we left off at the end of Chapter 2; with his wife buried and his girl(s) in the care of his mother-in-law, Maclaine again found himself at a crossroad in his life. At this time he engaged in conversation with a needy neighbour, a fellow Irishman by the name of William Plunket (1725–1791), an apothecary [chemist] by trade, whose business in London had recently failed. These two had come to know one another well as Plunket had attended to Maclaine's wife during her illness. They may have also been acquainted back in Ireland, as it transpires later that Plunket came from the small village of Glennan, within the Parish of Donagh, in County Monaghan, a few miles from Monaghan where Maclaine was brought up.

Knowing some of Maclaine's past and guessing his future intentions, Plunket spoke candidly to his friend: *"Honey"*, he said, *"Tho' he had lost a good Wife, yet, as she was gone, it was no Purpose to grieve much about the Matter, since it might in the End turn out the most lucky Incident in his Life, for it would allow him to go Snips with him in the Future;"* he would, *"help him to a Woman, worth at least ten thousand Pounds in her own Possession."*[10]

It was these words that gelled so firmly in Maclaine's mind. Once again he became quickly obsessed with the idea of *"getting suddenly rich, by marrying a Fortune,"*[11] as he had always considered himself entitled to *"by the speciousness of his behaviour, the gracefulness of his person, and the elegance of his appearance."*[12] With Plunket's help, fulfilling the role of his Master's footman, he could pose as the super-rich 'Squire Maclaine'. What Lady could possibly fail to fall for his considerable charms?

The two men set about putting Maclaine's £85 to best effect and invested in their new images. Maclaine dressed himself *"in lac'd Cloaths, and a Hat and Feather."*[13] This alone was a serious investment in its own right as the finest clothes in 1748 were about ten times as expensive as they are now. He sold his shop in Welbeck Street and moved to the more upmarket Dean Street, Soho Square, where he hired apartments at 15 shillings a week. There *"his morning dress was a crimson damask* [silk from

Damascus] *banyan* [a sort of 18th Century dressing gown, influenced by Persian/Asian clothing styles], *a silk-shag* [course, rough-woven silk] *waistcoat trimmed with lace, black velvet breeches, white stockings and yellow Morocco slippers.* "[14] He was often seen in this neighbourhood, visiting Coffee Houses (see above) and travelling in chaises, the 18th Century equivalent of a Hackney cab.

It is hard to make comparisons between the value of money today and that of money back in the mid-18th Century. According to the National Archives' "ready-reckoner" £1,000 in 1750 would equate to approximately £85,000 today. In 1750 wages for a skilled worker such as tailor or carpenter were in the order of 20 shillings a week or £50 per annum. A coach driver could earn maybe £12 per annum and a footman £8 whilst a decent grade housekeeper could earn between £20 and £30. Purchasing power was also quite different in 1750; one penny would buy a loaf of bread or provide enough gin to get drunk on; threepence would buy a dinner of bread, cheese and beer and fourpence would afford you a boat ride across The Thames.

To distance himself from his mother-in-law Maclaine relocated his lodgings from Dean Street to Downs Street, near Hyde Park Corner; just a stone's throw from where Plunket was stabling their horses. From their new base the two travelled far and wide to all the fashionable assemblies they could find, both in the capital and beyond. They went as far as Bath in Somerset to Tunbridge Wells in Kent; always on the lookout for a rich heiress. They spent many evenings visiting the Vauxhall and Ranelagh Pleasure Gardens (see above) and other such expensive places. Initially they were quite encouraged by their seeming success; Maclaine at some point apparently even coming near to becoming engaged to the younger sister of the Duke of Newcastle, Thomas Pelham-Holles (1693–1768), Leader of the House of Lords from 1744 to 1756 and thereafter Prime Minister until 1762, and stepsister of the then Prime Minister, Henry Pelham (1696–1754).

On another occasion the pair put high hopes and sustained effort into a certain young lady who was not only very beautiful but thoroughly loaded. They invested their capital and bribed their way into the confidences of her waiting-maid, her milliner and her haircutter, and followed her to Kilbourne Wells, another Pleasure Garden at modern-day Kilburn, just to the Northwest of London. The scene was set: Squire Maclaine was *"passing for a Man of Fortune, and in every Part of his Dress and Equipage appeared as such. Plunket acted his Footman."[15]* As they locked onto their target with *"the 'Squire himself was dancing, and 'ogling himself into the good Graces of the young Lady,"[16]* Maclaine unfortunately took that moment to take *"some Liberties at the Wells with an Apothecary, whose Quarrel was taken up by half-pay Officer, who kicked our Adventurer out of Company, and carried his Resentment so far, as to say publickly, that he knew the Rascal a footman but a few Years ago."[17]* The whole assemblage stopped dancing and stood in shock as the argument between Maclaine and his accuser unfolded. Eventually *"the 'Squire, and his Footman Plunket, was obliged to decamp without the Ceremony of taking Leave of their Friends."[18]*

This failed excursion had the effect of bringing the new partnership to its financial knees. When the two got back to London they found that they had just 5 guineas [a guinea in 1750 was a gold coin worth 21 shillings] left between them which in no way could support them in their current grandeur. They also had the fear of being the talk amongst the gossips of the town following their recent embarrassment. With Squire Maclaine's reputation shot to pieces, he just wanted to get away from London and resolved once more that he should sail to Jamaica where he felt he would have a chance to put his accountancy skills into practice to support himself, whilst he romanced the plantation owners' daughters and widows. A stroke of luck brought about a chance meeting with a friend and fellow countryman of his, who had also been familiar with Maclaine's fortune-hunting schemes. When he heard how Maclaine had so cruelly suffered with his latest disappointment he offered to discuss his predicament with some more of his own friends, some of whom were also acquainted with Maclaine's brother. When he came back it was with 60 guineas that had been raised between them to fit their worthy friend out for Jamaica and he gave Maclaine the money in good faith. To top it off he also managed to procure him *"Letters of Recommendation from some Merchant of Note to their Correspondents in that Island."*[19] Perhaps this was the "odious" Lauchlan Macleane whom we met in Chapter 2?

Maclaine paid part of the money for his passage in advance and procured some clothing fit for the climate of the West Indies. With a few weeks to go before the ship was due to sail, he found himself with time on his hands. At some point in time during this period *"he was tempted to go to a Masquerade, to take Leave, he said, for the last Time of the bewitching Pleasures of London."*[20] As Maclaine soaked up the atmosphere, *"the noise of the Gamesters drew his attention to Gambling-Table, where the quick Transition of large Sums from one Hand to another awaken'd his Avarice, and lull'd his Prudence asleep."*[21] As he had his stock with him in his pocket he felt comfortable trying his luck with some of it. Within half an hour he was up 100 guineas and feeling on top of the world. He broke off from the tables at that point to protect his winnings but, *"after taking a Turn or two round the Room, he again returned, and* [with]*in a few Minutes was stripped to his last Guinea."*[22]

Sick to his stomach after losing such an immense sum at the table, Maclaine was completely beside himself. Of all the disappointments that had befallen him in his time, this by far, hurt the most. Not only had he been so foolish to let himself down, but he had betrayed all those friends who had put their faith and trust in him. After this disaster he did not have the courage to show his face. In this sorry state he sent for Plunket to discuss his predicament and if possible raise his spirits, *"and from this Moment his Ruin commenced; for that Wretch, who had lived all his Lifetime on the Sharp, had no Notions of Honour, and a Stranger to all Ties or Principles of Religion or Honesty, took the Opportunity, when his Friend was agitated almost to Despair, to propose at first, by distant Hints, and at last in plain English, going upon the Highway for a Recruit."*[23] Maclaine must have passed on the actual words Plunket had used on that occasion, when he recalled them later (at a time when he was in an even sorrier state) to the Chaplin of Newgate: *"I thought Maclane* [sic] *had spirit and resolution, with some knowledge of the world. A brave man cannot want. He has a right to live, and need not want the conveniences of life. While the dull, plodding, busy knaves carry cash in their pockets, we must draw upon them to supply our wants. Only impudence is necessary, and the getting the better of a few idle scruples. Courage is scarcely necessary, for all we have to deal with are mere poltroons."*[24]

Initially horrified at the mere mention of highway robbery, Maclaine remained engaged in conversation with Plunket while they considered the pros and particularly the cons of the proposition. Some of their thought processes may have covered the following matters:

- There was no organised police force in 1748. Although there were thief-takers, night watchmen and wardens who might at any stage pop up and capture a highwayman, they were not organised in any meaningful way. Despite what was occurring in other European countries at the time, the British Government saw the establishment of a police force as an affront to civil liberties and something to be resisted.
- Turnpikes, which were spiked gates that shut off sections of roads for the purposes of raising taxes to fund improvements, were increasing on all the major routes in and out of London and highwaymen were being frequently trapped by the operators and / or their pursuers.
- In that time there were hundreds of crimes carrying the death penalty, but universally to be caught and found guilty of any sort of crime against property, no matter how small, for instance stealing any goods worth 5 shillings or more, would lead to a certain death sentence. Several Acts of Parliament such as the Highwayman Act of 1662 and the Waltham Black Act of 1723 had combined to add hundreds of crimes carrying the death penalty to the already full Statute Books. These were just part of what was to become later known as 'The Bloody Code' under which the ruling, property-owning classes of the 18th Century, attempted to control the mass population and ensure that any crime committed against property was dealt with in the severest manner. The intention behind the Acts and their application was always to deter others and to ensure the people obeyed the laws, or else!

- The updated Highwayman Act of 1693 aimed to pit highwayman against highwayman as it offered a reward of £40 and an amnesty to any accomplice who was prepared to impeach two or more of his confederates, leading to their convictions.
- Gibbets were hung on posts in areas associated with the crime of highway robbery and would contain the rotting corpses of those who had not escaped the rigours of the Law; thus reinforcing the message of intolerance.
- Maclaine, with his religious upbringing, would have dreaded the thought of bringing shame and dishonour upon his family and of betraying the Laws of God.

Perhaps "the clincher" would have come when Plunket suggested that if they were fortunate enough to get a speedy result, then Maclaine's friends might never find out he had gambled with and lost their money; he could surely still catch his ship and save himself from their utter contempt? Whatever, *'at length the pair entered into a solemn agreement to abide by each other in all adventures, and to share the profit of their depredations to the last shilling.'*[25] Whether Maclaine believed it was to be a "one off" event or if he knew it would lead to more robberies is unknown. However, we have now reached the point where it is necessary to temporarily break off from Maclaine's predicament and properly introduce the subject of **Highway Robbery**; remind ourselves of the appalling state of the late 17th/ early 18th Century **King's Highway** i.e. the scene of such crimes, and take a look at some of history's most celebrated **Highwaymen**. We can then return to examine Plunket's and Maclaine's highway exploits in more detail.

Highway Robbery

Highway robbery flourished in England between 1650 and 1800. César de Saussure, the Swiss traveller whom we met earlier in the Coffee Houses of London, left us the following contemporary description of highway robbery, in another of his letters home:

Highwaymen are generally well mounted; one of them will stop a coach containing six or seven travellers. With one hand he will present a pistol, with the other his hat, asking the unfortunate passengers most politely for their purses or their lives. No one caring to run the risk of being killed or maimed, a share of every traveller's money is thrown into the hat, for were one to make the slightest attempt at self-defence the ruffian would turn bridle and fly, but not before attempting to revenge himself by killing you. If, on the contrary, he receives a reasonable contribution, he retires without doing you any injury. When there are several highwaymen together, they will search you thoroughly and leave nothing. Again, others take only a part of what they find; but all these robbers ill-treat only those who try to defend themselves. I have been told that some highwaymen are quite polite and generous, begging to be excused for being forced to rob, and leaving passengers the wherewithal to continue their journey. All highwaymen that are caught are hanged without mercy. [26]

King's Highway

There would have been no highway robbery without a King's Highway on which to practice it. Whilst highway robbery was able to flourish on the appalling, badly maintained roads of the 17th Century the introduction of turnpikes at the beginning of the

18th Century was making some huge strides towards their improvement. Daniel Defoe (1660–1731), the famous English writer, journalist and spy, whose most popular novels were 'Robinson Crusoe' (1719) and 'Moll Flanders' (1722), wrote several passages about the turnpikes in his 1727 publication 'A Tour thro' the Whole Island of Great Britain' [Published in 1727]; below are two such passages:

> *The great Road from London…towards Ipswich and Harwich, is the most worn with Waggons, Carts and Carriages; and with infinite Droves of Black Cattle, Hogs and Sheep of any Road in England…These Roads were formerly deeply rutted, in times of flood dangerous, and at other times in Winter scarce passable, they are now so firm, so safe, so easy to Travellers, and Carriages as well as Cattle…This was first done by the help of a Turn-pike, set up by Act of Parliament, about the year 1697…* [27]
>
> *Turn-pikes or Toll-bars have been set up on the several great Roads of England, beginning at London, and proceeding thro' almost all those dirty deep Roads, in the Midland Counties especially; at which Turn-pikes all Carriages, Droves of Cattle, and Travellers on Horseback, are oblig'd to pay an easy Toll; that is to say, a Horse a Penny, a Coach three Pence, a Cart four Pence, at some six Pence to eight Pence, a Waggon six Pence, in some a Shilling, and the like; Cattle pay by the Score, or by the Head, in some Places more, in some less; but in no Place is it thought a Burthen that ever I met with, the Benefit of a good Road abundantly making amends for that little Charge the Travellers are put to at the Turn-pikes.* [28]

In 1736, writing from his home in Kensington, Lord Hervey (1696–1743), 2nd Baron Hervey; the famous English courtier

(Vice-Chamberlain of the Household for the year 1750), political writer and memoirist, had this to say about the condition of the roads:

The road between this place [Kensington] *and London is grown so infamously bad that we live here in the same solitude as we should do if cast on a rock in the middle of the ocean; and all Londoners tell us there is between them and us a great impassable gulf of mud.* [29]

Also in 1736 Robert Phillips produced his 'Dissertation Concerning the Present State of the High Roads in England, Especially those near London' in which he described the wretched conditions of the roads as follows:

In Summer the roads are suffocated and smothered with dust; and towards the Winter, between wet and dry, there are deep ruts full of water with hard ridges, which make it difficult for passengers to cross by one another without overturning; and in Winter they are all mud. [30]

Highwaymen

Unlike their counterparts in Europe, the mass population regarded the English highwaymen as heroes as they were seen to rob the rich and openly defy the oppressive authorities; this at a time when any theft of property would lead to the culprit's certain death, if caught. Stories of their daring robberies, as we shall shortly see, were highly popular with the English lower classes. Highwaymen were seen as the gentlemen amongst thieves, being a class apart (see Chapters 6 and 7) from the lowly regarded street robbers or "footpads", who were far more numerous in the almost completely unpoliced society.

Two more prominent foreign travellers left us their descriptions of Highwaymen in the "the Golden Age" of such robbers i.e. the 18th Century.

The first was Jean-Bernard le Blanc [a.k.a. Abbé le Blanc] (1701–1781), a famous French antiquarian and man of the church who often wrote of the differences between the English and the French ways of life. On his travels through England in 1737 he wrote the following passage on how highwaymen were perceived by those Englishmen he met:

> *...who were not less vain in boasting of the success of their highwaymen than of the bravery of their troops. Tales of their address, their cunning, or their generosity, were in the mouths of everybody, and a noted thief was a kind of hero in high repute.* [31]

The second, Johann Wilhelm von Archenholz (1741–1812), a Prussian historian and publicist, made the following observations on English highwaymen:

> *...generally very polite; they assure you they are very sorry that poverty has driven them to that shameful recourse, and end by demanding your purse in the most courteous manner.* [32]

Writing in hindsight in the 19th Century two famous Englishmen gave us the benefit of their wisdom by identifying the attributes that would have combined to produce successful exponents of this form of crime. The first was Thomas de

Quincey (1785–1859), the famous opium-eating English author and intellectual, who wrote that they:

> ...*required more accomplishments than either the bar or the pulpit, since it presumed a bountiful endowment of qualifications: strength, health, agility, and excellent horsemanship...The finest men in England, physically speaking, throughout the last century, the very noblest specimen of man, considered as an animal, were the mounted robbers who cultivated their profession on the great roads. When every traveller carried firearms the mounted robber lived in an element of danger and adventurous gallantry.* [33]

The second, [Lord] Thomas Babington Macaulay (1800–1859), 1st Baron Macaulay, whose 'History of England from the accession of James II' (Published in 1848 and 1855) contained the following description of what was required to make a successful highwayman:

> *It was necessary to the success and even to the safety of the highwayman that he should be a bold and skilful rider, and that his manners and appearance should be such as suited the master of a fine horse. He therefore held an aristocratical position in the community of thieves, appeared at fashionable coffee houses and gaming houses, and betted with men of quality on the race ground. Sometimes, indeed, he was a man of good family and education. A romantic interest, therefore, attached and perhaps still attaches, to the names of freebooters of this class. The vulgar eagerly drank in tales of their ferocity and audacity, of their occasional acts of generosity and good nature, of their amours, of their miraculous escapes, and of their manly bearing at the bar and in the cart.* [34]

The following ten highwaymen are the most notorious of all such protagonists:

• Captain James Hind [a.k.a. James Brown] (1616–1652) –'The Highwayman Adventurer' – Born in Chipping-Norton, Oxfordshire, Hind was first apprenticed to a butcher, before running away to London, where he very quickly, due to his association with a prostitute pick-pocket, found himself locked up in the Poultry Compter. There he met one Thomas ('Tom') Allen, a practiced highwayman, who took him under his wing and to Shooter's Hill to start him in a different profession. The two had some successes before they attempted to rob Oliver Cromwell (1599–1658) [the infamous English military and political leader who overthrew the monarchy and set England up as a republican Commonwealth (with himself as Lord Protector of England, Scotland and Ireland) for the years 1653 to 1658] whom they despised over the latter's treatment of King Charles I. Cromwell was well guarded and in the skirmish Tom Allen was taken and soon after executed. Hind escaped and apparently rode his horse so hard in the process that it collapsed and died under him.

From that moment he worked the roads alone and built a reputation for only robbing regicides (or republican supporters), many of whom he would lecture on the error of their ways, and sparing any royalists. On one occasion he shot through the head a man by the name of George Sympson whom he mistakenly thought was pursuing him and so, wanted for murder as well as robbery with violence, he resolved to hide himself away in the vast metropolis of London. He lodged under the assumed name of James Brown with a barber, who owned a shop beside St.

Dunstan's Church in Fleet Street, but was given away by a close friend. Having been tried for robbery and acquitted at the Old Bailey due to lack of evidence he was transferred from Newgate to Reading Jail to face the charge of murder. There he was found guilty but spared due to the coincidental timing of the passing of an Act of Oblivion providing an amnesty against all previous crimes bar those against the State.

Hind was finally transferred to Worcester Jail and tried for high treason. He was condemned and hanged, drawn and quartered, with his head being set upon Bridge Gate above the River Severn, as it passes through Worcester.

- John Cottington (1614–1655) – "Mull Sack" – Born in Cheapside, London, and the youngest of 19 children, Cottington was apprenticed to a chimney sweep from a young age. He later frequented 'The Devil's Tavern' in Fleet Street, opposite St. Dunstan's Church where he is said to fallen in love with and soon married what turned out to be a famed hermaphrodite by the name of Aniseed Robin. Cottington was known for only drinking sack, a Spanish wine so strong and rough that it needed to be sweetened by mixing with spice and at the same time mulled or warmed up; hence his nickname of "Mull Sack". He first thrived as a pickpocket before progressing to highway robbery and was probably one of the most successful highwaymen from the 17th Century. He achieved some large sums and some well-known victims and was known for the audacious and ingenious methods he employed in his robberies. He held up Oliver Cromwell and, after fleeing England on account of shooting dead his mistress's husband, he added the name of none other than King Charles II to his list of conquests, whilst the latter was in exile in Cologne.

- Claude Duval (1643–1670) – "The Gallant Highwayman" – Born in Domfront, in Normandy, France, Duval began his working life as a footman and travelled to England shortly after the Restoration of King Charles II. He quickly took to highway robbery, as the easiest method of supplying the funding needed for his gambling, whoring and drinking. By 1666 he was so notorious for his robberies in the Holloway, Islington and Highgate areas that his was the first name listed in a Proclamation identifying England's most wanted highwaymen.

Duval's most famous exploit involved robbing a Lord and his Lady with his gang on Hounslow Heath. He well knew the Lord was carrying £400 with him, but before relieving him of any of it he took time out to dance a coranto (or courant) with the Lady whilst one of his comrades played a flageolet [a 17th Century flute] to accompany them. When Duval asked his Lordship to pay for the music, the latter handed him only £100 so he told the Lord he could keep the remaining £300 that he was certain was secreted in the coach on the basis that the £100, given so generously, was worth ten times that sum taken by force. He had made his point and from that moment on he was the hero of every lady in England.

At one point Duval returned to France (to Paris) to escape his pursuers. Not long after his return he was taken, quite drunk, at 'Mother Maberley's Inn', at 'The Hole In The Wall' in Chandos Street [just to the North of Cavendish Square and immediately to the West of the present Langham Hotel] in London. An abundance of ladies tried to get him pardoned, as did the King, but the latter gave in when his Judge, Sir William Morton (1605–1672), threatened to resign. After his execution his body was carried to 'The Tangier Tavern' in St. Giles and laid in state, where hundreds of people, particularly ladies, came to see it. In his pocket was discovered a "dying speech" he had intended on delivering, but for some reason had not. It was very much "a thank you" to his female following and an extract is as follows:

It does not, however, grieve me that your intercession for me proved ineffectual; for now I shall die with a healthful body, and, I hope, a prepared mind. My confessor has shown me the evil of my ways, and wrought in me a true repentance. Whereas, had you prevailed for my life, I must in gratitude have devoted it to your service, which would certainly have made it very short, for had you been sound, I should have died of a consumption; if otherwise, of a pox. [35]

Duval was buried under the central aisle of St. Paul's Church in Covent Garden with the following inscription engraved on a white marble slab over him, as an epitaph:

Here lies Du Vall, Reader, if male thou art,
Look to thy purse. If female, to thy heart.
Much havoc has he made to both; for all
Men he made to stand, and women he made to fall.
The second Conqueror of the Norman race,
Knights to his arm did yield, and ladies to his face.
Old Tyburn's glory; England's illustrious Thief,
Du Vall, the ladies' joy; Du Vall, the ladies' grief. [36]

• William [a.k.a. John] Nevison (1639–1684) – "Swift Nicks" / "The Yorkshire Highwayman" – Born at Promfret in Yorkshire [other sources say Wortley, near Sheffield], Nevison ran away from home at a young age having stolen cash and a horse from his father. Arriving just outside London he cut the horse's throat, lest it gave rise to his discovery. He found work as an apprentice to a brewer, of whom he eventually robbed £200 and fled to Holland. He joined the Army and rose to the rank of Lieutenant-General before coming back to England 'and bought himself a horse and arms, and resolved for the road, and perhaps a pleasant life, at hazard of his neck, rather than toil out a long remainder of unhappy days in want and poverty which he was always averse to'.

Nevison was captured several times and always managed to escape, sometimes by the most audacious manner. On one particular occasion he got a friend to paint blue spots over his face and body, convincing his jailers that he had caught the plague, and pretended to be dead until they allowed him to be removed in a coffin.

Daniel Defoe (see above) in his 1727 publication 'A Tour thro' the Whole Island of Great Britain', was responsible for recording the event that makes Nevison remembered to this day. It relates to how Nevison literally went "out of his way" to create an alibi after committing a robbery where he was convinced his victim had recognised him:

At 4 am one summer morning in 1676, a traveller at Gads Hill in Kent, England was robbed by John Nevison. The highwayman then made his escape on a bay mare, crossed the River Thames by ferry and galloped towards Chelmsford [in Essex]. *After resting his horse for half an hour, he rode on to Cambridge and Huntingdon, resting regularly for short periods during the journey. Eventually, he found his way to the Great North Road where he turned north for York.*

He arrived in York at sunset after a journey of more than 200 miles, a stunning achievement for both man and horse. He stabled his weary horse at a York inn, washed and changed his travel-stained clothes, then strolled to a bowling green where he knew the Lord Mayor was playing bowls. He engaged the Lord Mayor in a conversation and then laid a bet on the outcome of the match – and Nevison made sure the Lord Mayor remembered the time the bet was laid – 8 pm that evening.

Later, Nevison was arrested for the robbery in Gads Hill and in his defence, produced the Lord Mayor of York as his alibi witness. The Lord Mayor could prove Nevison was in York at 8pm on the day of the robbery and the court refused to believe that a man would have committed a robbery at that time in Kent and ridden to York by 8 pm the same day. He was found not guilty of that crime and emerged as a folk hero, even impressing the King of England*. [37]

*Nevison apparently enjoyed recounting this tale to King Charles II in person. When he told him that "Old Nick" [The Devil] could not have made the journey any faster, the King promptly nicknamed him "Swift Nicks".

Nevison had a reputation for being charming and polite, whether robbing alone or in a gang of up to six confederates; and always charitable to the poor. His one blemish came when he shot dead a constable who tried to arrest him. Not long after one Captain Hardcastle and a group of bounty-hunters ("thief takers"), tipped off by his landlady for the reward money, captured him whilst he was drinking at 'The Magpie (or The

Plough) Inn' at Sandal, near Wakefield, swiftly removing him to York Jail for what turned out to be his last visit there.

•	William Davis (1627–1690) – "The Golden Farmer" – Born in Wrexham, in Denbighshire, North Wales, Davis moved at a young age to Salisbury, in Gloucestershire. Here he followed the life of a regular farmer and never raised suspicions about his extra curricula activities even though he got his nickname for always paying his debts in gold pieces. He robbed alone on the Salisbury Road and was once recorded as letting off a tirade of foul abuse at one of his lady victims, a Quaker, who had not complied with his instructions to hand over her valuables as her other female travelling companions had. His carefully chosen words were recorded for posterity as follows: *"You canting bitch! If you dally with me at this rate, you'll certainly provoke my spirit to be damnably rude with you. You see these good women here were so tender-hearted as to be charitable to me, and you, you whining whore, are so covetous as to lose your life for sake of mammon. Come, come, you hollow-hearted bitch, unpin your purse-string quickly, or else I shall send you out of the land of the living."[38]* The poor Quaker passed over a purse of guineas, a gold watch and a diamond ring, in double-quick time!

When Davis held up the coach of Lady Albemarle, he deliberately discharged a number of pistols wounding all four of her livery servants, before roughly removing her rings and watch, all the while swearing at her. On another occasion he deliberately shot the horse of his victim, one Sir Thomas Day, from under him. He was eventually captured after an outstandingly long career as a highwayman when he was cornered in Salisbury Court, off Fleet Street, but not before shooting dead one of his intended captors. Having been tried and executed his body was hung in chains in a gibbet on Bagshot Heath.

- John [a.k.a. Jack] Sheppard (1702–1724) – "The Great Escaper" / "Gentleman Jack" / "Jack The Lad" – Born in White's Row, Spittlefields, in London, and apprenticed to a carpenter in Drury Lane from a young age, Jack was quick to fall into bad company and become a shoplifter, burglar and pickpocket. The first time he was arrested he had been informed upon having committed a burglary with his brother Thomas and his girlfriend / wife Elizabeth Lyons.

It took him less than three hours to break out of St. Giles Roundhouse and escaping was to become his hallmark as he was quite the Harry Houdini (1874–1926) of his time. In fact he escaped from Newgate Prison on three occasions; each time after the guards had thought they had secured him better than before. On the third occasion he was put in the strong room, or 'The Castle', was handcuffed and manacled in leg-irons, and chained to an iron staple in the floor, but still they could not hold him. He became quite a folk hero, renowned for his breakouts and whenever he was taken people flocked to see him (whilst they could!). For further details of his great escapes I would recommend the reading of 'The Thieves Opera' by Lucy Moore [1999; Penguin Books].

For his highway robbery antics on the Hampstead Road, Jack teamed up with one Joseph, a.k.a. "Blueskin" Blake (1696–1724), who was captured and executed just a week before his partner. Blueskin managed to slit the throat of Jonathan Wild (1683–1735), the self-styled 'Thief Taker General of England and Ireland', but the latter was fortunate enough to survive the attack. Wild was probably the most famous criminal of London. When the authorities eventually found him out over his "double-crossing" antics he was hung at Tyburn on 25 May 1735.

- Richard [a.k.a. Dick] Turpin [a.k.a. John Palmer] (1705–1739) – "The Bandit of Epping Forest" – The most famous of all highwaymen; largely thanks to William Harrison Ainsworth (1805–1882) [the prolific British historical novelist] who included him and his mare, Black Bess, as secondary characters in his romantic novel 'Rookwood' [1834; Routledge & Sons]. If it had not been for Ainsworth then it is more than likely that Claude Duval and William Nevison would be the best known highwaymen of all time; certainly they were the only two included in Thomas Babington Macaulay's 'History of England…etc', as quoted earlier. Ainsworth himself had been inspired by Edward [George Earl] Bulwer-Lytton (1803–1873), 1st Baron Lytton, the English novelist, playwright and politician who is perhaps best remembered for coining the phrase, *'The pen is mightier than the sword'*, amongst many others, who in 1830, published his own novel about an elegant and charming highwayman, 'Paul Clifford' [1830; George Routlege & Sons], which opened with the immortal line, *'It was a dark and stormy night…'*[39]

Dick Turpin was born in Hempstead, near Saffron Walden, in Essex. He was apprenticed to a butcher in Whitechapel in London, before setting himself up in the same line of business in Buckhurst Hill, Essex. Rather than buy in his stock young Turpin liked to steal his sheep and cattle and when found out he hid away in the remotest caves on the East Anglian coast and in the depths of Epping Forest. From the latter location he soon became acquainted with and joined the 'Gregory Gang" (or 'Essex Gang'); a band of ruthless thieves involved in poaching the Royal game from the forest, house-breaking and robbery with plenty of violence. It was not long before the name Dick Turpin was associated with highway robbery and a price of £50 put on his capture.

When the Gregory Gang ran into trouble and started breaking up, Turpin teamed up with another highly wanted highwayman from Essex called [Captain] Tom King (−1737). As his behaviour to their victims was quite the opposite to that of his more brutal partner, King went on to gain himself the reputation of being a 'Gentleman Highwayman'. Turpin meanwhile shot and killed a man who tried to arrest him at Fairmead Bottom, near Loughton in Essex and shortly after stole the thoroughbred horse he nicknamed 'Black Bess'. Bess was so unique that she was easily traced to where Turpin stabled her at 'The Red Lion Inn' at Whitechapel. When the authorities went to reclaim the horse and take Turpin, there was an almighty gunfight in which Turpin somehow managed to shoot Tom King by accident before fleeing the scene. King subsequently died of his wound but not before letting on the hiding places where Turpin might shelter.

Too wily to go where he might he might be looked for Turpin decided to leave the area altogether and went to Lincolnshire and on to Yorkshire where he changed his name to John Palmer and started afresh as a horse dealer. Resorting to his old ways he would of course steal the horses he was selling. Not long into his new life Palmer managed to get himself arrested on a petty charge of shooting a game-cock that belonged to the landlord at 'The Green Dragon Inn' near York and enquiries into his background soon revealed that he had been stealing horses in Lincolnshire. When he wrote to his brother-in-law for help in getting a character reference for himself his handwriting was recognised by his old school master in Hempstead, John Smith, who travelled personally up to York to identify him and at the same time pocket what had now become £200 reward money.

Turpin was tried at York Assizes, not for murder or highway robbery, but for horse rustling, was found guilty and sentenced to death. The Hangman on duty at York Knavesmire [the site of the present day York Racecourse] on the day of his execution was one Thomas Hadfield, a former friend and member of the Gregory Gang, who had been pardoned for his past sins when he agreed to become a Hangman. Apparently Turpin was seen stamping his right leg down to stop it shaking before he climbed the ladder of the scaffold and threw himself off.

- William Page (1730–1758) – "The Master of the Roads" – Born at Hampton in Middlesex, young William first went to work for his cousin at the latter's haberdashery shop in London. Having been caught "with his hand in the till" he was quickly dismissed. He then tried a career in acting, before becoming a livery servant and ultimately "taking to the Road". Page was a meticulous planner of his robberies; he even took the trouble to draw up his own map of all the roads within a twenty-mile radius of the City.

According to The Newgate Calendar write up on Page, *"In his excursions for robbery he used to dress in a laced or embroidered frock, and wear his hair tied behind; but when at a distance from London he would turn into some unfrequented place and, having disguised himself in other clothes, with a grizzled or black wig, and saddled one of his horses, ride to the main road and commit a robbery. This done, he hastened back to the carriage* [He was renowned for riding a 'phaeton' which was a lightly sprung carriage with large wheels], *resumed his former dress, and drove to London.*[40]

Page teamed up with an old school friend by the name of Darwell and together they committed perhaps as many as 300 robberies in 3 years. Eventually Darwell "shopped" his old friend for the reward money and told the authorities where they might find Page. He was taken at 'The Golden Lion Tavern', near Hyde Park, and found about his person were three loaded pistols, his wig and his map. Initially he was acquitted of committing a couple of specific robberies due to lack of evidence, but on the third attempt his prosecutor from Rochester in Kent "made his case stick" and Page was shortly afterwards executed at Maidstone.

- John [a.k.a. Jack] Rann (1750–1774) – "Sixteen-String Jack" – Born near Bath in Somerset, John started his working life as a stable boy, a driver of post-chaises and a coachman in Portman Square in London. In the latter role he was often seen sporting breeches with eight strings or ribbons at each knee, earning him his nickname. Dressing in a flamboyant style was his trademark ever after. He was arrested several times but each time released due to lack of evidence and his victims' inability to match the figure of the highwayman that robbed them with the fine gentleman before them.

Jack Rann's downfall came when he and his partner, William Collier, robbed a Doctor of a distinctive watch in a tortoiseshell case. It was his girlfriend Eleanor Roche that arranged to take it to a pawnbroker in Oxford Road who, suspicious of its background, happened to take it to a watchmaker in Russell Street, Covent Garden, who recognised it as the one that he had personally made for the Doctor. At his trial at the Old Bailey,

Jack wore a brand new pea green suit with a round hat tied with silver bows. His confidence was shattered when the Jury found him guilty as he had felt he had as strong a chance of "getting away with it" as at any of his previous examinations or trials. In Newgate, on a Sunday, the week before his execution date, he apparently dined with seven ladies of ill repute. At least he would have gone to Tyburn with a smile on his face!

- Lewis Jeremiah Avershaw [a.k.a. Jerry Abershaw] (1773–1795) – "The King of the Roads" / "The Laughing Highwayman" – Born at Kingston-upon-Thames in Surrey, Jerry became a post-chaise driver from a young age, but by the age of 17 he was already a gang-leader of a bunch of thieves and highwaymen who terrorised Kennington Common, Hounslow Heath, Bagshot Heath and Wimbledon Common. He soon had a price on his head but managed to avoid capture for almost 5 years. Eventually he was cornered by two Bow Street Runners in 'The Three Brewers Inn' at Southwark, one of whom he shot in the gut and who subsequently died, and the other whom he shot in the head, but somehow survived to give evidence at his trial which was then for murder and intent to murder, not just robbery with violence.

Jerry was highly agitated throughout his three minute trial and constantly shouted at the Judge and Jury that he himself should not be condemned to suffer 'murder' on the evidence of just one witness. The Jury duly found him guilty and as the Judge put on the traditional black cap to pronounce sentence Jerry mimicked him causing much hilarity in the court.

Apparently whist in his condemned cell he used the juice of black cherries to draw on the walls, depicting several scenes from his robberies. His "gallows humour" at Kennington Common was legendary; at one point he raised a laugh by kicking off his boots on the basis that he was determined to disprove his mother's theory that he would die with them on. Having so entertained the crowd his would have been described by them as a "good death" (see Chapter 6). His body was taken to Putney Heath and hung in chains to rot; apparently he was the last ever highwayman to be 'gibbeted' in this way. So popular had he been that thieves from across London would make a gruesome pilgrimage to see the corpse of their hero, taking the bones from his fingers and toes as souvenirs to use as stoppers for their tobacco-pipes!

Once more returning to Maclaine's story, and with the decision made between him and Plunket to commit to highway robbery, the latter hired two horses, and furnished two pistols *"for this was not his first Entrance upon Business of that kind,"*[41] and they set out the evening after the Masquerade to lie in wait for passengers on their way to Smithfield Market. For this first expedition they chose a location renowned for its history of highway robbery, Hounslow Heath, a vast area of wasteland covering approximately 25 square miles to the southwest of London. Two main roads crossed the Heath, the Bath Road and the Exeter to Staines Road; both heavily used by wealthy visitors who would travel down to Bath to partake of the mineral waters and by courtiers coming up for an audience with the King at Windsor. For two centuries Hounslow Heath had the reputation for being the most dangerous place in the British Isles. Claude Duval (see above) undertook many of his robberies on Hounslow Heath. The next morning, between three and four o'clock, they stopped a grazier on his way home from the Market. They were wearing Venetian style masks (as they did on all such occasions) that covered the upper part of their faces, but even this could not instil any courage in Maclaine; apparently he sat back, did not utter a word and did not even draw his pistol. *"The least Resistance on the Part of the Countryman, would have given Wings to his Heels, and he had certainly left his Accomplice in the Lurch."*[42] Plunket, however, having more than enough resolve for two, *"suddenly enlightened as to Maclaine's want of nerve, took the conduct of the incident firmly in hand at once, or the result might have been disastrous for both."*[43] Plunket managed to relieve the farmer of between sixty and seventy pounds and sent him on his way.

As they left the scene Maclaine apparently found his pangs of guilt so intolerable that he rode behind Plunket for some miles without speaking at all. Eventually, when they were about ten miles away, they pulled up at an inn and Maclaine *"called for a Room, and was afraid of every Shadow he saw, for Fear it should be Justice in Pursuit of him. His Agonies of Mind and Conscience was so great, that Plunket was afraid his Folly would raise Suspicion in the House."*[44] Plunket was all for returning to London straight away, but Maclaine refused to stir from his room before dusk, *"so great was his Dread of Discovery,"*[45] and the two stayed there, laying low, for two more days. Despite, with his share of the spoil, Maclaine having re-couped some of his losses at the gaming table, he proposed to his friend that they should stay out of town and go to the country for a week or two whilst things cooled down. The latter was not opposed to the idea *"especially as he was to direct the Rout, and had some Intelligence of a Prize coming that day from St Albans, towards which Place they set out."*[46] After they had travelled some miles Plunket imparted his plans, which Maclaine initially refused to have anything to do with until he was persuaded by the former's hints at his cowardice.

It was eventually agreed Maclaine would ride up to the coach that contained their booty and present his pistol from one side and that Plunket would likewise follow up to rob the passengers from the other. Maclaine apparently prepared himself for the attack with the expression: *"He Needs must whom the Devil drives; I am over Shoes, and must over Boots."*[47] but whilst he rode up to the jehu, several times, with the intention of shouting the highwayman's traditional command of "Stand and deliver!", he found himself unable to do it. Jehu (c. 842–815 BC) was a commander of chariots, who later became King of Israel, noted for his furious chariot attacks; The Bible notes Jehu "drives furiously" (II Kings 9:20). Thus a "jehu" was a *"driver, especially of a coach; one who drives fast or recklessly."*[48] The term is still in occasional use today. If Plunket had not again taken charge of the situation they would have lost their prey altogether. They took from the lady and gentleman in the coach two gold watches and about £20 in cash. Travellers in these perilous times often set out with two purses, one to keep hidden with their true wealth inside and the other to give up if they were unfortunate enough to be stopped by a highwayman. The wiser highwaymen of course would know this and things could on occasion get rather bloody; but never in any such case have we understood with Plunket and Maclaine, as they of course always acted as perfect gentlemen. They would become renowned for never taking more from a lady than she was prepared to part with. They immediately left off the St. Albans road and headed for Richmond where they put up before morning. Again Maclaine *"had no Rest, no Peace of Mind, and staid here two or three Days sullen, sulky and perplexed, what Course to pursue."*[49]

By the time they returned to town, having ridden via Hampton Court and other towns in that area, they found that Maclaine's ship had already sailed, just two days prior to their arrival. Disappointed as he was, Maclaine at least had cash in his pocket and was able to make excuses to his friends and financiers. He promised them he would leave on the next available ship. That of course was not for some time and all the while the "bewitching Pleasures" were ever present. Needless to say he continued to gamble and lose his money and to fritter the remainder on fancy clothes, whores and any other diversions that came his way. Gambling particularly *once more stripp'd him of his Cash; and his evil Genius Plunket was ready to suggest the former Method of Supply, which he now complied with, with much less Reluctance than before.*[50] However, Plunket did put it firmly to Maclaine that he could no longer just sit *shivering in cowardice in the background,*[51] and that *he was unfit for his business,*[52] if he was unable to pull his weight. These words had such a profound effect on Maclaine that he went out alone that same night and robbed a gentleman, returning home to share the plunder with his partner.

Not long after, the pair headed out for a further "Recruit" and took to the road [a.k.a. "the High Toby"] towards Portsmouth where they practiced their trade until Maclaine's confidence grew a little stronger. The General Advertiser of 20 September 1748 touched briefly on their exploits in the following article:

Last week several robberies were committed on the Portsmouth Road, by two highwaymen well mounted, who made a considerable booty. – The great number of robberies we continually hear of on the several roads, and in this City and Suburbs, and the probability of

*their encreasing in the winter season, requires the strictest regard of
all people to prevent them. – Many schemes have been propos'd, but
none seems more likely to answer the purpose, than that of all people
who lett lodgings should be obliged to give an account of all inmates, their business, &c.*

The General Advertiser, 20 September 1748 [53]

To avoid being teased by his friends about going to Jamaica
and to get another step further from his mother-in-law, Maclaine
then moved from his lodgings to the first floor of a tradesman's
(a Mr. Dunn's) house in St. James's Street (see Illustration (x) –
Jean [a.k.a. John] Rocque's (1709–1762) 'Map of London 1746').
This house was beside White's Gentleman's Club (see above);
still there in St. James's Street (although maybe not in the exact
same location) and thriving to this day. Mr Dunn's was directly
opposite the 'Old Bagnio', a well-known brothel, where many a
wealthy gentleman would stay when visiting London. Therefore
Maclaine had chosen an excellent location to base himself as he
was able to continue to gather information about people's worth
and their travel plans. All the while his appearance kept him
above suspicion. At Mr. Dunn's he *"presented a gorgeous figure to
morning callers."*[54] Apparently *"he was even more gorgeous in the
evening, when he frequented places of public entertainment, and
obtained the freedom of some fashionable houses."*[55] This no doubt
included White's, next door.

Illustration (x) — A small segment of 'John Rocque's Map of London 1746' (1746) — John Rocque (1709–1762)

Plunket at the time had lodgings at a shoemaker's in Round Court along The Strand. When his landlady became suspicious of his movements late at night she unlocked the door to his room and found two pistols and a mask hidden in his trunk. [Perhaps she had read and was following up the General Advertiser's September advice?] On this discovery he immediately relocated to 'Bab-Mase-Meuse' in Jermyn Street, St James's, ideally positioned to support his 'Master'. Jermyn Street on John Rocque's Map was clearly labelled as Great Germain Street, see Illustration (x), so must have been re-named after Henry Jermyn (1605–1684), 1st Earl of St. Albans, shortly after the Map was produced. Maclaine meanwhile explained away his flamboyance by claiming he owned a large estate in Ireland that brought him in £700 a year. During all this time, we learn that he seldom visited his child(ren), *"and when he did, would not sit down,"*[56] nor stay long; no doubt to avoid giving his mother-in-law enough time to ask him any awkward questions about his apparent new found affluence.

About this time there was an incident worth recounting concerning Maclaine and a gentleman who unwittingly fell foul of him. As we have already learned Maclaine was fond of spending time at Coffee Houses (see above), particularly Button's on the south side of Russell Street in Covent Garden. Daniel Button's Coffee House was famous for being the centre of the free press. Newsletters were handwritten and distributed throughout the other Coffee Houses by its reporters. It is said that the periodical publications 'The Tatler', 'The Spectator' and 'The Guardian' all started there. Here he paid special attention to the barmaid, daughter of the landlord. This became obvious to all the patrons of the establishment including a Mr Donaldson, who knew Maclaine, and took the opportunity of warning the girl's father of his real character. The father duly cautioned his daughter, but rather foolishly let slip the name of his informant. She naturally passed it on to the engaging Maclaine. *"On the next occasion when Donaldson visited Button's, and while he was sitting in one of the boxes, Maclaine entered, and in a loud voice, and the pronounced Irish brogue that was ever on his tongue, said: "Mr. Donaldson, I wish to spake to you in a private room". Mr. Donaldson being unarmed and naturally afraid of being alone with such a man as he knew Maclaine to be, said that as there could not possibly be anything pass between them that the whole world was not welcome to know, he begged leave to decline the invitation. "Very well", rejoined Maclaine, "we shall meet again."*[57]

Sure enough, within a few days, while Mr Donaldson was out walking near Richmond in the evening, he saw Maclaine approaching him on horseback. When the latter perceived it was his prey in the distance, he spurred the animal on causing Mr Donaldson to take to his heels. Fortunately Maclaine was distracted by a gentleman's carriage crossing his path, which he immediately rode after. Donaldson hastened into the protection that the streets of Richmond town afforded. *"It is probable that, but for this timely diversion, Maclaine would have shot the man who dared tell the truth about him."*[58]

Over the next few months, sometimes separately, mainly in company together, Plunket and Maclaine committed some fifteen or sixteen robberies, many in Hyde Park, not far from where Plunket stabled their horses at Hyde Park Corner, *"near Mary le Bon,"*[59] and other places, all within twenty miles of London. They got away with some rich prizes but still the money seemed to go as easily as it came. Plunket, *"like Captain Cottle was all for love, and a little for the bottle,"*[60] spent his share that way. Plunket's favourite tipple was whisky, unlike most of the rest of the London population at the time that was in the middle of a "Gin Craze" and consuming it in vast quantities. Of the 15,000 drinking establishments in London in 1750, over half were gin shops. Gin was originally invented in Holland and used the juice of juniper berries; the French (soldiers) called it "eau de genièvre" ("juniper water"), which in English translated as Geneva or "gin" for short. Maclaine, as always, was *"doatingly fond of gay Cloaths, Balls, Masquerades, Etc at all which places he made a gay and impudent Figure."*[61] His main aim remained fortune hunting and he continued at every opportunity to push himself *"into the Companies of Women, and made Love to some of all Ranks, and was* not unsuccessful, for we find amorous Epistles both from Maids, Wives and Widows, directed to him."[62] These private letters were no doubt passed on to the Fleet Street reporters when Maclaine's trunk was broken into following his arrest.

Some of the above mentioned letters were published, by way of examples of the many others of a similar kind, by one reporter, or "hack-writer", in one of the many "grub ballads" to be sold shortly after his death. These were short stories written about the lives of renowned convicted criminals, in readiness to be sold at their hanging. The hack writers of the time were notoriously located in Grub Street; nowadays Milton Street (which links Silk Street to Chiswell Street). The "hack" included the epistles of one particular lady with whom Maclaine had an affair purely to get to his real target, *"a young lady, not quite seventeen, who had a considerable Fortune."*[63] He *"knew she visited at a Gentleman's House, who was either married to or kept a very gay, coquettish Lady, whose real Name we shall disguise under the fictitious Name of Selinda."*[64] Maclaine evidently *"saw Selinda's Foible, that she lov'd a Gallant, made his Address to that Quarter, and was soon well received, by which means he got an Acquaintance with the lady of fortune he was in Quest of, and then gave over his Assiduity to Selinda, whose amorous Epistles take as follows, that is, as many of them as are legible."*[65]

From: SELINDA to Mr MACLEAN [sic].

L E T T E R I.

S I R,

I Expected the Favour of a Line from you this three Weeks, I swear three Years; for it is so by my Calculation, since you gave me your Word and Honour of writing to me; but you fine Gentlemen of this Town mind no more your Honour than you do your Words: Excuse the Freedom I take by calling your Honour in Question; but Freedom, in my Opinion, is a Mark of Friendship, and true Friendship the surest Mark of Esteem. I don't know, whether I deserve either Friendship or Esteem from you, when I recollect the Night's Adventure we had together, which gives me the utmost Contempt of myself: But I desire you to think as favourably as possible of me; for, when any such scurvy Thoughts interrupt the favourable Ideas, that I would willingly have you to have of me, look immediately in the Glass, and think of the Softness of our Hearts, when we see a pretty Fellow. Don't imagine, that I write this long Scrawl with a View of seeing you, which I absolutely don't intend, for two Reasons; the one, because I have not Impudence enough; and the other is, that I have not — But I will not tell you; only I may say, as a great Author* says,

> *How gladly would I from myself remove,*
> *And at a Distance send the Thing I love;*
> *My Breast is warm'd with such unchaste Fire,*
> *I wish him absent whom I most desire.*

Now I suppose you think I am over Head and Ears in Love, but I an't though; I do not know what another Sight of you may do, in your Morning-Gown and yellow Slippers. But to be serious; I hope you are very well, and in high Spirits, as you was on Saturday Morning; for, by your Looks, you have not taken half a Dozen Doses of Physick** since I saw you. You run much in Miss ---'s Head, for your Name is never out of her Mouth. You are dangerous Company for such young Creatures. Well, I think it Time to have done, so wish you a bon Repose. Adieu

Sunday Night, 12 o'clock.   *SELINDA.* [66]

*The *"great Author"* quoted by Selinda was an illustrious Roman poet by the name of Publius Ovidius Naso [a.k.a. Ovid] (43BC–AD17) who wrote on the topics of love, abandoned women and mythological transformations. It was the latter that spawned the quoted lines, from 'The Story of Narcissus' in 'Book The Third' of his epic 'Metamorphoses' (AD8).

** *"half a Dozen Doses of Physick"* in late 1748 would probably been enough to kill anyone. There was at that time no real understanding of the causes of the most common diseases and therefore the various concoctions sold as remedies were at best placebos and at worst toxins, making the underlying illnesses worse. The Gentleman's Magazine of August 1748 listed the names and prices of over 200 commonly available medicines or "Nostrums and Empirics" of the day in a "Pharmacopoeia Empirica" that would claim to cure all manner of Agues (fevers), Bladders-stones, Broken-winds, Consumptions, Corns, Gleets (abnormal discharges), Gouts, Impotencies, Itches, Nervous disorders, Poxes, Rheumatism, Ruptures, Toothaches and Warts.

L E T T E R II. From the same.

My dear Jemmy,   *Wednesday Noon, 1 o'Clock*

THE Moment I set out to come to you, Mr ---------- came Home, and I came off very badly. He swears, if I go out any more, that The Moment I come Home he will murder me; so, if you have that Love for me you pretend, endeavour to release me from the Man I hate, as soon as possible. God knows when I shall see you again, but till I do, pray, my Dear, keep honest. I should be glad to hear from you, if you can send any-body about Eleven o'Clock, and let them deliver the Letter to me, and No-body else: Till when, my dear Love, believe me to be,

                                        Your Sincere Friend
                                        SELINDA. [67]

L E T T E R III. From the same.

Dear Jemmy,

I AM so very ill I can hardly hold my Pen; but if I am any thing better by Monday, I will see you at your own House, for there is no Place here I can trust. Pray God send we may get over all our Difficulties, and that I may have the Pleasure once more to be happy, for I am very far from it at present: Till when, believe me to be what you really wish.

                                        SELINDA. [68]

LETTER IV. From the same.

SIR

IT is hard, and very unfortunate, that I should come so far, and not see you; but I find you are so much taken up with that despicable Girl, that you have no time to think of any Body else. But I deserve it, since it was by my Means you got acquainted with the silly Trifler, and might have known what Faults the Hopes of a Fortune would conceal. If you think it worth your while to be at Home To-morrow Morning, I will be at your House by Nine o'Clock: Till when, I am,

Your humble Servant.
Monday, 10 o'clock

SELINDA. [69]

As the correspondence ended after the fourth printed letter, it is not possible to know if the lady got access to Maclaine at the time appointed. It is likely that she did not as his grand design for the young lady of fortune was soon to fall apart. Another gentleman who knew Maclaine *"in all the Scenes of his life he had gone through"*[70] advised a relation of the "despicable Girl" what she might be getting involved with, and that was the end of that.

As the time spent with Selinda and the "silly Trifler" was not time spent on the road, Maclaine had not had the *"Opportunity of making any Excursions on the Road, and to "supply his expenses."*[71] He had however taken on more cost by taking country lodgings in Chelsea. He had also apparently *"borrowed from a Citizen's Wife, with whom he had an Intrigue, about twenty Pounds, which he promised faithfully to repay before her Husband should return from the*

Country to miss it."[72] When her husband was due home this lady pressed hard for the return of the cash, *"lest the Want of that should lead to a Discovery of an Embezzlement of a worse Nature."*[73] Maclaine invited the lady to Chelsea to collect the money *"but took care that his Friend Plunket should ease her of the Trouble of carrying it Home, by way-laying her in the Five Fields."*[74] The Five Fields most probably are situated in modern day Pimlico and Belgravia.

With a supply of ready cash now needed the pair took off on the Chester Road where Plunket had been planning an excursion for some time. In three days, between Stony Stratford, near the modern town of Milton Keynes, and Whitchurch, both in Buckinghamshire, they committed five robberies; some on their own countrymen and *"one of them an intimate Acquaintance, by whom Maclean [sic] had been very handsomely entertained but two Days before they left the Town."*[75]. Stony Stratford was one of the most important coaching towns on the road from London to Liverpool. The town had many inns along its High Street, two of which were particularly renowned for being excellent places to catch up with fresh news from all parts of the country. These were 'The Cock Inn' and 'The Bull Inn'. The two establishments developed a rivalry as to which could furnish the most outrageous stories; hence the saying "a load of old Cock and Bull". Whilst their haul from all five hold-ups only amounted to about £30 in cash, they had watches, rings and other jewellery to a much greater value.

The same evening of their return to London they gained knowledge that an Officer of the East India Company, having received a large sum of money, was due to return from London to Greenwich. They rode out after him and managed to stop and rob him on Shooter's Hill, near Woolwich. Shooter's Hill may well be the highest point in South London, but in the 18th Century it was certainly the lowest point on anyone's journey between London and Dover. In those days there was much forestry on the Hill that allowed highwaymen the advantage of cover for an ambush. They would watch the comings and goings from 'The Bull Inn' at the crest of the Hill which itself was the first/last post house where coaches stopped to change their horses. To deter highway robbery the Hill was long used as a site for hanging corpses of executed highwaymen. Samuel Pepys (1633–1703), the infamous 17th Century diarist, made the following diary entry concerning his journey along the Dover Road on Thursday 11 April 1661: *"under the man that hangs upon Shooter's Hill, and a filthy sight it is to see how his flesh is shrunk to the bones."*[76] Dick Turpin (see earlier) undertook some of his robberies on Shooter's Hill, a decade before Plunket and Maclaine. It was however the latters' most successful robbery ever and the two were both in such fear of being discovered that within three days of committing it, they both made arrangements to leave the country. Having shared all the money, they then carefully divided all the watches and jewellery to take with them for sale on their respective travels where they felt this could be achieved with greater safety. Maclaine left for The Hague on the pretext of holidaying with his brother, whilst Plunket headed for Ireland to see family and friends.

Chapter 3 – References

[1] Anonymous. *'A COMPLETE HISTORY of James Maclean [sic], THE GENTLEMAN HIGHWAYMAN, who was executed at TYBURN on Wednesday, October 3, 1750, for a Robbery on the Highway'*. [1750; Printed for Charles Corbett, London]. Page 17

[2] *THE COFFEE HOUSES OF OLD LONDON'*. Retrieved 18/10/11

[3] Van Muyden, Madame. *'A FOREIGN VIEW OF ENGLAND IN THE REIGNS OF GEORGE I. & GEORGE II. The Letters of Monsieur César de Saussure to his Family'* [1902; John Murray, London].

[4] *The Gentleman's Magazine*, 21 April 1749.

[5] Cunningham, Peter. *'The Letters of Horace Walpole, Earl of Orford'*. *Volume II*. 1749–1751. Page 77

[6] Ibid. Page 78

[7] Wright, John and Ellis, George Agar (1797–1833), 1st Baron Dover. *'THE LETTERS of HORACE WALPOLE, EARL OF ORFORD'*. *Volume I*. (1735–1745) [1840; Printed by Richard Bentley, London]. Page 353

[8] Steinmetz Esq'., Andrew (1816–1877). *'The Gaming Table; Its Votaries and Victims'*. *Volume II*. [1870; J. Tinsley Brothers, London]. Page 78

[9] Cunningham, Peter. *'The Letters of Horace Walpole, Earl of Orford'*. *Volume II*. 1749–1751. Page 87

[10] Anonymous. *'A COMPLETE HISTORY of James Maclean [sic], THE GENTLEMAN HIGHWAYMAN, who was executed at TYBURN on Wednesday, October 3, 1750, for a Robbery on the Highway'*. [1750; Printed for Charles Corbett, London]. Page 14

[11] Ibid. Page 13

[12] Knapp, Andrew and Baldwin, William. *'THE NEW Newgate Calendar BEING INTERESTING MEMOIRS OF NOTORIOUS CHARACTERS,*

Who have been convicted of Outrage on THE LAWS OF ENGLAND, DURING THE SEVENTEENTH CENTURY, BROUGHT DOWN TO THE PRESENT TIME'. Volume II. [1810; Printed for J. and J. Cundee, London]. Page 336

[13] Anonymous. '*A COMPLETE HISTORY of James Maclean [sic], THE GENTLEMAN HIGHWAYMAN, who was executed at TYBURN on Wednesday, October 3, 1750, for a Robbery on the Highway'.* [1750; Printed for Charles Corbett, London]. Page 14

[14] Anonymous. '*A Genuine Account of the Life and Actions of James Maclean [sic], Highwayman, to the time of his trial and receiving sentence at The Old Bailey, containing his Robberies, Gallantry at Public Places, with other remarkable transactions; together with some account of Plunket his companion'.* [1750; Printed for W. Falstaff, London].

[15] Anonymous. '*A Genuine Account of the Life and Actions of James Maclean [sic], Highwayman, to the time of his trial and receiving sentence at The Old Bailey, containing his Robberies, Gallantry at Public Places, with other remarkable transactions; together with some account of Plunket his companion'.* [1750; Printed for W. Falstaff, London].

[16] *Ibid. Page 15*

[17] *Ibid. Page 15*

[18] *Ibid. Page 15*

[19] *Ibid. Page 16*

[20] Anonymous. '*A COMPLETE HISTORY of James Maclean [sic], THE GENTLEMAN HIGHWAYMAN, who was executed at TYBURN on Wednesday, October 3, 1750, for a Robbery on the Highway'.* [1750; Printed for Charles Corbett, London]. Page 17

[21] Ibid. Page 17

[22] Ibid. Page 17

[23] Ibid. Page 17 and 18

[24] Knapp, Andrew and Baldwin, William. '*THE NEW Newgate Calendar BEING INTERESTING MEMOIRS OF NOTORIOUS CHARACTERS, Who have been convicted of Outrage on THE LAWS OF ENGLAND, DURING THE SEVENTEENTH CENTURY, BROUGHT DOWN TO THE PRESENT TIME'. Volume II.* [1810; Printed for J. and J. Cundee, London]. Page 336

[25] Ibid. page 336

[26] Van Muyden, Madame. '*A FOREIGN VIEW OF ENGLAND IN THE REIGNS OF GEORGE I. & GEORGE II.* The Letters of Monsieur César de Saussure to his Family' [1902; John Murray, London].

[27] Defoe, Daniel. '*A tour thro' the whole island of Great Britain, divided into circuits or journies*'. [1927; JM Dent and Co., London].
[28] Ibid.

[29] Webb, Sidney (1859–1947) [1st Baron Passfield] and Webb, [Martha] Beatrice Potter (1858–1943) [Lady Passfield]. '*English Local Government; The Story of the King's Highway*' [1913; Longmans, Green & Co., London]. Page 72

[30] Phillips, Robert. '*Dissertation Concerning the Present State of the High Roads in England, Especially those near London*' [1737; printed by L. Gilliver and J. Clark, London]

[31] Mackay, Charles (1814–1889). '*Memoirs of Extraordinary Popular Delusions and the Madness of Crowds*'. *Volume I.* [1841; Harmony Books, New York].

[32] von Archenholz, Johann Wilhelm (1741–1812). '*England und Italien*' *Volume I* [1785; Leipzig]

[33] de Quincey, Thomas (1785–1859), '*Memorials and Other Papers*' [1891;]

[34] Macaulay, [Lord] Thomas Babington (1800–1859). '*History of England from the Assession of James II*' [1848]. Page 298

[35] Anonymous. *'ANNALS OF CRIME, AND NEW NEWGATE CALENDAR' Issues 1–53*. No 20 'Life, Trial, and Execution, of Claude Du Vall, A Celebrated Highwayman' [1833; Printed by W. Barnes, London] Page 157

[36] Ibid. Page 157

[37] Defoe, Daniel. *'A tour thro' the whole island of Great Britain, divided into circuits or journies'*. [1927; JM Dent and Co., London].

[38] Knapp, Andrew and Baldwin, William. *'THE NEW Newgate Calendar BEING INTERESTING MEMOIRS OF NOTORIOUS CHARACTERS, Who have been convicted of Outrage on THE LAWS OF ENGLAND, DURING THE SEVENTEENTH CENTURY, BROUGHT DOWN TO THE PRESENT TIME'. Volume II*. [1810; Printed for J. and J. Cundee, London].

[39] Bulwer–Lytton, Edward [George Earl] (1803–1873), *1st Baron Lytton. 'Paul Clifford'* [1830; George Routlege & Sons, London]

[40] Knapp, Andrew and Baldwin, William Lee. *'THE NEWGATE CALENDAR; COMPRISING INTERESTING MEMOIRS OF NOTORIOUS CHARACTERS, Who have been convicted of Outrage on THE LAWS OF ENGLAND, SINCE THE BEGINNING OF THE EIGHTEENTH CENTURY'. Volume II*. [1825; J. Robins and Co., London]. Pages 228 and 229

[41] Anonymous. *'A COMPLETE HISTORY of James Maclean [sic], THE GENTLEMAN HIGHWAYMAN, who was executed at TYBURN on Wednesday, October 3, 1750, for a Robbery on the Highway'*. [1750; Printed for Charles Corbett, London]. Page 18

[42] Ibid. Page 18

[43] Harper, Charles George (1863–1943). *'HALF-HOURS WITH THE HIGHWAYMEN, Picturesque Biographies and traditions of the "Knights of the Road"*. [1908; Chapman & Hall Limited, London]. Page 281

[44] Anonymous. *'A COMPLETE HISTORY of James Maclean [sic], THE GENTLEMAN HIGHWAYMAN, who was executed at TYBURN on Wednesday, October 3, 1750, for a Robbery on the Highway'*. [1750; Printed for Charles Corbett, London]. Page 19

[45] Ibid. Page 19

[46] Anonymous. *'A COMPLETE HISTORY of James Maclean [sic], THE GENTLEMAN HIGHWAYMAN, who was executed at TYBURN on Wednesday, October 3, 1750, for a Robbery on the Highway'*. [1750; Printed for Charles Corbett, London]. Page 19

[47] Ibid. Page 19

[48] *Collins English Dictionary* [2010; HarperCollins]

[49] Anonymous. *'A COMPLETE HISTORY of James Maclean [sic], THE GENTLEMAN HIGHWAYMAN, who was executed at TYBURN on Wednesday, October 3, 1750, for a Robbery on the Highway'*. [1750; Printed for Charles Corbett, London]. Page 20

[50] Ibid. Page 20

[51] Harper, Charles George (1863–1943). *'HALF-HOURS WITH THE HIGHWAYMEN, Picturesque Biographies and traditions of the "Knights of the Road"*'. [1908; Chapman & Hall Limited, London]. Page 282

[52] Knapp, Andrew and Baldwin, William. *'THE NEW Newgate Calendar BEING INTERESTING MEMOIRS OF NOTORIOUS CHARACTERS, Who have been convicted of Outrage on THE LAWS OF ENGLAND, DURING THE SEVENTEENTH CENTURY, BROUGHT DOWN TO THE PRESENT TIME'*. Volume II. [1810; Printed for J. and J. Cundee, London]. Page 337

[53] *The General Advertiser*, 20 September 1748

[54] Harper, Charles George (1863–1943). *'HALF-HOURS WITH THE HIGHWAYMEN, Picturesque Biographies and traditions of the "Knights of the Road"*'. [1908; Chapman & Hall Limited, London]. Page 282

[55] Ibid. Page 282

[56] Knapp, Andrew and Baldwin, William. *'THE NEW Newgate Calendar BEING INTERESTING MEMOIRS OF NOTORIOUS CHARACTERS, Who have been convicted of Outrage on THE LAWS OF ENGLAND, DURING THE SEVENTEENTH CENTURY, BROUGHT DOWN TO THE PRESENT TIME'. Volume II.* [1810; Printed for J. and J. Cundee, London]. Page 337

[57] Harper, Charles George (1863–1943). *'HALF-HOURS WITH THE HIGHWAYMEN, Picturesque Biographies and traditions of the "Knights of the Road"*. [1908; Chapman & Hall Limited, London]. Pages 285 and 286

[58] Ibid. Page 286

[59] Anonymous. *'A COMPLETE HISTORY of James Maclean [sic], THE GENTLEMAN HIGHWAYMAN, who was executed at TYBURN on Wednesday, October 3, 1750, for a Robbery on the Highway'.* [1750; Printed for Charles Corbett, London]. Page 21

[60] Seccombe, Thomas (1866—1923). *'LIVES OF TWELVE BAD MEN; Original Studies of Eminent Scoundrels by Various Hands'* [1894; T. Fisher Unwin, London]. Page 254

[61] Anonymous. *'A COMPLETE HISTORY of James Maclean [sic], THE GENTLEMAN HIGHWAYMAN, who was executed at TYBURN on Wednesday, October 3, 1750, for a Robbery on the Highway'.* [1750; Printed for Charles Corbett, London]. Page 21

[62] Ibid. Page 21

[63] Anonymous. *'A COMPLETE HISTORY of James Maclean [sic], THE GENTLEMAN HIGHWAYMAN, who was executed at TYBURN on Wednesday, October 3, 1750, for a Robbery on the Highway'.* [1750; Printed for Charles Corbett, London]. Page 21

[64] Ibid. Page 21

[65] Ibid. Page 21

[66] Ibid. Pages 22 and 23

[67] Ibid. Pages 23 and 24

[68] Ibid. Pages 24

[69] Ibid. Pages 24

[70] Ibid. Pages 25

[71] Ibid. Pages 25

[72] Ibid. Pages 25

[73] Ibid. Pages 25

[74] Ibid. Pages 25

[75] Ibid. Pages 26

[76] Wheatley, Henry B[enjamin] (1838–1917) FSA. *'The Diary of Samuel Pepys, 1661'*

Chapter 3 – Suggested Further Reading

In addition to the above:

The Memoires of Monsieur Du Vall; Containing the History of his Life and Death: whereunto are annexed his Last Speech and Epitaph. Intended as a severe reflexion on the too great fondness of English Ladies towards French footmen; which, at that time of day, was a too common complaint... Pope, Walter and Pope, William (Printed for Henry Brome, London, 1670)

Inns and Taverns of Old London, Shelley, Henry Charles (Isaac Pitman & Sons, London, 1909)

A Hundred Years of Quarter Sessions, The Government of Middlesex from 1600 to 1760, Dowdell, Eric George; Holsworth, Sir William Searle and Hazeltine, Harold Dexter. (Cambridge University Press, Cambridge, 1932)

Imortal Turpin: The Authentic History of England's Most Notorious Highwayman, Dash, Arty and Day, Julius Edgar. (Staples Press, London, 1948)

Highwayman's Health: The Story in Fact and Fiction of Hounslow Heath in Middlesex, Maxwell, Gordon Stanley. (The Middlesex Chronicle, Middlesex, 1949)

Stand and Deliver. The Story of the Highwaymen, Pringle, Patrick (Museum Press, London, 1951)

Henry Fielding, His life, Works and Times, Dudden, Frederick Holmes (Claredon Press, Oxford, 1952)

Hogarth's England. A Selection of the Engravings with Descriptive Text, Cruikshanks, Eveline (Folio Society, London, 1957)

Highwaymen, Hibbert, Christopher (Weidenfeld and Nicolson, London, 1967)

Evil London. The Dark Side of a City, Aykroyd, Peter (Wolfe, London, 1973)

Stagecoach and Carriages. An Illustrated History of Coaches and Coaching, Sparkes, Ivan (Spurbooks Limited, Bourne End, 1975)

"Smash Annual, 1976" (IPC Magazines Limited, London, 1976)

Hero on a Stolen Horse. The Highwayman and His Brothers-In-Arms the Bandit and the Bushranger, Evans, Hilary and Mary. (Frederick Muller Limited, London, 1977)

The Crimson Book of Highwaymen, Newark, Peter (Jupiter Books Limited, London, 1979)

Highwaymen and Outlaws, Gilbert, John (Pan Books Limited, London, 1991)

The English Highwayman: A Legend Unmasked, Haining, Peter (Robert Hale, London, 1991)

The London Dungeon Book of Crime and Punishment, Byrne, Richard (Little Brown and Company, London, 1993)

Hanging in Judgement: Religion and the Death Penalty in England from the Bloody Code to Abolition, Potter, Harry (SCM Press Limited, London, 1993)

Discovering Highwaymen. A Gallery of Rogues, Ash, Russell (Shire Publications Limited, Princes Risborough, Buckinghamshire, 1994)

Horace Walpole: The Great Outsider, Mowl, Timothy (John Murray Publishers, London, 1996)

Highwaymen and Outlaws, Billett, Michael (Arms & Armour Press Limited, London, 1997)

The Thieves' Opera. The Remarkable Lives and deaths of Jonathan Wild, Thief-Taker, and Jack Sheppard, House-Breaker, Moore, Lucy (Penguin Group, London, 1998)

City of Sin. London and Its Vices, Arnold, Catherine (Longman, London, 1999)

Disorderly Women in Eighteenth-Century London: Prostitution and Control in the Metroplois, 1730–1830, Henderson, Tony (Longman, London, 1999)

Farman, John. 'The Short and Bloody History of Highwaymen' [2000; Red Fox, London]

Stand and Deliver! A History of Highway Robbery, Brandon, David (Sutton Publishing Limited, Gloucestershire, 2001)

London's Pleasures: From Restoration to Regency. Two Centuries of Elegance and Indulgance, Cameron, David Kerr (Sutton Publishing Limited, Gloucestershire, 2001)

Con Men and Cutpurses. Scenes from the Hogarthian Underworld, Moore, Lucy (Penguin Group, London, 2001)

Outlaws and Highwaymen. The Cult of the Robber in England from the Middle Ages to the Nineteenth Century, Spraggs, Gillian (Pimlico, London, 2001)

Sin City: London in Pursuit of Pleasure, Emerson, Giles (Andre Deutsch, Granada Media, 2002)

Dr. Johnson's London: Coffee-Houses and climbing Boys, Medicine, Toothpaste and Gin, Poverty and Press-gangs, Freakshows and female Education, Picard, Liza (St. Martins Griffin, London, 2002)

Highwaymen, Outlaws and Bandits of London, Elborough, Travis (Watling Street Publishing, Gloucestershire, 2003)

London's Underworld. Three centuries of Vice and crime, Linnane, Fergus (Robson Books Limited, London, 2003)

London 1753, O'Connell, Sheila, Roy Porter, Celina Fox, and Ralph Hyde, (David. R. Godine Publisher, London, 2003)

Gin: The Much-Lamented Death of Madam Geneva: The Eighteenth-Century Gin Craze, Dillon, Patrick (Justin, Charles and Company, Boston, 2004)

Down and Out in Eighteenth Century London, Hitchcock, Tim (Hambledon and London, London, 2004)

Madams: Bawds & Brothel-Keepers of London, Linnane, Fergus (Sutton Publishing Limited, Gloucestershire, 2005)

CHAPTER 4

'THE GENTLEMAN HIGHWAYMAN'

Rev. Archibald Maclaine was delighted to see his brother and full of fraternal affection towards him. He was completely taken in by James's tale as to how he had nurtured the fortune of his late wife and how her father, who had recently passed away, had also left him a considerable legacy. Archibald rejoiced in his brother's good fortune and introduced him to the *"politest of his Aquaintance"[1]* in The Hague. James *"behaved with great Gallantry, making Balls, and giving handsome Treats; for which it has been since surmised, that he had the Art to make some gold Watches and Purses of his guests bear the Charge, though no suspicion fell upon him till his Commitment here."[2]*

Maclaine stayed in The Hague until he thought that it was safe to return and the plot being developed by him and Plunket, alluded to in the following exchange of letters between them, was ripe for execution. Again many names were deliberately omitted when these letters were printed, no doubt, to protect the innocent:

LETTER I

From Mr Plunket to Mr Maclean [sic].

My Dear Fellow   *London, March 12, 1749*

BY *his Time I hope you are pretty well acquainted at the Hague, and doubt not, but you have for some Time expected an Answer to your kind and affectionate Letter from Harwich, which the Uncertainty of my Departure from London prevented. My Intention of going in Company with Mr ------, on Monday last, was prevented by a Letter from ---- ------, at ------, acquainting me, that he lay very ill of a Disorder which made his Life to be despaired of; and desired, as his last Request, to see me. This I could not think of refusing; for laying aside all Friendship for him, yet his Friends in Ireland would take it very ill, if I were to leave him in such a Condition: However, he is now better, and To-morrow is the Day peremptory fixed for my turning out. To comfort you a little, and I am sure I want a little Comfort too, I have not been quite idle since I see you; for having my Nose quite sharp set, I picked up a Trail, which I pursued four Miles below ----, where I espyed a Doe of forty Thousand, enclosed in a Park, with an old stern Fellow at the Gate; yet there were some Breaches in the Wall, whereby I thought it practicable to steal in, and catch the Fawn napping. However, I shall not content myself here, for you may depend upon it I shall use both my Ears and Eyes, as well as my Nose, on my Journey.*

I have, out of pure Obedience to your Commands, said a very few good natur'd Things to Miss ----; which I assure you was contrary to my Inclination; and the more so, that you declare a Love for her. This you may think ill-natur'd, but I can foresee where this Love will end: Why, it will be in your Time and Money spent; the Girl's Virginity and Reputation lost, our Schemes neglected, and your humble Servant half starved.

Your Advice with Regard to Presents I am determined punctually to observe for to be plain, it is out of my Power to do otherwise. You know we talk'd of a Sattin Waistcoat, with a slight Lace, but when it came to be made, the Lace grew broad, and all together it is too good to go to Ireland, so it is laid up in Lavender; and the only Pleasure it gives is, that I hope to see it wore under the embroidered Saxon Blue Coat, by Way of a Change, at ----, or elsewhere. I have likewise bought a Mare, in whose Praises I shall be short, only wish we were this Day on our journey to -----, and my Lord no better mount'd than on her Back. Your Sister Ann-Jane wrote to you,

and I opened the Letter, which indeed is a very sensible affectionate one, but nothing in it that you may not hear soon enough at our meeting. Your Mother-in-Law defers Administration till after Easter. I have opened the Trunk, taken out the Coat, and done it up with the same Lock faster than ever. I have left my Trunk in good Order, and made the Bonfire you desired. Though I am unwilling to confess all with Regard to Miss ----, yet I must tell you, that I am convinced that she is as willing to receive your Addresses as you are to make them.

I hope you will write to me to Monahan as soon as you receive this, and let me know how long you intend staying in Holland; for my Delay in Ireland shall be determined by yours at the Hague.

Direct for me at Mr Rogers's, at Monahan, not to be opened if absent.

I have omitted all Complaisance, Gratitude, and that Warmth of Affection that my Zeal for your Welfare prompt me to; being, ever since I left you, in very low Spirits. However, believe me to be as much as ever the Man who has your Happiness at Heart; and am,

> *Your humble Servant,*
> *WILLIAM PLUNKET.*

Directed to Mr James Maclean [sic], to the Care of Mr Maclean [sic], Minister of the English Church, at the Hague. [3]

LETTER II

From Mr Plunket to Mr Maclean [sic].

Dear Jemmy   *Monahan, April 12, 1749*

IN Answer to Yours from Harwich, I wrote to You from London. The most material Part of my Letter was to convince you, that I continued in the same Resolution you left me in, and had made some Progress in the Task you laid upon me at parting; and as my Delay in the Country was to be fix'd by yours at the Hague, I desir'd a Letter from you directed to Monahan, which I'm convinc'd would not have been open'd till I came.

Now what your Reason was for not answering it, I'm greatly at a Loss to find out; whether my Letter never came to your Hands, whether you were afraid to write to Monahan, for fear of a

Discovery, or whether you were determined to pursue the Affair no further, I can't guess; however, be the Case what it will, I shall give a short obscure Account of my Proceedings since I left London.

On my Way I met with a good deal of Diversion, and was at Chester and Liverpool several Days, at Assemblies, etc. much to my Satisfaction; I had a good Passage to Dublin, but on my Journey near Dundalk, I unfortunately fell from my Mare, and disjointed my Shoulder, and was otherwise very much bruised; this detained me some Time at Dundalk; and another Day, between New Mills and Lowart, going over a Stile, I slipt the Joint again, and am now at the Mills, waiting for Doctor Wedderby to have it settled a second Time.

Notwithstanding my Misfortune, I can justify myself with Regard to my Duty to my Lord and Master, for I was at Market-Hill, before I was at Lowart, delivered the Letters there, and saw your Aunt and Sister Ann-Jane; she and all your Friends there are well, Betty is in Bellfast.

I'm a little afraid to talk freely to you upon some Affairs, lest it should fall into the Hands of our Enemies, but would be glad to hear your Determination, which you may be as plain and open in as you please, because I have fixed Matters so, that no Letter directed to me at Monahan is to be delivered to any one but myself; and if I should even be set out for London, I can have them sent after me. I have been thinking of late, that if you were to bring over some Lace, etc. for the Use of the Ladies, that I could in some Country Places sell it to Advantge, and by that Means introduce myself into other Business. This by all Means would I have you do, and you will find at meeting that the Scheme is good.

You remember, I was to have bought two Horses in Ireland, for the Use of a Gentleman; but that I must confess I am not able to do, without a Remittance.

I'm divided whether I shall direct this to the Hague, lest you are set out for London, or inclose it first to London, and if you are not come there, have it directed to the Hague; the last Scheme is best, so I'll enclose it to Mr ----. I beg, for the Sake of the strictest Ties of Friendship, that you may as soon as possible satisfy me with Regard to your Intentions, and be assured that I am ready at a Day's Notice, and am as firmly as ever,

Your unchangeable Friend,

And most obedient Servant,

WILL. PLUNKET. [4]

LETTER III
Mr Plunket to Mr Maclean [sic].

My dear Fellow,   *Lowart, April 29, 1749*

SINCE I came Home, I have been very impatient on Account of my not hearing from you as I desired, and at last about ten Days ago wrote to you, but very prudently inclosed the Letter to Mr ---- if in Case you were come Home to be delivered to you, if not to be forwarded to the Hague; but if you have set out for London according to your Resolution, you I hope have met the Letter in London; however, that is a Matter to be doubted, and as the Style was somewhat ambiguous, I shall run over the Particulars in short, and with less Disguise: First then the ---- Doe, I'll venture to call Miss ----a young Lady of 40,000l* [£40,000], *independent, in some small Measure despicable in Person, desirous of being married, but confin'd by a rustic old Father of great Fortune, who has no Ambition for Places of Trust or Power, nor Taste for Pleasures; which Temper confines not only himself, but likewise his whole Family at Home; where there is no Gentleman of Fortune or Spirit enough to Court the Girl. I met with her Maid at my Mama ---- 's, and found Means, without Suspicion, to hear so much of her as I have told you; but was not myself at ----. On my Road to Chester, I met with nothing remarkable, and in Chester and Liverpool, I saw abundance of fine Ladies of extensive Fortunes, these being Places of Spirit, where they have Assemblies, etc.*

In my last, I advised you to bring some Lace, etc. from Holland, for the Use of the Ladies; which I thought I could sell to the Ladies, and say, I had been in Holland and France, with my Lord; and after puffing a little, perhaps have Sharp's good

Fortune**, by being brib'd by the Ladies to assist them in seducing my Master.

The Poor Mare has by her Journey got a dry Blindness, to such a Degree, that she scarce sees enough to ride along the bad Roads, about Lowart, and without she is better before I set out, I shall lose considerably by her; and in short, unless I can both sell her and the two Watches, of which I see no Prospect at present, I shall not be able to pay ten Guineas I owe here; which I absolutely must, much less buy a Gelding or two, with other Necessaries.

As to Miss ----- you may be assured, there is nothing of the kind, that would give you Pleasure, that I would not assist you in; but as I cannot be of any Use in that Case, except what is to be done by ----- Means, and even then, thro' her Perverseness, no Certainty of succeeding. I am sure, you'll excuse me, when I tell you, that my either sending to her a Message, or writing to – would do me the greatest Injury, be quite over-turning a Scheme I have laid, of being off with her; for which End, I wrote her a long, formal, lying Letter lately, and if her knowing, that you were in Town could be easily avoided, I should be glad on't.

In my Journey from Dublin, I got an accidental Fall, which disjointed my Shoulder, bruis'd and hurt me very much; of all which, I am pretty well recover'd, except the Weakness in my Shoulder, which has very much obstructed my Happiness, since I came Home particularly with Regard to my Cousin; ---- ---- the ---- ---- Daughter, who is now at ---- ----, and has a thousand Pounds certain, in her own Power, and without a Joak, I believe, it might be possible to carry her off; but enough of this.

I have been the more plain and particular, both with Regard to what Success I have had in tracing, and concerning my own Circumstances, that you may be the able to give me your Sentiments, what is to be done; by which, be assured, I shall be determined, and let me beg you'll loose no Time in answering me. Look not for a Multiplicity of Words to convince you of my Constancy, that being the Method of those, who endeavour to deceive; but in all Times and Places, I am semper eadem [as always].

WILLIAM PLUNKET. [5]

*The "l" in "40,000l" stands for libra pondo, the Latin words meaning "pound weight" and libra was the name of an ancient Roman weight equivalent to a pound and hence somehow adopted in the Kingdom of Great Britain to refer to monetary pounds.

**"Sharp's good Fortune" was most probably a reference to James Sharp (1613–1679) who had a meteoric rise through the Scottish Church to become Archbishop of St. Andrews (1661–1679).

LETTER IV

Mr Maclean [sic] *to Mr. Plunket; taken from a Copy written on the Back of the Former*

Dear Billy,   *Hague, May 15, 1749*

I Receiv'd your two kind Letters, and am much pleased with your Diligence, to promote our mutual Interest. The Doe is tempting, and the Circumstances not unfavourable to our Designs; I think, if we can get Access, we cannot fail of Success. The Thoughts of it has determined me to leave this Place the Day after Tomorrow, where the Pleasures of the Place would tempt me to a longer Stay; but I haste to meet you at London, that we may proceed on Schemes, that may, if rightly conducted, make us both happy for Life, and save me from the Horrors, that haunt me in the Midst of the greatest Gaiety. Your Proposal as to the Lace would do, but the India Stock is too low, to be encroach'd upon; for I have but sixty Pounds left, how the rest went, for Particulars I refer to our Meeting. I am, Dear Billy,

     Yours, &c.
     JAMES MACLEAN [sic]. [6]

LETTER V

I Receiv'd Yours, of the 15th of May, and think it unnecessary to mention my last to you, in Answer to Yours, from the Hague; because I am almost convinc'd, you have before this Time received it, and now to be short, let me first assure you, that my Dispositions, towards our intended Expedition, are as good as ever; but I am sorry to find, that the India Stock is so low, especially considering the State of Affairs with myself, which frankly is as follows: My fine Mare, worth thirty Guineas, is like to go blind, and consequently not marketable; so that I must turn her to breed, and my two Watches are still undisposed of. I am twenty Pounds in Debt in this Country, and not one Guinea in my Pocket. Now, what is to be done in this Case, I shudder at the Thought; but to convince you, that I am as well affected as ever, and I beg, you may believe me to be so, if you send me a Bill of ten Pieces, I'll endeavour to wait on you as soon as possible; but without that, by G ---- I am Storm-sted, not to mention Horse, Cloaths, etc. I am now fretting by Guts to Fiddle Strings, and tho' I have been very elegantly entertain'd since I came here, yet, I have a good deal of Trouble in keeping my Countenance, in any Sort of Gaiety, and nothing I long so much for, as to see my dear Jemmy once more.

You have seen, and I hope gained your Desire in seeing Miss ---- ----, which would give me great Pleasure; but I hope in the mean Time, you will f---- -----y for after all, I find that must be the Way for me to get rid of her.

My dear Friend, I am almost drunk, but rather than lose one Post, I chuse to trouble you with this Scrawl, which I hope you will excuse, and believe it to be the real State of the Case. I have avoided letting any of your Friends or mine know of your being in London, for certain Reasons.

I could say a great deal more, but the Whiskey is in my Head, and the Post waits; but G---- d---- me, my Dispositions for Business of any kind are as strong as ever, notwithstanding I am a Cripple, God bless you.

WILLIAM PLUNKET. [7]

LETTER VI

Mr Maclean [sic] *to Mr Plunket; taken from a Copy on the Back of the Former*

Dear Billy,   *London, May 25, 1749*

I just receiv'd your Letter, which at the same Time gave me Concern and Surprize, every Part of it being so different from what I have seen and expected from you. I am sorry you had not one sober Hour to spare to write to me in; for I think being drunk a very bad Apology for the imperfect Stile of your Letter, which, I dare say, you would blush to see, just now with the Eyes that I do, being out of a sick Bed, full of melancholy Reflections. However, it is from Will. Plunket, which prevents my saying any more on the Subject.

I now begin where I before left off; for in my former Letter, I told you, I had sixty Pieces left, twenty of which, I lost at the late Jubilee Masquerade*. My late illness, that I am just recovering out of, and my Expences otherwise, since I came to Town, has borrowed sixteen more; so that I declare, my whole Capital does not exceed 25l. [£25] which we might do something with, if you were here; but by sending ten Pounds to you, the Remainder we could never expect to do any Good with. You must have been very extravagant in your Expences, to spend what you had, and run so much in Debt. But that is a Thing, I have no Right to charge to your Account, as I have been too guilty of it myself. I wish to God you could by any Means come over, where with the small remaining Stock, and good Economy, we might put our Designs in Execution about Miss ---- - but if you stay much longer, the Money will be all gone; and I, at last, must march off to Jamaica, which I am resolved shall be my next Recourse, *if I can do nothing before the Cash is all gone; as I am resolved, what kept me before from it never shall again; you know what I mean.*

All that I can say, is that, there is to be a Masquerade at Marybon**, in eight Days, where, for the last Time, I am resolved to try my Fortune; if I am successful, you may depend on a Remittance, the next Post after, which if at all will be in ten Days after the Receipt of this. I am,

Yours, &c.

JAMES MACLEAN [sic]. [8]

* The "late Jubilee Masquerade" to which Maclaine refers in LETTER VI was held at Ranelagh Gardens, see earlier and Illustration (xi) below, at the order of King George II, partly in celebration of some sustained peace in the Wars of the Austrian Succession. Horace Walpole (see earlier) was also there and wrote of his own experience of the event as follows:

May 3, 1749- We have at last celebrated the peace, and that as much in extremes as we generally do everything, whether we have reason to be glad or sorry, pleased or angry. Last Tuesday it was proclaimed: the King did not go to St Paul's, but at night the whole town was illuminated. The next day was what was called "a jubilee-masquerade in the venetian manner" at Ranelagh: it had nothing Venetian in it, but was by far the best understood and the prettiest spectacle I ever saw: nothing in a fairy tale ever surpassed it. One of the proprietors, who was a German, and belongs to Court, had got my Lady Yarmouth [Amalie Sophie Marianne Wallmoden (von Wendt) (1704–1765); mistress of King George II; to whom he bequeathed £6,000 which was found in his desk drawer shortly after his death] *to persuade the King to order it. It began at three O'clock, and, about five, people of fashion began to go. When you entered, you found the whole garden filled with masks and spread with tents, which remained all night very commodely. In one quarter, was a May-pole dressed with garlands, and people dancing around it to a tabor and pipe and rustic music, all masqed, as were all the various bands of music that were disposed in different parts of the garden; some like huntsmen with French horns, some like peasants, and a troop of harlequins and scaramouches in the little open temple on the mount. On the canal was a sort of gondola, adorned with flags and streamers, and filled with music, rowing about. All round the outside of the amphitheatre were shops, filled with Dresden china, japan, etc. and all the shop-keepers in mask. The amphitheatre was illuminated; and in the middle was a circular bower composed of all kinds of firs in tubs from twenty to thirty feet high: under them orange trees, with small lamps in each orange, and below them all sorts of the finest auriculas in pots; and festoons of natural flowers hanging from tree to tree. Between the arches too were firs, and smaller ones in the balconies above. There were booths for tea and wine, gaming-tables* [no doubt with one where Maclaine was losing his money] *and dancing, and about two thousands persons. In short, it pleased me more than anything I ever saw...* [9]

Illustration (xi) — 'BY HIS MAJESTY'S COMMAND. The JUBILEE
BALL after the Venetian manner, Or MASQUERADE at Ranelagh
Gardens April the 26th, 1749.' (1749) — Anonymous

**The Masquerade Ball noted at the close of LETTER VI no
doubt took place at Marylebone Gardens that were opened in
1738 by the proprieter of the adjacent 'Rose of Normandy
Tavern'; one Daniel Gough. These Pleasure Gardens were also
famous for concerts, gaming, cock-fightng, bear-baiting and
boxing.

LETTER VII

Mr PLUNKET to Mr MACLEAN [sic].

I Receiv'd Yours of the 25th of May, and notwithstanding, I must acknowledge several Parts of it are not quite so kind, as I should have expected from the Person, who was always so liberal in his Declarations of Friendship. Yet, the melancholy Account of your Health, and the dismal State of your Purse, gives me as much Concern as my own present Circumstances. And now, as well to shew you, that I am not willing to be at Enmity with my once dearest Friend, as to vindicate and justify myself from the Accusation, you a little too warmly charge me with, I shall beg Leave to give you my Remarks on your severe Letter.

I acknowledged myself drunk, allow it to be so, I am sure, I wrote nothing but Facts; and I hope said nothing affronting, except, that I wanted to beg a Favour. I would be glad to know, what you mean by saying, It is Will. Plunket, that disappointed you. I am very sorry, I can say in Return, that James Maclean [sic] *has disappointed me, and shall say no more on that Subject. Next, as to my Expences, I have been so far from being extravagant, that I have been quite the Reverse; for this Debt, that I owe, was not contracted since I came Home, nor am I push'd for it at present; but what I wanted ten Pounds for, was to bring me to London, being disappointed in the Sale of two Watches, and a Mare, which I intended should bring me over; and poor as I am at present, were I in London to Night, I could pay ten Guineas by Tomorrow Night; so that I assure you, I had no View to be complimented with that Sum. Your losing Money at the Masquerade, I am not at all chargeable with, because I am convinced, had I been on the Spot, I* could not have prevented your being there, but might likely have shared the same Fate.

I confess, I am as anxious to see London once more, as you can be for what you most wish for, and will be as ready to wait of you to any Part of England, as ever I profess'd; but cannot by any Means, under my present Circumstances, get away from here before three Weeks; so that I suppose, you will make your Journey to ---- - --- before then; and without you carry a Servant, I am afraid of your Success, as they are People in a very high Station.

The best Account I can give of Mr ---- ---- is, that he is a Gentleman, who lives four Miles beyond -------- has one only Daughter of 40,000l. [£40,000] independent, besides a good deal more to be expected. She is ugly, little, and desirous of being married to a handsome, tall Gentleman; she is confined at Home very much; so that I think, if a Gentleman of Figure and Fortune were accidently to meet her at Church, and would promise to bring her to her beloved London, he might have a Chance for the Prize. And now, dear Jemmy, I'll swear, it grieves me not to accompany you, and if you could, by any Means, put off going till I hear from you, send me the Bill, and upon my Honour, you shall be paid the Day I come to Town. Besides, I have a Chance of bringing a good handsome Gelding over with me, belonging to Robin; but, I owe him ten Pounds, and without I pay him that, he will not trust me the Horse.

If you cannot come into this Scheme, I hope you'll write to me; and in the sincerest Manner, I pray God send you good Success. And am, in Spite of Fate,

Your sincere Well-wisher,
WILLIAM PLUNKET.

p.s. For Safety of Keeping, I pawn'd my Watch, at ---- Three Balls ---- ---- for two Guineas, and foolishly not thinking to stay so long in Ireland, gave him a Title to sell it at the End of three Months, if not released; therefore, beg you'll speedily release it, and pawn it again for the same; he will give it upon the under Note. Here followed an Order in common Form. [10]

LETTER VIII

Mr Maclean [sic] *to Mr Plunket; taken from a foul Copy, without Date or Subscription.*

Dear Billy,

WHEN Friends like you and I write, a scrupulous Scrutiny into the Meaning and Import of Words ought to be avoided; we know each other too well and too long, and our Interest is too much connected, to leave Room for Enmity or Suspicion on either Side. Believe me, I am as sincerely Yours as ever, and not to delay any Thing, that can give you Pleasure, know that I had a little Success at the Masquerade, and now send you the Bill for ten Pounds. For God's Sake make haste over, as we have now Cash; if you were here, I should look upon this Doe as our own. I shall do nothing till you come; but I hope to have some Amusement with Miss ---- ---- I have as good as an Assignation with her Tomorrow Night; so that I find, what you told me in one of Yours to be true, viz. that she was almost as willing to receive my Addresses, as I was to make them: But I assure you, my Affair with her shall neither take up much Time, nor Money; nor interfere with our Schemes, much less shall it half starve my Friend as you pretend to prophecy.

I am,   &c. [11]

It is difficult to understand the exact means by Plunket's and Maclaine's correspondence fell into the hands of the Press. By the fact that some of Maclaine's are written on the reverse of some of Plunket's one might assume that they were passed on by the latter in exchange for money after the former's arrest, but that of course does not explain them all. Another possible explanation crops up later in our story (see Chapter 6).

The partnership continued to carry out robberies through the summer of 1749 to fund their continued extravagance and in preparation for their grandest fortune hunting scheme; the one they had schemed up whilst apart. At some point during this period they apparently added the scalp of Sir Thomas Robinson (1695–1770); 1st Baron Grantham; who rose to fame as the English ambassador to Vienna from 1730 to 1748. When he returned to England in 1748 to represent Christchurch in Parliament he also had the misfortune of being another of their victims. Also, according to one of Horace Walpole's letters, a Mrs [Catherine] Talbot [nee Chetwynd] (1731–   ), second wife of John Talbot (1720–1756) M.P., fell prey to the pair. In the meantime Maclaine continued his own fortune hunting and romancing in London.

The following letters from a young lady; probably the one referred to in the highwaymens' earlier correspondence, were also published. After the third letter Maclaine's biographer gave her the fictitious name of 'Marian' for the following three more letters, but as you will read it was way too late of him to be trying to protect her innocence!

LETTER I

Miss ---- ---- to Mr MACLEAN [sic]

N.B. No Address.

AS I had not the Pleasure to see you the other Day, I must beg Leave to take Course to Pen and Paper, to let you know I shall be glad to see you To-day, in the Park, at three o'Clock, if agreeable to you; please to sit upon the Bench by St. James's-Gate, I'll meet you, to speak a Word or two once more. It shall be the last Time of troubling you, tho' the greatest Pleasure I have at present, is in thinking of dear Mr M ---- and I believe, it is a Displeasure to you when I come into your Thoughts. Oh! Poor me, unhappy as I am, but the Pleasure of seeing you Today, will be Life. I shan't keep you long, I shall tell you the Reason when I see you; once more send me a Line, because I shall know you are not angry with me for taking this Liberty of troubling you with my Scrole. Dear Sir, let me see you; which will be esteemed as a great Favour done to, dear Mr M.

Your most obedient humble Servant

Friday Oct 12, 1749.[12]

LETTER II

From the same to Mr Maclean [sic].

SIR,

YOUR Goodness will excuse my not seeing you; for I am so sick with Fright, I have not seen my Mama, nor No-body of the Family. Dear Sir, let me know what to do, if you will be my Friend, as promised; for I have said a great many Things about what you know. I said I was at the Play with a Lady, and I went to the Tavern with her, and was so late before it was done. I hear no more about the Marriage. From

Your disconsolate Friend.

P.S. I pray a Line from you. I am almost mad. It is impossible for me to go out, I am so confin'd. Burn this when you receive it. [13]

LETTER III

From the same to Mr. Maclean [sic].

SIR,

FOR God's Sake tell me what to do, for my Mama has got a Warrant out for to take them up where I said I was all Night. If you do not stand my Friend, and tell me what to do, I shall be lost for ever. Oh, dear Sir, remember what you promised me before I left my Papa's House. O Christ! Sir, send me a Line this Moment, for I am raving mad: From

Your dear Friend, ----. [14]

LETTER I

MARIAN to Mr MACLEAN [sic].

SIR,

UPON second Consideration of what we was talking of last Night, I think it must be on Thursday; I must put off my Engagement, though with Difficulty, and forge some Story, that I am obliged to go into the City to see a Place; so desire you will not fail coming: For, I assure you, I was forced to put my Wits to work, to contrive to be here; but as to that, it is not the first Lye I have been forced to tell on your Account – God forgive me. You know where I am now, so my Cousin gives her Compliments to you. --- Pray do not fail coming; if you do,

Wednesday Morn.   *Farewel for ever.* [15]

LETTER II

MARIAN to Mr MACLEAN [sic].

SIR,

*I W*as much surprised that you did not come on the Thursday in the Afternoon, when you urg'd it so very much, which I complied with, though with a deal of Difficulty; and after I had staid the utmost Time I could, found you did not come. --- You are not sensible of the Uneasiness it gave me, - so desired to see you in the Morning; when I went with much ado, and waited patiently till the Hour of Eleven, ---- then till Night, and finding you did not come --- Oh! You have not Tenderness enough to sympathize with me in what I underwent in my own Mind; for I plainly see you have not, nor never had, any Regard for me: If you had, you would behaved otherwise to me that you have done; for you nor No-body knows what Trouble you have brought me into, but myself: But yet, through my own Unthinkingness, you have often said to me, as well as to others, that you would do something for me, ---- though I never asked it of you; no, I have a Heart that scorns a Thing so mean, ---- but thought you had Honour and Generosity enough to have done it without, ---- but find you have neither; ---- so should be glad if you would consider seriously with yourself, not as a Man of the World, ---- but as a Man of some Gratitude, whether you think it reasonable or no; for all what I suffer now you are the Cause of. ---- I desire only to have an Hour's Talk with you, if you think it worth while: But, alas! you will think you have had what you wanted, and I may go to the Devil now, for what you care. ---- If I had no more Goodness in me than you have, I should have went otherwise to work with you than I did. ---- But now let me have a Proof of your Goodness, and let me know if you will speak to me or no; if you will not, send me a few Lines and enclose it to Mrs A--- - P----, at you know where; she said she told you. ---- So, if you will send me a few Lines, then I will let you know where I will see* *you, and when. Pray write the direct Post, for I am almost mad. - ---- No-body knows of this; pray burn it. ---- I brought it myself.*

To Mr Maclean [sic].   *Monday Night.* [16]

LETTER III

MARIAN to Mr MACLEAN [sic].

SIR,

I Suppose you received a Letter from a Friend of mine last Tuesday, but sent no Answer; – so think proper to write myself, for I find you take no Notice of the unhappy Situation you have involved me in. – You said it was in your Power to make me happy; if it is, for God's Sake do it now, for I am quite miserable at present. – Oh! Sir, had you but half that Weight upon your Mind that I have, – if you had no Love, no Honour left, yet Pity (yes, I say Pity) would move you to compassionate my Distress: – For, oh! consider what you have forced from me. You robbed me of what was always dearer to me than Life, – Yes, you know you forced it from me. – Had you robbed me of all I had in this World, but what you did, I should not have cared, for then I could have got my Living any where with an easy Mind; but now, where shall I go? Oh! Where shall I fly for Comfort? – Oh! Consider in what an unhappy Situation you left me in that fatal Night. – Oh! Why did you not take my Life, rather than what you did; then you would have done a charitable Act, and I only should have been eased of my Grief a little sooner; for you will have my Death to answer for; -- for now

I die by Inches; -- for I find it so firmly fixed upon my Spirits never to be removed, -- without you remove it. – So, Sir, for Heaven's Sake, think of something to do for me directly, for I must not stay where I am long; and where I shall go, God only knows, for I do not –

Oh! Sir, you know my Innocence, you know you forced from me what, if you had loved me, you would have scorned to have done! Oh! Man, cursed, deceitful Man, what have you all to answer for, in ruining poor, innocent, young Creatures as you do? It was your Tongue that led me into my Ruin; Oh! Wretched Creature that I am! – Oh! What can you ever do to make me Amends for what I undergo? --- if you can, do, make me easy --- if you can make me your Wife, or will, I should make it my daily Study for you never to have Cause to repent it. --- For I am sure I could not be so vile as ever to have a thought of having any Body else, for no other Man has any Right to me, but yourself --- but you never must think of having me upon other Terms, for you never shall --- no, I will first go to the farthermost Part of the World, and never think of cursed Man ---- My Inclinations are as virtuous as ever --- so, Sir, consider my Distress, and think of some Relief – before I go hence, if you do not, there is a just God that will right the Innocent, and punish the wrong Doer --- You may say any Thing to this good Gentleman, for he lives in the House, and heard all the Noise the next Morning, he is a very good Friend of mine, so you may write to me, or send by Word of Mouth which you please, for one I do expect --- Good Heaven defend me, I shall go distracted, for I hardly know what I say or do --- I could say a great deal more, but the Gentleman waits; if the Paper should be wet, it is with the Tears from my Eyes – so must conclude myself the most unhappy and wretched of my Sex.

To Mr Maclean [sic].

N.B. He told a Friend of hers that he had burnt this Letter, but it appears he did not. [17]

L E T T E R IV

MARIAN to Mr MACLEAN [sic].

SIR,

I Wonder that after writing such a Letter to you, you should take no Notice of it, but to say I had used you ill, and did not know what to make of it. Alas! Sir, I think it was I that was used ill; for what you accused me of in that Respect I know nothing of --- and as to my Letter, you know it was Truth, and all from my Heart; and there is not one Word but I can stand to; but one Word I am sorry I put in, and that is --- Wife --- Oh! Sir, I thought your Nature was more humane and tender than I find it is, for you are sensible how barbarously you used me in so short a Time, and must think what I must suffer by it, which I must keep to myself as long as I can ---.

Oh! My God, never was Girl betray'd and ruin'd in such an unthinking Manner as I was; had you perswaded or bribed me to it, then I should not have minded it so much as I do now --- But, Oh! Your Honour --- but why should I talk of Honour to one that

knows not what it is, but yet may know what Gratitude is, though
you do not practice it --- my Hand trembles, so I don't know if you
can read it, but must take it as it is --- I am at Miss --- now, and
set down to write, to ease my Mind --- they wonder they never see
you of so long ---- As you burnt the other letter for your own
Pleasure, I conjure you to do the same by this for mine --- I desire
to hear what you have to say to me, and send it where I am now --
- burn this for God's Sake, for no Body knows of it, nor would I
have them for ever so much. In Haste,

    From your uneasy,
    And injured Girl [18]

Maclaine appears not to show this "*injured Girl*" the slightest interest. Judging by the date of the first letter from her, being Friday 12 October 1749, we can estimate that the remaining correspondence took the pair at least through the next two months. This was a very busy time for Maclaine. It was to be a particular robbery he undertook in November 1749 that above all others brought him the reputation of being 'The Gentleman Highwayman'.

On Wednesday 8 November 1749 Plunket and Maclaine lay waiting for prey in the shadows of Hyde Park. At about ten o'clock they stopped the coach of none other than Horace Walpole whom we met earlier at Vauxhall, Ranelagh and White's (see Chapter 3). If the robbery had gone at all smoothly we would probably know very little about it, however Maclaine was the 'acting man' that night and with his nervous disposition, something went wrong. Plunket stopped the coach driver by holding a blunderbuss [18th Century equivalent of the sawn-off shotgun] to his head, whilst Maclaine leaned through the window to rob the passenger. We do not know if Walpole had been their specific prey that night or just in the wrong place at the wrong time. Maclaine had taken Walpole's purse and was still waiting for his watch and other valuables when quite by accident he discharged his pistol. The shot went through the roof of the carriage, but as he had been holding the pistol so close to his victim, the force of it pushed Walpole backwards and left him quite stunned. The two robbers grabbed what they could, including the coachman's watch and Walpole's sword and fled through Kensington Gate, lest the shot should have aroused the neighbourhood.

The London Evening Post, 9–11 November 1749, picked up on the story and published the following report of the robbery:

On Wednesday night last, as the Hon. Mr Horace Walpole, Brother to the Right Hon. the Earl of Orford, was returning from Holland-House*, between Nine and Ten, he was stopt in Hyde-Park by Two Men on Horseback, mask'd, one of which held a Blunderbuss to the Coachman, while the other came up to the Chariot, and, thrusting a Pistol into it, demanded Mr Walpole's Money and Watch; he gave the Fellow his Purse, and as he was giving him the Watch, the Pistol, which was held close to his Cheek, went off; but, tho' it was so near that the Force struck Mr Walpole backwards, the ball luckily miss'd him, and went thro' the Corner of the Chariot just above his Head, only scorching his Face, and leaving several marks of Powder. The Coachman started, and said, What is that? The Man with the Blunderbuss swore he would shoot him, if he spoke, bid him give him his Watch, and then riding up to *the Chariot, they took Mr Walpole's Sword, and some Silver from the Footman, and rode off to Kensington Gate. Besides the two Highwaymen who attacked the Chariot of Horace Walpole, Esq: there were three more at a Distance, who waited the Event, very strongly arm'd.*

The London Evening Post, 9–11 November 1749 [19]

"Holland-House" was the home of Henry Fox (1705–1774), 1st Baron Holland of Foxley, a leading British politician.

When Walpole advertised the loss of his watch, money [*"about eight guineas,"*[20]] and seals in the General Advertiser of 10 November 1749 with a reward of 20 guineas for their safe return, Maclaine took the very unusual step of writing directly to his victim, apparently on gilt-edged paper, offering to return them for twice that amount. His letter (see below) offered a rendezvous at Tyburn Gallows (see Chapter 6), between seven and eight o'clock i.e. well after dark, on the evening of Monday 13 November 1749. Maclaine would of course have another appointment at the same venue within a year and for quite a different purpose! His letter was as follows:

Sir   *Friday Evening [Nov. 10, 1749].*

> *seeing an advertisement in the papers of to Day giveing an account of your being Rob'd by two Highway men on wedensday night last in Hyde Parke and during the time a Pistol being fired whether Intended or Accidentally was Doubtfull Oblidges Us to*

take this Method of assureing you that it was the latter
and by no means Design'd Either to hurt or frighten
you for tho' we are Reduced by the misfortunes of the
world and obliged to have Recourse to this method of
getting money Yet we have Humanity Enough not to
take any bodys life where there is Not a Nessecety for it.
we have likewise seen the advertisem[en]t offering a
Reward of twenty Guineas for your watch and sealls
which are very safe and which you shall have with your
sword and the coach mans watch for fourty Guineas
and Not a shilling less as I very well know the Value of
them and how to dispose of them to the best advantage
therefor Expects as I have given You the preference that
you'll be Expeditious in your answering this which
must be in the daily advertiser of monday; and now
s[i]r to convince you that we are not Destitute of
Honour Our selves if you will Comply with the above
terms and pawn your Honour in the publick papers
that you will punctually pay the fourty Guineas after
you have Rece[ive]d the things and not by any means
Endeavour to apprehend or hurt Us I say if you will
agree to all these particulars we Desire that you'll send
one of your
Serv[an]ts on Monday Night Next between seven and
Eight o clock to Tyburn and let him be leaning
ag[ain]st One of the pillers with a white hankerchif in
his hand by way of signall where and at which time we
will meet him and Deliver him the things All safe and
in an hour after we will Expect him at the same place
to pay us the money Now s[i]r if by any Means we find

186

that you Endeavour to betray Us (which we shall goe prepaird against) and in the attempt should even suceed we should leave such friends behind us who has a personall knowledge of you as would for ever seek your Destruction if you occasion ours but if you agree to the above be assured you nor none belownging to you shall Receive any or the least Injury further as we depend upon your Honour for the punctual paym[en]t of the Cash if you should in that Decieve us

the Concaquence may be fattall to you– if you agree to the above terms I shall expect your answer in the following words in Mondays Daily Advertiser– Whereas I Rece[ive]d a letter Dated friday Evening last sign'd A:B: and C:D: the Contents of which I promise in the most sollemn manner upon my Honour strictly to comply with. to which you are to sign your name–if you have anything to object ag[ain]st any of the above proposalls we Desire that you'll let us know them in the Most Obscure way you Can in mondays paper but if we find no notice taken of it then they will be sold a tuesday morning for Exportation._____

A:B: & C:D:

P:s:

    the same footman that was behind the Chariot when Rob'd will be Most Agreeable to Us as we Intend Repaying him a triffle we took from him–

Addressed: To
  The Hon[oura]ble Horatio Walpole Esq[ui]r[e] [21]

Apparently there was a second letter from Maclaine to Walpole as they negotiated over Maclaine's [extortionate] price. The Gentleman's Magazine for the month of November 1749 also published the story of the robbery and the resulting correspondence (see below); this caused quite some speculation in the capital as to the identities of 'A:B: and C:D:' Who were these 'Gentlemen Highwaymen'?

The Hon. Horatio Walpole, brother to the Earl of Orford, who was robbed by two men on the 7th in Hyde Park, when a pistol going off shot through the coach, and scorched his face, received a letter from the robbers, intimating their concern for the accident, and their apprehension of the consequences at that time; and that, if he would send a place named, a person would be there to deliver his watch, sword and coachman's watch, if he would, on his honour, send 40 guineas in less than an hour to the same place, with threats of destruction if he did not. But he did not comply, though he afterwards offered 20, the sum they fell to in a second letter.

The Gentleman's Magazine, November, 1749. [22]

Walpole himself, writing for the 103rd Edition of 'The World' magazine on Thursday, 19 December 1754, said of his robbery *"that the whole affair was conducted with the greatest of good breeding on both sides"*[23] He also wrote about the episode some years later within the memoirs of his life:

One night in the beginning of November, 1749, as I was returning from Holland House by moonlight, about ten at night, I was attacked by two highwaymen in Hyde Park, and the pistol of

one of them going off accidentally, razed the skin under my eye, left
some marks of shot on my face, and stunned me. The ball went
through the top of the chariot, and if I had sat an inch nearer to the
left side, must have gone through my head.
Horace Walpole [24]

Of Maclaine's letters, Walpole said that whilst they had *"less*
wit than the epistles of Voltaire, [they] *had ten times more natural*
and easy politeness in turn of their expression." [25] Voltaire was the
pen name of Francois Marie Arout (1694–1778) whose
intelligence, style and wit combined to make him one of France's
greatest writers and philosophers of all time. When Maclaine was
at the height of his fame, Arout was living in Potsdam, near
Berlin, at the invitation of Frederick II (1712–1786], King of
Prussia, "Frederick the Great".

Plunket and Maclaine must have felt the time was now ripe
for their much-awaited excursion to the country in pursuit of the
"Doe of 40,000l". They could happily leave the conjecture behind
them and probably explained their absence by 'Squire Maclaine
returning home to Ireland to attend to financial matters of his
estates. Maclaine's biographer advises that at the start of the
excursion *"it was the Season of Cocking,"* [26] which helps us place it
in time. The season of pheasant shooting nowadays is from 1
October to 1 February (however very few estates consider
pursuing the birds before late October), and it will have been
roughly the same period in the 18th Century. Therefore their
expedition, which lasted for approximately three months, will
have been from December 1749 to February 1750.

They had left London in high spirits, with cash in their pockets, astride two fine geldings, handsomely *"equiped with very grand Furniture."[27]* Maclaine was to assume the title of a Lord and Plunket the role of his valet. When they first reached the area where they knew the Fawn to lay [hopefully napping!], they had no acquaintance with anyone connected with the family apart from a waiting maid with whom Plunket had spoken some eight months previously. *"However, that was but a trivial Discouragement to Men of their enterprizing Spirit."[28]* They put up at an inn in the next-door village and began working out how they were going to get an introduction to the young lady. As we know, it was the season of cocking, so they came up with the stratagem that "my Lord" should pretend to be fond of the sport of shooting pheasant. He *"borrowed a Gun of the Landlord of the Inn, and sent his Man with an impudent, formal Compliment to the Lord of the Manuor* [sic], *the stern old Fellow that watched the Doe, desiring to shoot in his Enclosures."[29]* They had two hopes from this; firstly to get the family acquainted with the assumed title and secondly to allow Plunket to gain access to the servants. Both succeeded; leave to shoot was granted, and *"my Lord went a shootin, shot a Brace of Cocks, and sent them as a present to the Squire, who received them in but a surly Manner,"[30]* but at least Plunket was building up a rapport with the butler and the Waiting Maid. The latter gave them great encouragement by agreeing to fall into the scheme.

At this stage everything seemed to be going very well but they needed to do better, so *"My Lord went to Church on the Sunday, dressed fine enough for a Birth-Day, drew the Eyes of the whole Congregation on his Person and Finery, and made no small Impresion on the Object to whom this gawdy Show was addressed."[31]* The next day they heard from their emissary, the Waiting Maid, that he had certainly made the young lady's heart flutter and his name was scarce from her lips for the rest of the day.

On the following Sunday, after sermon, my Lord was so bold as to invite himself into the Squire's company, *"but the stern old Fellow who hated Court and Courtiers, as much as he did Debt or Taxes, suspecting his Lordship of some Court-Intrigue relating to Election, returned the Complement he made him in the Church-yard, in such gruff terms, that Impudence was dashed, and he durst not proceed to invite himself to Dinner."*[32] He decided to bide his time and did not push for an appointment, *"however, he bowed to the little ugly Miss, saw Corn, Wine, and Oil in her Countenance, and a kind of an approving Languor in her Eye, that made great Amends for the unpolite Behaviour of the Rustic her Father."*[33]

Despite their continued efforts, the pair found it almost impossible to extend the "Breaches in the Wall" of protection around the girl. Over the course of three months they really got not much further than their "successes" of the first two weeks. Time and again, my Lord would send amorous notes via the Waiting Maid, begging for the opportunity to meet with his Love, either inside or outside her Father's land, but these were never answered. At last, as their patience was wearing thin *"and their Purse drained to the last Guinea, and my Lord's Horses in some Danger of being in Tribulation at the Inn."*[34] Maclaine received a short note from the Waiting Maid; it was not good news… *"her Master had discovered his Lordship's Business in that Country, said publickly at Table, that he was a sharping Scoundrel, and no Lord, and before two Days would have him in the stocks, dressed in one of his best Suits."*[35] She went on to warn Maclaine that her Master *"was a malicious, testy old Fellow where he took a Pique, and valued a Lord no more than a Louse."*[36] My Lord did not need any more convincing; he *"packed up his Awls that very Night,"[37]* and set out for London in deep despair and anger.

Maclaine conveniently forgot his resolution made in his second letter to Plunket (Letter VI, dated 25 May 1749 from London), that he would "march off for Jamaica", which he had described as his next recourse if the scheme failed. The two highwaymen set about replenishing their severely depleted funds in the manner that had been all too successful for them in the past. Maclaine had by degrees become bolder in his behaviour during the course of each robbery. He had convinced himself that he was in some way untouchable and *"he became every day more free to commit robbery, and less apprehensive of detection, for he imagined that Plunkett's [sic], turning evidence could alone affect him; and he had no doubt of the fidelity of his accomplice."[38]*

He continued to romance the ladies of London, attending Coffee Houses, balls and masquerades, always on the look-out for any Lady of Fortune. He had another "set-to" with a gentleman who nearly exposed him, while he was courting a fine Lady of Chelsea. Maclaine was so maddened by yet another disappointment that he went looking for the fellow, a Captain M_____, demanding satisfaction. Maclaine caused a scene at Kilbourne Wells whilst in pursuit of him and finally caught up to confront him at Putney Bowling Green. Captain M_____ refused him the honour of a duel on the basis *"that he was not obliged to fight every Scoundrel, and that he was no Gentleman."[39]* Maclaine immediately wrote to Colonel Richard Tonson of Dunkettle whom we met in Chapter 2. When a letter returned confirming his status he made an arrangement to meet Captain M_____ at Hyde Park; renowned at the time for the fighting of duels. Captain M_____ refused to accept the letter as genuine *"which induced Maclean* [sic], *who happened to have his Whip in his Hand, to shake it over his Head, as if he were going to discipline him; but Company coming up, soon interposed, and prevented any further Consequence."*[40]

The incident with Captain M_____ was the last of worthy note before the final robberies undertaken by Plunket and Maclaine. On the night of Monday 25 June 1750 Maclaine was determined to go out on Hounslow Heath to rob one Alexander Montgomerie (1723–1769), 10th Earl of Eglinton, who had effectively thrown down a gauntlet to any highwayman daring enough to attempt to rob him, by making it widely known that he travelled with an armed guard and a blunderbuss of which he was not afraid to use. Eglington was at the time the Grand Master of the Grand Lodge of Scotland and very well-known across the British Isles. Maclaine's bravado was riding on a high and he wanted the satisfaction of belittling the Lord. It was he who proposed this excursion to Plunket, *"who was at the Time indisposed, and very unwilling to turn out, but Maclean* [sic] *impelled by an uncommon Impulse, urged him so earnestly, that he complied."*[41]

At two o'clock the following morning, Tuesday 26 June 1750, the two, on their way to intercept Lord Eglinton, and apparently on the spur of the moment, stopped the Salisbury Flying Stage Coach. They were between Turnham Green and Brentford *"at the Place where the Horses usually stale."*[42] As it was at such an early hour, the passengers were at a particularly low ebb and allowed themselves to be robbed without putting up the slightest resistance. Five men and one lady were on board and Plunket, as acting man on this occasion, bid all the men to stand outside the coach, while he robbed them one by one. The first, a Mr. Thomas

Lockyer, conversed with Plunket whilst the latter searched him; he said he did not carry much since being robbed of a gold watch some six months prior. That did not stop Plunket taking all he had including his wig and a very fine whip. A Mr. Josiah Higden was wearing an exceptionally fine waistcoat that Maclaine took an instant shine to, as he was quite a connoisseur in such garments, and bade him remove it. From a Roman Catholic priest they took some linen in a cloth bag and his crucifix. Plunket then put his pistol in his pocket so as not to frighten the lady as he robbed her whist she remained in the coach, asking from her *only what she chose to give,*[43] and did not search her further. As an afterthought they went back for the portmanteaux [18th Century suitcases] stored away in the boot; *each of them took one of them before him and made off, bidding a Polite Adieu to the Passengers, and riding as deliberately as if they had been guilty of no such Thing.*[44]

Neither of them had time or inclination to give this unscheduled robbery a second thought for it was not much later the same morning when they reached Hounslow Heath and very quickly spotted Lord Eglinton approaching them in his post-chaise. As anticipated he had two guards on horse with him, but as they were about half a mile behind, he might as well have been alone. The Gentlemen Highwaymen executed Maclaine's pre-planned stratagem to perfection. Maclaine deliberately approached the post-chaise from the front [note: other sources say it was Plunket; see Illustration (xii)] and shielded himself from his Lordship's direct aim by keeping the Post-boy, whom he threatened with his pistol and made stop, between himself and his prey. His gamble paid off as Lord Eglinton did not dare shoot his blunderbuss and endanger the lad; not that he had much time to aim, as Plunket pushed his pistol through the glass at the back of the post-chaise and threatened to *"blow his Brains out through his Face,"*[45] unless he threw the gun down. *"The danger of the situation rendered compliance necessary, and his Lordship was robbed of his money and a surtout coat."*[46] *"Maclean* [sic] *declared in the Gatehouse that they took from his Lordship but seven Guineas in Cash, though the News-Papers made their Booty amount to forty Guineas."*[47] *"After the carriage drove forward, Maclane* [sic] *took up the coat and blunderbuss, both of which were found in his lodgings when he was apprehended; but when he was afterwards tried for the offence which cost him his life Lord Eglinton did not appear against him."*[48] Lord Eglinton in 1769 came to his own sticky end when he was shot by a poacher on his own property at Ardrossan, in Scotland, and after lying languishing for fourteen hours, died. The culprit was an Excise Officer by the name of Mungo Campbell (–1770), another veteran of the Battle of Dettingen. To avoid an ignonimous death Campbell hung himself on 28 February 1770 the day after he was sentenced to death for murder.

Illustration (xii) – 'An Exact Representation of MACLAINE the
Highwayman Robbing LORD EGLINTON on Hounslow Heath on the
26th June 1750'. (13th August 1750) – Charles Mosley (fl. 1737–1765)

The two highwaymen returned to Maclaine's lodgings that
night with their substantial plunder and smuggled it inside in
their usual way: *"the Master and Mistress of the House being in Bed,*
they called up the Boy who lay in the Shop to let them in, and then sent
him for some Liquor, while they carried the Baggage up Stairs."[49]
Those who examine the sources of old sayings have started to
agree that the saying "[to be] as p_____d as a newt" most probably
stemmed from the 18th Century. When gentlemen spent much
time in gaming houses etc. they would leave their horses in the
care of young boys, or 'Newts" as they called them. It was
customary, particularly on cold nights, to send out a warm-up
drink or two, only to find the boys quite inebriated by the time
they collected their horses later! There was nothing out of the
ordinary concerning the robberies they had committed that

morning; indeed they had been totally successful. It was what Maclaine did next that was the problem…

Chapter 4 – References

[1] Anonymous. '*A COMPLETE HISTORY of James Maclean [sic], THE GENTLEMAN HIGHWAYMAN, who was executed at TYBURN on Wednesday, October 3, 1750, for a Robbery on the Highway*'. [1750; Printed for Charles Corbett, London]. Page 27

[2] Ibid. Page 27

[3] Ibid. Page 27 to 29

[4] Ibid. Pages 30 and 31

[5] Ibid. Pages 32 to 34

[6] Ibid. Pages 34 and 35

[7] Ibid. Pages 35 and 36

[8] Ibid. Pages 36 and 37

[9] Wright, John and Ellis, George Agar (1797–1833), 1st Baron Dover. '*THE LETTERS of HORACE WALPOLE, EARL OF ORFORD*'. *Volume I*. (1735–1745) [1840; Printed by Richard Bentley, London]. Pages 267 and 268

[10] Anonymous. '*A COMPLETE HISTORY of James Maclean [sic], THE GENTLEMAN HIGHWAYMAN, who was executed at TYBURN on Wednesday, October 3, 1750, for a Robbery on the Highway*'. [1750; Printed for Charles Corbett, London]. Pages 38 to 40

[11] Ibid. Pages 40 and 41

[12] Ibid. Pages 41 and 42

[13] Ibid. Page 42

[14] Ibid. Pages 42 and 43

[15] Ibid. Page 44

[16] Ibid. Pages 44 and 45

[17] Ibid. Pages 46 and 47

[18] Ibid. Page 48

[19] *The London Evening Post*, 9–11 November 1749

[20] *The General Advertiser* 10 November 1749

[21] Paget Toynbee, Helen (–1910). '*Supplement to the Letters of Horace Walpole*' Volume III [1918–1925; Clarendon Press, Oxford]. Pages 132 to 135

[22] *The Gentleman's Magazine*, November 1749

[23] The World No 103; Thursday 19 December 1754. Page 316

[24] Paget Toynbee, Mrs Helen (–1910). '*Short stories of My Life; The Letters of Horace Walpole' Volume I* [1903–1905; Clarendon Press, Oxford]. Page x1

[25] *The World* No 103; Thursday 19 December 1754. Page 317

[26] Anonymous. '*A COMPLETE HISTORY of James Maclean [sic], THE GENTLEMAN HIGHWAYMAN, who was executed at TYBURN on Wednesday, October 3, 1750, for a Robbery on the Highway*'. [1750; Printed for Charles Corbett, London]. Page 49

[27] Ibid. Page 49

[28] Ibid. Page 49

[29] Ibid. Page 49

[30] Ibid. Page 49

[31] Ibid. Page 50

[32] Ibid. Page 50

[33] Ibid. Page 50

[34] Ibid. Page 50

[35] Ibid. Pages 50 and 51

[36] Ibid. Pages 51

[37] Ibid. Pages 51

[38] Knapp, Andrew and Baldwin, William. '*THE NEW Newgate Calendar BEING INTERESTING MEMOIRS OF NOTORIOUS CHARACTERS,*

Who have been convicted of Outrage on THE LAWS OF ENGLAND, *DURING THE SEVENTEENTH CENTURY, BROUGHT DOWN TO THE PRESENT TIME'.* Volume II. [1810; Printed for J. and J. Cundee, London] Page 338

[39] Anonymous. '*A Genuine Account of the Life and Actions of James Maclean [sic], Highwayman, to the time of his trial and receiving sentence at The Old Bailey, containing his Robberies, Gallantry at Public Places, with other remarkable transactions; together with some account of Plunket his companion'.* [1750; Printed for W. Falstaff, London]. Page 15

[40] Ibid. Page 16

[41] Anonymous. '*A COMPLETE HISTORY of James Maclean [sic], THE GENTLEMAN HIGHWAYMAN, who was executed at TYBURN on Wednesday, October 3, 1750, for a Robbery on the Highway'.* [1750; Printed for Charles Corbett, London]. Page 52

[42] Anonymous. '*A Genuine Account of the Life and Actions of James Maclean [sic], Highwayman, to the time of his trial and receiving sentence at The Old Bailey, containing his Robberies, Gallantry at Public Places, with other remarkable transactions; together with some account of Plunket his companion'.* [1750; Printed for W. Falstaff, London]. Page 11

[43] Harper, Charles George (1863–1943). '*HALF-HOURS WITH THE HIGHWAYMEN, Picturesque Biographies and traditions of the "knights of the Road"'.* [1908; Chapman & Hall Limited, London]. Page 286

[44] Anonymous. '*A COMPLETE HISTORY of James Maclean [sic], THE GENTLEMAN HIGHWAYMAN, who was executed at TYBURN on Wednesday, October 3, 1750, for a Robbery on the Highway'.* [1750; Printed for Charles Corbett, London]. Page 52

[45] Anonymous. '*A Genuine Account of the Life and Actions of James Maclean [sic], Highwayman, to the time of his trial and receiving sentence at The Old Bailey, containing his Robberies, Gallantry at Public Places, with other*

remarkable transactions; together with some account of Plunket his companion'. [1750; Printed for W. Falstaff, London]. Page 14

[46] Knapp, Andrew and Baldwin, William. *'THE NEW Newgate Calendar BEING INTERESTING MEMOIRS OF NOTORIOUS CHARACTERS, Who have been convicted of Outrage on THE LAWS OF ENGLAND, DURING THE SEVENTEENTH CENTURY, BROUGHT DOWN TO THE PRESENT TIME'*. Volume II. [1810; Printed for J. and J. Cundee, London] Page 339

[47] Anonymous. *'A COMPLETE HISTORY of James Maclean [sic], THE GENTLEMAN HIGHWAYMAN, who was executed at TYBURN on Wednesday, October 3, 1750, for a Robbery on the Highway'*. [1750; Printed for Charles Corbett, London]. Pages 52 and 53

[48] Knapp, Andrew and Baldwin, William. *'THE NEW Newgate Calendar BEING INTERESTING MEMOIRS OF NOTORIOUS CHARACTERS, Who have been convicted of Outrage on THE LAWS OF ENGLAND, DURING THE SEVENTEENTH CENTURY, BROUGHT DOWN TO TH E PRESENT TIME'*. Volume II. [1810; Printed for J. and J. Cundee, London]. Page 339

[49] Anonymous. *'A Genuine Account of the Life and Actions of James Maclean [sic], Highwayman, to the time of his trial and receiving sentence at The Old Bailey, containing his Robberies, Gallantry at Public Places, with other remarkable transactions; together with some account of Plunket his companion'*. [1750; Printed for W. Falstaff, London]. Page 17

Chapter 4 – Suggested Further Reading

In addition to the above:

As per Chapter 3

CHAPTER 5

CAPTURE / EXAMINATION / TRIAL

One of Maclaine's biographers, when at his most moralising, noted: *"all human Prudence is in vain to Stop the Hand of Justice, when once the Measure of our Iniquity is full, our closet Secrets take Air we know not how, our Precaution serves to betray us and our Folly acts the Part of Informers to satisfy offended Justice. The crisis of Maclean's* [sic] *fate was at Hand; he had run his Course, and must now attone for his Depradations on the Public."*[1] And so it was to be that Maclaine's own folly would bring him down. He missed the *"Snares and Precipices"* that lay before him as clear as *"the Sun at Noon-day"* to use the expressions that his own brother would later adopt (see Chapter 6) in writing to him after his condemnation.

Just two weeks after the robberies of the occupants of the Salisbury Flying Coach and of Lord Eglinton, Maclaine, needing a further supply of ready cash, decided to dispose of the stolen property. He stripped the lace from the fine waistcoat of Mr. Higden who had been on the Coach and, by a sheer and very unfortunate coincidence, happened to take it for sale to the exact same laceman who had sold it to Mr. Higden in the first place. The laceman had heard of the robbery through advertisements taken out in the public papers [a practice noted by César de Saussure when describing English Coffee House culture in

Chapter 3] and recollected the pattern of the lace. He did not buy the lace at that time as there was some strong haggling over the price, Maclaine feeling that he could get a much better price elsewhere.

The laceman immediately told Mr. Higden of what had happened and that he knew the gentleman with the lace as he had sold some to him before. Mr. Higden told the laceman that should the lace be offered again that he must buy it at any price and have the gentleman followed. Sure enough Maclaine did return to the shop saying that he would prefer to sell the lace to someone known to him rather than a stranger, albeit at a much lesser price that its true worth. When he left the shop he was duly followed. Whether he realised this or not, Maclaine managed to give "the slip" to the person on his tail by darting in and out of the various courts along The Strand.

Maclaine was however still so much off his guard that on Thursday 19 July 1750 he visited the shop of a Mr. William Loader, a Jew dealer, of Monmouth Street, offering clothes for sale. He invited the shopkeeper to his lodgings later that day so that he might properly see all the items he had available. When Mr. Loader viewed the clothes he said, *"Sir, these were not made for you; but received for Answer, that they were left by a Relation who died."*[2] Mr. Loader bought the clothes for £4.10s. He later showed them to a Mr. W___ler, who had kept the shop before him, who recognised them from the description in the papers following the robbery of the Salisbury Stage Coach. Mr. Loader said: *"I can shew you where, and of whom I bought them."*[3] When Mr. W___ler showed Mr. Higden the clothes he confirmed them as his own, and applied to the Justice of the Peace, Thomas Lediard, for a warrant to seize Maclaine.

On the morning of Friday 27 July 1750, the constable, Mr. W___ler, together with Pat Henly, the Turnkey of The Westminster Gatehouse, went to St. James's Street. They could see that Maclaine was at home and was dressing; they decided to wait rather than risk a shoot out. Maclaine left the house and turned into Ryder Street and on towards Bury Street [perhaps he had been intending to see Plunket in Jermyn Street or was just heading to St James's Square?] where they came up behind him, one to each arm, whilst the third took his sword. They walked him back to St. James's Street where they put him a coach and took him to Justice Lediard's house in New Palace Yard.

News of the arrest of 'The Gentleman Highwayman' quickly spread and many people came to identify him as being the highwayman that robbed them but no one would swear to it. Maclaine initially strongly protested his innocence and stressed his indignation at being a gentleman arrested for theft; what should a gentleman such as he know of highway robbery? No confession was sought at that time and Maclaine was therefore due to be allowed to go to The Gatehouse. The Westminster Gatehouse was situated opposite the West end of Westminster Abbey. Built it 1370, it once kept Sir Walter Raleigh (1552–1618), the famous explorer, historian, poet and courtier of Queen Elizabeth I (1533–1603), on the eve of his execution in Old Palace Yard in October 1618. Samuel Pepys, whom we met, admiring the gibbets on Shooter's Hill in Chapter 3, was held there for three weeks in 1690 on suspicion of supporting the exiled King James II. It was eventually demolished in 1776 but not before Dr Samuel Johnson, writing in 1761, described it as *"a disgrace to the present magnificence of the capital, and a continual nuisance to neighbours."*[4] Maclaine would have been entitled to travel without handcuffs; however, Pat Henly said to him: *"Countryman, Indeed, but I must put your Ruffles on."*[5] Justice Lediard then commanded a full search of Maclaine's lodgings. *"where was found a remarkable coat of Lord Eglinton's, embroidered with Silver, His Lordship's Blunderbuss, Mr Lockyer's Whip with his Name on it, some of the Priest's Linen, Whip, Shoes, etc. taken out of the Portmanteaus. There were also a great many rich Suits of Cloaths belonging to himself, and in the Pockets of a Frock were found, two Pistols, not Fellows, loaded* [Perhaps Maclaine could add "cross-dressing" to his growing list of crimes?!]; *two Powder-Horns, and some Ball. In searching his Drawers, above twenty different Sorts of Purses were found cramm'd into one: and a great Variety of Rings and other Effects of Value, which they had taken in their several Robberies."*[6] A *"Mrs M____t____e, one of his Ladies, had the Assurance to stay there all the while, very little concern'd!"*[7] In total the haul from Maclaine's lodgings was estimated at approximately £200 of stolen goods. At the Gatehouse Maclaine immediately began to attract many visitors including *"Lord Mountford* [sic], *at the head of half White's."*[8] One of Maclaine's aunts is also recorded as being present that day and therefore must have been staying in London at the time.

I cannot be certain of it but I believe that the assured and "very little concerned", "Mrs M____t____e" was one Lady Mary Wortley Montague (1689–1762), née Pierrepont; divorced spouse of Sir Edward Wortley Montague (1678–1761); who was himself famous for being appointed British Ambassador in Turkey and also being one of the earliest champions of the copyrighting of books. She was a famous early feminist, poet and travel writer who is also credited with bringing back from Turkey the knowledge of the Ottoman way of fighting smallpox by inoculation [a.k.a. variolation]. The British medical profession at the time was sceptical of a foreign treatment and one championed by a woman but were made to listen when she gained the backing of Queen [Wilhelmina Charlotte] Caroline (1683–1737) of Brandenburg-Ansbach; queen consort of King George II. Mary herself had survived, but at the same time had been quite disfigured by the disease in December 1715; even to the extent of losing her eyelashes. Her "discovery" later influenced the work of Edward Jenner (1749–1823), 'The Father of Immunology', as he developed a smallpox vaccination from cowpox. Lady Mary was originally betrothed to one Clotworthy Skeffington (1660–1714) who later became the 3rd Viscount Massereene in Ireland before she eloped with her future husband. Alexander Pope (1668–1744); the famous English essayist, satirist, poet and critic whose long poem 'An Essay on Criticism' included the now infamous lines: "*a little Learning is a dang'rous Thing*" [often misquoted as "a little knowledge.."]; "*To Err is Human, to Forgive Devine*" and "*For Fools rush in where angels fear to tread*"[9] fell in love with her in 1731 but their relationship ended very publically and very acrimoniously. She visited Horace Walpole in Florence in 1740 whilst he was on his Grand Tour (see Chapter 3), the latter taking an instant dislike to her particularly due to her slovenliness. Apparently, according to one of her biographers, "*She did not care a straw whether she was being named in all sorts of grimy liaisons because men came and went in her house, and sometimes stayed. ...it is hard to conceive of an aging slattern* [an untidy, dirty woman] *who did not look in her glass for eleven years being very much concerned about lovers...*"[10]

The Whitehall Evening Post, 26–28 July 1750, described Maclaine as a "*very genteel, tall young fellow, and very gay in his*

207

dress."[11] This publication was a London newspaper started in September 1718 by Daniel Defoe, whom we met on the King's Highway in Chapter 3, which had three issues a week until 1801. We do not know at what stage William Plunket found out that his friend had been taken, but he quickly disappeared and was never captured. Perhaps he knew there was a real danger of Maclaine impeaching him. He was never heard of again …or was he? (see Chapter 8). When his rooms were searched a lady was found there, wearing little other than Mr. Higden's ribbons!

On Monday 30 July 1750, Justice Lediard visited Maclaine at The Gatehouse as he had heard that the latter *"was desirous of making a Confession."[12]* The Justice would only ask how many accomplices were involved; when Maclaine insisted only one, he said that if he had *"any View of serving himself by Impeaching; the naming of one only would be of no signification."[13]* (see reference to The Highwayman Act in Chapter 3). The Justice told Maclaine to dwell on this for an hour, after which time he would return to see if he wished to proceed.

Maclaine would not have been aware of it, but Justice Lediard was also interviewing other witnesses put forward by Mr. Higden, such as William Loader, the laceman and his own tailor. *"The following Circumstance contributed greatly to prove his Guilt; which was, That the Taylor who made the Waistcoat and trimm'd it, being ready to swear before Justice Lediard, that if the Lace produced before him was Mr Higden's Property, that the Piece sewed on the left Sleeve was longer by an Inch than that sewed on the right, owing to a Mistake in the Taylor's Foreman, who had carelesly cut the Lace too long, which he had sewed on the left, the Master himself having sewed the Lace on the right Sleeve* [sounds like the Master was the one who actually got it wrong!]; *and upon the Lace being measured before the Justice, it appeared to exactly match what the Taylor asserted."[14]*

On Wednesday 1 August 1750, Maclaine was taken before the Justice in a coach with a file of musketeers and hundreds of people following behind. During the next one and a half hours, with persons of Quality present, Maclaine *"behaved with utmost pusillanimity, confessing with continued Tears the robbing of the Honourable Horatio Walpole, Esq; in Hyde Park, of his Watch and Money; and declared that the Pistol was not fired intentionally, but went off by Accident."[15]* He went on to say that if his shot had found its billet in Walpole's head, then he would surely have put another through his own. He had written out a confession that included details of all the robberies that he had undertaken with Plunket, but at that meeting he was not pressed to sign it. *"were present Lord M[ontfor]d* [Henry Bromley (1705–1755) 1st Lord Montfort of Horseheath*], Lord Edg[com]b[e]* [Sir George Edgecombe (1720–1795*)], Lord S____l, Sir G. O___n, Lady P[etersha]m, Lady T_____, who has since said, he had often been about her House, and she never miss'd any Thing; Miss S_____, Miss A___k, Mrs W_____pe. The major Part of whom, especially the Ladies, not only shew'd a Concern for him, but shed Tears in abundance."[16]*

Elsewhere others are recorded as being present that day including: John Ponsonby (1713–1789) [Lord Duncannon], Philip Dormer Stanhope (1694–1773) [4th Earl of Chesterfield, whom we met earlier at Ranelagh Gardens in Chapter 3] and Miss Ashe [*"The Pollard Ashe,"[17]* as Walpole referred to her, singing her way to Vauxhall in Chapter 3]. By their own testimonies at Maclaine's later trial, both Mr. Higden and Mr. Loader were also present. When Maclaine asked Justice Lediard to obtain for him two and half guineas from a box in his room, as he now needed it in his current circumstances [see Chapter 6], this, *"occasioned several Persons to make him considerable Presents."[18]*

Maclaine *"was remanded to the Gatehouse with a Serjeant's Guard attending him, for Fear of a Rescue."[19]* At the end of his examination into the facts presented to him, Justice Lediard committed Maclaine for trial at the Old Bailey. He bound over Mr. Higden and Mr. Loader as witnesses for the Prosecution. During his stay at The Gatehouse, Maclaine apparently had thousands of visitors. One gentleman accused him of robbing him but described him as being on foot at the time, to which Maclaine replied that he had never robbed on foot in his life. The gentleman then commented *"it was common talk that he was a meer Poltroon, an errant Coward, who had never dar'd shoot a Pistol in his Life."[20]* Maclaine replied: *"Sir, I have as much personal Courage in an honourable Cause, as any man in Britain: But as I knew I was committing Acts of Injustice, so I went about them half loth and half consenting; and in that Sence, I own I am a Coward indeed."[21]* One Reverend Minister burst into his cell demanding to see the highwayman that had robbed him, but Maclaine's friends ridiculed him so much that he never got to make his voice heard above their laughter. Many of Maclaine's visitors were from the highest of society including his friends and acquaintances from White's Club [no doubt they would have wagered on the outcome of his up and coming trial] and gave him much money. Captain M_____ also came; Maclaine apparently greeted him with the words: *"Ah, M_____! You are glad to see me here, and triumph over me now"[22]*

Horace Walpole wrote to one of his closest friends, Horace Mann (1706–1784); the British ambassador at Florence with whom he had stayed whilst on his Grand Tour, the following letter expressing his thoughts at the time:

To Horace Mann, Strawberry Hill, Aug. 2, 1750

I have been in town for a day or two, and heard no conversation but about M'Lean [sic], a fashionable highwayman, who is just taken, and who robbed me among others; as Lord Eglinton, Sir Thomas Robinson of Vienna, Mrs Talbot, &c. He took an odd booty from the Scotch Earl, a blunderbuss, which lies very formidably upon the justice's table. He was taken by selling a laced waistcoat to a pawnbroker, who happened to carry it to the very man who had just sold the lace. His history is very particular, for he confesses everything, and is so little of a hero, that he cries and begs, and I believe, if Lord Eglinton had been in any luck, might have been robbed of his own blunderbuss. His father was an Irish Dean; his brother is a Calvinist minister in great esteem at the Hague. He himself was a grocer, but losing a wife that he loved extremely about two years ago, and by whom he has one little girl, he quitted his business with two hundred pounds in his pocket, which he soon spent, and then took to the road with only one companion, Plunket, a journeyman apothecary, my other friend, whom he has impeached, but who is not taken. M'Lean [sic] had a lodging in St James's Street, over against White's, and another at Chelsea; Plunket one in Jermyn Street; and their faces are as known about St James's as any gentleman who lives in that quarter, and who perhaps goes upon the road too. M'Lean [sic] had a quarrel at Putney bowling-green two months ago with an officer, whom he challenged for disputing his rank; but the captain declined, till M'Lean [sic] *should produce a certificate of his nobility, which he has received ... There was a wardrobe of clothes, three-and-twenty purses, and the celebrated blunderbuss found at his lodgings, besides a famous kept mistress*. As I conclude he will suffer, and wish him no ill, I don't care to have his idea, and am almost single in not having been to see him. Lord Mountford* [sic]*, at the head of half White's, went the first day: his aunt was crying over him: as soon as they were withdrawn, she said to him, knowing they were of White's, 'My dear, what did the lords say to you? Have you ever been concerned with any of them?' Was it not admirable? what a favourable idea people must have of White's! – and what if White's should not deserve a much better! But the chief personages who have been to comfort and weep over this fallen hero are Lady Caroline Petersham and Miss Ashe: I call them Polly and Lucy, and asked them if he did not sing*

**Thus I stand like the Turk with his doxies around. [23]

*The "famous kept mistress" as I have conjectured was most probably Lady Mary Wortley Montague, see earlier.

**"Thus I stand like the Turk with his doxies around" is the first line of the final song of John Gay's (1685–1732) 'The Beggar's Opera'. It is sung by the highwayman Captain Macheath, whilst standing surrounded by his female conquests, which include Polly Peachum (his "fence's" [someone who knowingly buys stolen goods for later resale] daughter to whom he is married) and Lucy Lockit (his Gaoler's daughter, who is carrying his child).

Walpole's parallel between 'M'Lean' [sic] and Captain Macheath, in his closing remarks, is an interesting one on many levels. 'The Beggar's Opera' was well-known to satirise his own father's corrupt governmental administration, at the same time lampooning the then hugely popular Italian opera and showing up the moral degradation of London's society by depicting a pervasive underworld of thieves, prostitutes and robbers, some of whom were outwardly quite respectable. The original idea of the Opera came from Jonathan Swift (1667–1745); the Irish satirist and writer; probably most famous for his novel 'Gulliver's Travels' (1726), who wrote to Alexander Pope (see earlier, one lover of Lady Mary Wortley Montague) on 30 August 1716 asking, *"...what think you, of a Newgate pastoral among the thieves and whores there?"*[24] Their friend, Gay, decided that it should be a comedy rather than a pastoral.

Almost every reference to James Maclaine that touches on 'The Beggar's Opera', without exception, makes Maclaine out to have been the original highwayman on which the opera is based. As the Opera was written in 1716 and first performed on the London stage on 29 January 1728; at John Rich's Theatre Royal at Lincoln's Inn Fields where it ran for 62 consecutive performances, more than any other work known up until that time; this when Maclaine would have been just four years of age, we know that this could not possibly be the case. 'The Beggar's Opera' was "aped" almost 200 years later in 1928 in Germany by an alternate version produced by Bertolt Brecht (1898–1956) and Kurt Weill (1900–1950), under the title 'Die Dreigoschenoper' ('The Threepenny Opera').

The Gentleman's Magazine for September 1750, as well as printing Maclaine's defence statement, of which we shall see shortly, also published a letter written by Rev. Archibald Maclaine to a gentleman who had written to inform him, upon learning of his brother's arrest. This letter and another written by Rev. Maclaine to his "Unhappy Brother!" became very popular and were published widely. The first is as follows:

Utrecht, Aug. 17, N.S.* 1750
S I R,

I Receiv'd your melancholy Letter, but the dismal News it contained had reached me here before it arrived, as I have been happily absent from the Hague some Time.

I never thought any belonging to me would have loaded me with such heart-breaking Affliction, as the infamous Crimes of him whom I will call Brother no more, have brought upon me; how often, and how solemnly have I admonished him, of the miserable Consequences of an idle Life, and, alas! to no Purpose!

However that be, I have made all the Application possible for his Life, filled with Shame and Confusion, that I have been obliged to make Demands so contrary to Justice, and hardly knowing with what Face to do it, in the Character I bear, as a Minister of Truth and Righteousness.

It is the Interest of some Friends, I have made here, that can only save his Life: They have lost no Time in applying, and I hope their Endeavours will be successful; but I still hope more, that if Providence should so order Events, as that he escapes the utmost Rigour of the Law, and has that Life prolonged, he does not deserve to enjoy any longer, I hope, or rather wish, that in such a Case he may have a proper Sense and Feeling of his enormous Crimes, which lay ample Foundation for drawing out the wretched Remainder of his Days in Sorrow and Repentance.

With Respect to me, it would give me Consolation, if I could hope that this would be the Issue of his Trail; it would comfort me on his Account, as he is a Man, because I will never acknowledge him in any nearer Relation; and because, except such good Offices as former Ties, and present Humanity demands from me on his Behalf, I am never to have any further Correspondence with him during this mortal Life.

I have given Orders to look towards his Subsistence, and what is necessary for it.

I am obliged to you, Sir, for your Attention in communicating to me this dismal News, and shall willingly embrace any Opportunity of shewing myself, Sir,

Your most, &c.

P.S. If you see this my unhappy Brother, let him know my Compassion for his Misery, as well as my Indignation against his Crimes; an also that I shall omit nothing in my Power to have his sufferings mitigated; – he has, I fear, broken my Heart, and will make me draw on the Rest of my Days in Sorrow. [25]

*It is interesting to note the letters 'N.S.' included in the date of this letter. This stood for 'New Style'. On the Continent of Europe the Gregorian calendar had been in use for many years, while England lagged behind, in every sense, by adhering to the Julian calendar. In 1750 the English were eleven days behind their European counterparts. The month of September 1752 in

England was shortened by eleven days to allow us to catch up.

Archibald's letter betrays his confusion and turmoil at the time. On the one hand he disowns James: *"him whom I shall call brother no more,"* with all the righteousness of the pious Minister he was becoming; on the other he explains how he had done everything possible, through his contacts in Holland and England, to help have his life spared and misery in prison alleviated.

Shortly before Maclaine's trial, Horace Walpole wrote the following brief letter to his friend, Mann; clearly he had caught up with what Maclaine had said about his own robbery, probably from Lady Caroline Petersham:

To Horace Mann, Arlington Street, Sept. 1, 1750

My friend M'Lean is still the fashion: have I not reason to call him my friend? He says, if the pistol had shot me, he had another for himself. Can I do less than say I will be hanged if he is? They have made a print*, a very dull one, of what I think I said to Lady Caroline Petersham about him,

Thus I stand like the Turk with his doxies around! [26]

*See illustration (xvi) in Chapter 6.

On Friday 7 September 1750 Maclaine was transferred from The Gatehouse to Newgate (see Chapter 6 where a full description of that prison is included), to await his trial at The

Old Bailey, which was by then scheduled to be part of the Sessions [a batch of trials] due to commence on Wednesday 12 September 1750. The Old Bailey was the nickname for the Justice Hall or Sessions House that had been present in that street, in one guise or another, since at least 1539.

Before the Sessions could be called the Clerk of the Court was responsible for drawing up the indictments. This was apparently done to a set formula, based on information about the nature of the crime, the identity of the accused and the victim. The indictments were important, as the way in which the offence was defined would pre-determine the punishment the defendant might receive, if convicted. Before the case could proceed to the Old Bailey, there needed to be a sort of pre-trial in front of a Grand Jury, reviewing the indictment with the prosecutor (the victim of the alleged crime) and their witnesses (but not the accused; who had to second-guess what evidence would be put up against them) to see if there was sufficient evidence to try the case before a Jury. Those cases that were approved to go forward for trial were known as "True Bills"; whilst those that were rejected were considered "Ignoramus" (or "not found") and were kicked out at that stage.

In James Maclaine's case The London Metropolitan Archives in London still hold a hand-written parchment record of his indictment that contains slightly more detail than that which was finally printed in The Proceedings i.e. the official record of all the trials from each Session, written by the Recorder of the Court and printed for sale by M. Cooper, at the Globe in Paternoster Row, at four pence. The version below is from the former:

*The jurors of our Lord the King upon their oath present that
James Macklaine* [sic] *late of the parish of Chiswick in the County
of Middlesex Labourer on the 26 day of June in the 24th year the
reign of our Sovereign Lord George the second King of Great
Britain or with force and arms at the parish aforesaid in the county
aforesaid in the Kings Highway there in and upon one Josiah
Higden in the peace of God and our said Lord the King then and
there being feloniously did make an assult and* [putting] *him the
said Josiah in corporal fear and Danger of his life in the Kings
Highway aforesaid then and there feloniously did put and* [take]
*one Cloth Coat of the value of twenty shillings, one pair of Cloth
Breeches of the value of ten shillings, one wig of the value of thirty
shillings, one pair of pumps of the value of four shillings, five
Holland Shirts of the value of forty shillings, three Sewn Stocks of
the value of three shillings, one pair of Silk Stockings of the value of
six shillings, one pair of Worsted Stockings of the value of three
shillings, one pair of Thread Stockings of the value of two shillings,
one pair of Gloves of the value of six pence, one Linnen Towel of the
value of six pence, one pair of Silver Spurs the value of fifteen
shillings, one pair of Silver Shoe Buckles of the value of eight
shillings, one pair of Silver Knee Buckles the value of three shillings,
one half pound weight of Tea of the value of three shillings, two Tin
cannisters of the value of two pence, three yards Ribbon of the value
of twelve pence, three Linnen handkerchiefs of the value of two
shillings, one Leather Cloak Bag of the value of two shillings, two
pieces of Gold Coin of the proper Coin of this Kingdom called
Guineas, the value of forty-two shillings of the Goods Chattels and
Moneys of the said Josiah from the person and against the Will of
the said Josiah in the Kings Highway aforesaid then and there and*

feloniously did steal take and carry away against the peace of our said Lord the King his Crown and Dignity. [27]

The above document is annotated with the following words in the top right hand corner: *"Puts himself upon the County Jury... Guilty. Hanged by the neck until he be dead,"*[28] but this is so extremely faint and faded it is only possible to decipher it by comparison to the other surrounding indictments. It was signed on the back by the following list of people: Josiah Higden, William Loader, Peter Cappreol, Thomas Hughes, James Kentley, Thomas Humphryes and John Waddloy. Maclaine's indictment, when published within The Proceedings had altered the spelling of his name to Macleane [sic] and had, perhaps more understandably, shortened the list of stolen items.

"The Right Honourable John Blachford, Esq; Lord Mayor of the City of London, the Right Honourable the Lord Chief Justice Willes, and Richard Adams, Esq; Recorder, and others of His Majesty's Justices of Oyer [to hear] *and Terminer* [to determine] *of the City of London, and Justices of Gaol Delivery* [to deliver the gaol of its prisoners i.e. to hand over the prisoners to be tried to determine their innocence (or guilt)] *of Newgate, holden for the said City, and County of Middlesex,"*[29] were the judges who led the Proceedings of all of the trials within the Session starting on 12 September 1750. A total of 117 other prisoners were tried during the seven day September Sessions with the cases generally not lasting longer than half an hour each; Maclaine's case which started at approximately noon on Thursday 13 September 1750 is reported to have lasted about an hour and a half.

The juries had to be lined up well in advance and approved by the Sheriffs of both the City of London and of Middlesex. Jurors were always men of worth, gentlemen, tradesmen, professional, shopkeepers, artisans etc. Maclaine's case was heard before the Middlesex Jury which consisted of the following twelve gentlemen: Benjamin Timbrell, John Luttman, Richard Stenton (who, having fallen ill at some point during the Sessions, was replaced by one John Gilbert), William Perrett, John Wilkins, John Barlow, William Seccul, Thomas Blake, William Timbrell, Robert Morgan, Thomas Morris, and John Blacksley. The jurors sat in stalls to the defendant's right; sufficiently close together to be able to confer with one another and reach the speedy verdict that was demanded of them, without leaving the court to achieve it.

As the prisoners within Newgate were kept in such cramped, rancid conditions, disease would run rife from time to time, throughout the complex, which of course would include the Sessions House. The worst ever epidemic of "Gaol Fever" [typhus or typhoid] was at its height during one of the earlier Sessions of 1750; it apparently killed off the Lord Mayor – Sir Samuel Pennant (–1750), one Alderman – Sir Daniel Lambert (1685–1750), two judges, one of the Under Sheriffs of Middlesex and at least fifty other jurors and barristers. Subsequent to this, the Lord Mayor, Judges, Aldermen and Sheriffs relied on carrying nosegays and having aromatic herbs spread on the floors of the benches [this apparently still happens today], to keep down the stench and prevent infection[!].

Spectators frequently came to see the trials, and courthouse officials had the right to charge fees for entry to the galleries. At Maclaine's trial a great many "society folk" crammed into the galleries, the vast majority of them *fine ladies who had consorted with the accused.*[30] After the Clerk to the Court had read out

Maclaine's indictment, making it a formal charge against the defendant, he was asked to plead to which he replied *"Not guilty."[31]* This was important, and the Court would generally encourage this plea, as an admission of guilt at this stage would otherwise negate the need for any evidence to be heard and take away the Court's ability to be flexible with the punishment. In other words, if the Judges could hear and question all the evidence they could determine whether the defendant merited a lesser sentence or even a pardon.

First it was the turn of the Prosecution to state its case. Mr. Higden duly took to the Witness Box; where both Prosecution and Defence witnesses stood to testify, the layout of the Court being arranged so as to emphasise the conflict between the accused and the rest of the Court. He was therefore directly opposite Maclaine, who stood at 'the Bar', and made the following statement:

Mr. Higden: "On the 26th June, I was [a] passenger in the Salisbury flying Coach, going thither. There were four gentlemen and one gentlewoman with me. Betwixt Turnham Green and Brentford, betwixt the five and six mile stone in the parish of Chiswick, between 1 and 2 o'clock in the morning, a man came up to the side of the coach and put his pistol in, demanding our money; at the same time calling to his companion who lagg'd behind to come up. Then came up another person. They were both arm'd and mask'd. The second acted but little; he rather sat on horseback as a guard. I gave about twelve or fourteen shillings to the man that came up first. They declared that should not do, and ordered us out of the coach into the high-way. They took six shillings out of another pocket of mine, and four penny worth of halfpence out of my breeches pocket, and threaten'd to blow my brains out for concealing it. He on horseback I believe threatened as much as the other. After this, the person who came up first, declared he would see what was in the boot of the coach, and accordingly jump'd up, and by the help of the coachman, took out two cloak bags; one of which as my property. They made the coachman help them up before them, and each rode off with one.

Some of these things were found again in the prisoner's lodgings. I found there a light perriwig, three pair of stockings, a pair of double channel pumps, a handkerchief, two canisters without tea. They were found on the 27th July, the day the prisoner was taken, in his trunk, and they are my property, taken out of my cloakbag. I found also at Mr. Loader's a cloth coat and breeches, and a waistcoat, with the lace stripp'd off. The portmanteau was brought home three weeks after, said to be found in Kensington Gravel-pits. There were also two guineas in money.

I also heard the prisoner own the robbery before the Justice; he said he, and one William Plunket, did commit that robbery; and told me how they divided the cloaths; he wrote his confession down himself, but did not sign it." [32]

Whilst Maclaine had the unusual luxury for the time of having the assistance of a defence lawyer, he insisted on conducting his own defence. In the mid-18th Century there was no presumption of innocence. It was down to the defendant to disprove the evidence presented against them and establish their innocence. A common line of attack for a defendant, particularly one being advised by a lawyer, would be to take advantage of the opportunity to cross-examine the witnesses and to therefore question the motives of the prosecutor in bringing the action in the first place e.g. were they not trying to claim a reward of some sort? Maclaine tried to throw some tricky questions at Mr. Higden, mainly based on the answers the latter had given during the Judges' cross-examination (these were only ever rarely recorded in The Proceedings, and not at Maclaine's trial), but to little effect:

Maclaine: "When was the first time that witness ever saw me?"

Mr. Higden: "I have seen him pass my door several times before this."

Maclaine: "Did he hear me make any confession?"

Mr. Higden: "Yes I did."

Maclaine: "Did not Mr. Higden declare before the Justice he never saw me before?"

Mr. Higden: "No, My Lord, I did not."

Maclaine: "Did not Mr. Higden say, the man's voice that robb'd him did not agree with mine?"

Mr. Higden: "I said, I could not say it was the prisoner's voice."

Maclaine: "Did he never declare he would have my life, and hoped on that account to be made a great man?"

Mr. Higden: "No, I never declared any such thing. I said, I would go through with it in duty to my country." [33]

The only other witnesses that appear to have taken the stand on the prosecution side were William Loader and Justice Lediard, whose testimonies, under oath, with a final comment from Mr. Higden, were as follows:

William Loader: "The prisoner came himself to me, and desr'd I would come and look at some things he had to dispose of; I think this was the 19ᵗʰ of July, he lived with one Mr. Dunn in St. James's-Street; he shew'd me a light colour'd cloth coat and breeches, a waistcoat with the lace ripped off, I bought them of him with other things. Mr. Higden came to my shop some time after, and found the things on the counter and own'd them. I went and got a warrant for the prisoner in the name of Macleane [sic], the name he left with me of his own hand writing, for a direction for me to come to see the cloaths; he was taken, I was with him before the Justice and heard him confess taking these things from the coach, with the other things."

Mr. Higden: "These things were advertised in the publick papers several times, and there is the periwig maker that made the wig now in court."

Justice Lediard: "The prisoner and the things were brought before me, he denied the fact at first, he said if I would be of any service to him he would make a confession. I told him I could not admit him as an evidence, but if he had a mind to make a voluntary confession, I would hear it, but I would not at all press him to it: I gave him an hour's time to do it; I went down stairs and up again, and then he told me he had committed this and several other robberies in company with one Plunket; I bid him recollect, as nearly as he could, all the robberies he had committed, and come again the next day; he bought it me the next day in writing, I did not ask him to sign it, he gave it me to read, and said the contents of that paper were true. I left the paper in his hands and never ask'd it of him. [I rather suspect Maclaine ate it in any way!]. *He confess'd the taking of the two portmanteaus, and among the rest, the things that lay before him. He confess'd this when I went to him at the Gate-house, and likewise when he was examined by me the first of August."* [34]

Maclaine at this point desired to read out his defence statement. A mirrored reflector was positioned above 'the Bar' to shine light from the windows into the face of the accused. This would allow the Court to observe their facial expressions and form opinions on the validity of their testimonies. There was also a sounding board to amplify their voices. Sat directly in front of the accused, below the judges, were the clerks, lawyers and writers who took the notes in shorthand for production of The Proceedings. This is what Maclaine had to say for himself:

Maclaine: "My Lord, I Am persuaded from the Candour and Indulgence shewn me in the Course of my Trial, that your Lordship will bear with me with Patience, and make Allowance for the Confusion I may shew before an awful Assembly, upon such solemn an Occasion.

Your Lordship will not construe it Vanity in me, at this Time, to say, that I am the Son of a Divine of the Kingdom of Ireland, well known for his Zeal and Affection to the present Royal Family and happy Government; who bestowed an Education upon me, becoming his Character, of which I have in my Hand, a Certificate from a noble Lord, four Members of Parliament, and several Justices of the Peace, for the Country where I was born and received my Education.

About the Beginning of the late French War, my Lord, I came to London, with a Design to enter into the military Service of my King and Country; but unexpected Disappointments obliged me to change my Resolution; and having married the Daughter of a reputable Tradesman, to her Fortune I added what little I had of my own, and entered into Trade in the Grocery Way, and continued therein till my Wife died. I very quickly after her Death found a Decay in Trade, arising from an unavoidable Trust reposed in Servants; and fearing the Consequence, I candidly consulted some Friends, and by their Advice, sold off my Stock, and in the first Place honestly discharged my Debts, and purposed to apply the Residue of my Fortune in the purchase of some military Employment, agreeable to my first Design.

During my Application to Trade, my Lord, I unhappily became acquainted with one Plunket, an Apothecary, who by his Account of himself, induced me to believe, he had travelled abroad, and was possessed of Cloaths and other Things suitable thereto, and prevailed on me to employ him in attending on my Family, and to lend him Money to the amount of 100l. [£100] and upwards.

When I left off Trade, I press'd Plunket for Payment, and after receiving by degrees several Sums, he proposed, on my earnestly insisting that I must call in all Debts owing to me, to pay me part in Goods and part in Money.

These very Cloaths with which I am charged, my Lord, he brought to me to make Sale of, towards Payment of my Debt, and accordingly, my Lord, I did sell them, very unfortunately, as it now appears; little thinking they were come by in the Manner Mr Higden hath been pleased to express, whose Word and Honour are too well known to doubt the Truth.

My Lord, as the contracting of this Debt between Plunket and myself was a Matter of a private Nature, so was he Payment of it; and therefore, it is impossible for me to have the Testimony of one single Witness to these Facts, which as it is an unavoidable Misfortune I hope, and doubt not, my Lord, that your Lordship and the Gentlemen of the Jury will duly weigh.

My Lord, I cannot avoid observing to your Lordship, Is it probable, nay, is it possible, that if I had come by those Cloaths by dishonest Means, I should be so imprudent as to bring a Man to my Lodgings at Noon-day to buy them, and give him my Name and Place of Residence, and even write that Name and Residence myself in the Salesman's Book? It seems to me, and I think must to every Man, a Madness that no one, with the least Share of Sense, could be capable of. [Too true! We are still wondering that ourselves; even now!]

My Lord, I have observed in the Course of Mr Higden's Evidence, he hath declared, he could not be positive either to my Face or Person, the Defect of which, I humbly presume, leaves a Doubt of the Certainty of my being one of the two Persons.

My Lord, it is very true, when I was first apprehended, the Surprise confounded me, and gave me the most extraordinary Shock; it caused a Delirium and Confusion in my Brain, which rendered

227

me incapable of being myself, or knowing what I said or did; I talked of Robberies as another Man would do in talking of Stories; but, my Lord, after my Friends had visited me in the Gate-house, and had given me some new Spirits, and when I came to be re-examined before Justice Lediard, and then asked, if I could make any Discovery of the Robbery, I then alledged I had recovered my Surprize, that what I had talked of before concerning Robberies was false and wrong, and entirely owing to a confused Head and Brain.

This, my Lord, being my unhappy Fate; but unhappy as it is, as your Lordship is my Judge and presumptive Counsil, I submit it, whether there is any other Evidence against me than circumstantial.

First, the Selling of the Lace and Cloaths, which I agree I did; for which I account.

Second, The verbal Confession of a confused Brain; for which I account.

All this Evidence, I humbly apprehend, is but circumstantial Evidence.

It might be said, my Lord, that I ought to show where I was at this Time.

To which, my Lord, I answer, that I never heard the Time, nor the Day of the Month, that Mr Higden was robbed; and, my Lord, it is impossible for me, at this Juncture, to recollect where I was, and much more to bring any Testimony of it.

My Lord, in cases where a Prisoner lies under these Impossibilities of Proof, it is hard, nay, it is very hard, if Presumption and Intendment may not have some Weight on the Side of the Prisoner. I humbly hope, and doubt not, but that Doctrine will not escape your Lordship's Memory to the Jury.

My Lord, I have lived in Credit and have had Dealings with Mankind, and therefore humbly beg Leave, my Lord, to call about a Score to my Character, or more, if your Lordship pleases; and then, my Lord, if in your Lordship's Opinion the Evidence against me should be by Law only circumstantial, and the Character given of me by my Witnesses should be so far satisfactory, as to have equal Weight, I shall most willingly and readily submit to the Jury's Verdict." [35]

Maclaine called a total of nine people to testify to his good character. Such witnesses were especially useful, since if the defendant was found guilty, evidence of good character might lead to a lesser sentence. The Proceedings did not record the names of his witnesses; we know only that one was a Mr. Barlowe. A print was produced by T. Fox in the Old Bailey and sold for sixpence. Plain, one shilling. coloured, shortly after; showing Maclaine standing, with his legs shackled, at the Bar, see Illustration (xiii), holding his defence statement in his left hand, with his right hand resting on his chest in an expression of innocence. Beneath the picture was his defence statement printed out. Also in the picture, as well as ladies shedding tears in the gallery, is Lady Caroline Petersham (see below) in the Witness Box, answering the Right Honourable John Blachford Esquire's question: *"What has your L[adyshi]p to say in favour of the Prisoner at y'Bar?"* She replies: *"My L[or]d, I have had the Pleasure to know him well, he has often been about my House and I never lost any thing."*[36]

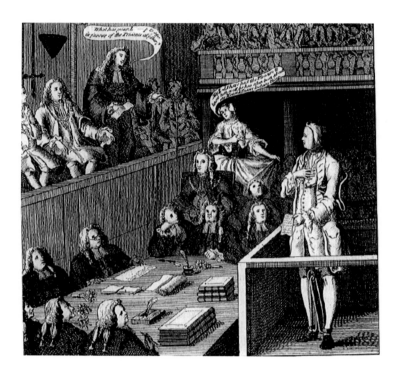

Illustration (xiii) – 'James Macleane [sic], the Gentleman Highwayman at the Bar'. (29ᵗʰ September 1750) – Anonymous

Lady Caroline Petersham (1722–1784), whom we met earlier at the centre of Horace Walpole's party at Vauxhall Gardens (see Chapter 3) and at Justice Lediard's house (see Chapter 5), was a daughter of Charles Fitzroy (1683–1757), 2ⁿᵈ Duke of Grafton. She was the wife of William Stanhope (1719–1779), Viscount Petersham and (eventual, 1765) 2ⁿᵈ Earl of Harrington, who was nicknamed "Peter Shambles" due to a peculiarity of gait, following an injury at the (lost) Battle of Fontenoy on 30 April

1745 (see Chapter 2). She was an energetic socialite, despite being the mother to three young daughters by 1749; a friend of Horace Walpole and "close acquaintance" of James Maclaine.

At the end of Maclaine's trial the Jury retired (or huddled together) to debate their verdict. They would have the choice of three possible outcomes: innocent, guilty, or a partial verdict i.e. the defendant would be found guilty of part of the charges only. It was no real surprise to anyone when the Foreman of the Jury pronounced Maclaine to have been found Guilty. He was returned to his cell in Newgate to await sentencing.

On Wednesday 19 September 1750, as The Sessions came to a close, Maclaine and all the other prisoners who had been found guilty were returned to the Justice Hall to hear their fates. It was traditional, if not a right, for defendants who had been convicted of capital crimes to be given the opportunity to address the Court, immediately before receiving their sentence. In the same way that he had prepared a defence statement for his trial, Maclaine had also written down a final plea for lenience that he intended to read out; it was certainly expected of him. Perhaps he was so shocked to hear the death penalty come down on so many of his fellow convicts or he had simply resigned himself to the inevitable helplessness of his situation, but when it came to the moment of truth, he found himself completely unable to deliver it. He could only utter the words: *"My Lord, I cannot speak."*[37]

My Lord, however, could speak. He donned his "Black Cap" and pronounced that Maclaine would *"be hanged by the Neck until he be Dead."*[38] Fifteen others from that Session were to receive the same fate, five were to be transported for fourteen years, thirty-two for seven years, two were to be branded, six were to be whipped; only one had their sentence respited [delayed] at that point in time. Therefore out of a total of 117 people committed for trial in the September 1750 Sessions, only a little over half (62) were found guilty.

Thinking for a moment what James Maclaine's sentence might have been if today's guidance to judges were to be applied; this comes from the Crown Prosecution Service under Section 8 of the Theft Act 1968 and has a maximum sentence of 'Life' (in prison). There are however a series of example length of sentences noted as well as the below list of 'Aggravating and Mitigating Factors' that might sustain or reduce such a sentence:

- Professional hallmarks – *yes*
- More than one offender or gang – *yes – two, with William Plunket*
- Detailed reconnaissance and planning – *yes – to some extent*
- Carrying firearm or ammonia – *yes*
- Firearm real – *yes*
- Disguise/balaclavas worn – *yes – Venetian masks*
- Substantial Gain – intended or obtained – *yes – sometimes such as the East India Company haul on Shooter's Hill*
- Firearm discharged or ammonia used – *yes – we know at least once*
- Injury caused to victim – *yes – slight injury to Horace Walpole*

Having reviewed the list one might argue that all applied to some extent in Maclaine's case and therefore he would probably have been recommended to receive either 18 years or 'Life'.

I have learnt recently of a little known fact about London in September 1750 whilst the focus of the Town was on Maclaine's trial. Apparently Bonnie Prince Charlie sailed from Antwerp to England and stayed secretly in a house in Essex Street, just off The Strand, where he met with Jacobite sympathisers and spies.

The poet Thomas Gray (1716–1771), the lover of Horace Walpole, who we met earlier on the Grand Tour (see Chapter 3), at the time of Maclaine's trial altered the wording of his poem 'The Long Story', a poem of 144 lines arranged in 36 verses of 4 lines each; written at the invitation of a Lady Cobham, Anne Halsey (–1769), of the Manor House at Stoke Poges, and widower of Sir Richard Temple (1675–1749), Viscount Cobham, to incorporate the following verse:

> *But soon his rhetoric forsook him,*
> *When he the solemn hall had seen;*
> *A sudden fit of ague shook him,*
> *He stood as mute as poor Macleane* [sic]. [39]

What Maclaine had intended to say was the next day published as follows:-

The following is a Copy of what he intended to say, if Sorrow had not denied him Utterance; from his own Hand-writing:

"My Lord, I shall not presume to trouble your Lordship with many Professions of Sorrow and Penitence; such from Men in my unhappy Condition, are too often considered to proceed more from Fear and Shame, than a Heart justly touched with a deep Sense and

Abhorrence of my past inexcusable Conduct------ Were the Sentiments of my Soul this Moment disclosed to the World in their in their true Light, I should have no Occasion to use any Expressions to move Compassion------ For the best of Men are the readiest to pity the Anguish o their Fellow-Creatures not hardened in Guilt. ------I might, perhaps, collect some Circumstances to mitigate the Execution of a Sentence I am now going to receive. ------But as I am sensible that nothing of that Sort on my Trial escaped the Penetration of the Court, so I am equally assured, that if there is room for Mercy, it will be recommended.

My Lord, it is for my Offences against Heaven and the Publick; it is for my Family disgraced, for a helpless Infant Daughter, that my Heart is weighed down with contrite Anguish, and dares not with Confidence apply to the Great and Good. And yet, my Lord, permit me to implore so Much mercy as will for ever remove me from being a Disgrace to those who once knew me worthy of a better Fate, and will enable me to pass the Remainder of my Days in Penitence and sorrowful Obscurity." [40]

As Maclaine never had the courage to read out these words we do not know if they would have had any effect at all on the Judges present at the time. Once again he was returned to his cell in Newgate, but this time to wait to hear when his end would come. His only thought now was a hope against hope that he might somehow receive a pardon. This may not have been a completely unrealistic prospect, as the punishments handed down by the Court were not always carried out. Cases could be referred to the King and his cabinet who had the power to award free or conditional pardons. It was the Recorder's job to prepare the Court's recommendation to the King and his Privy Council, indicating which prisoners should hang and which should have their sentence commuted (usually to transportation). The King and Privy Council would then sit in their "Hanging Cabinet" meeting and make the final determinations…

Chapter 5 – References

[1] Anonymous. *'A COMPLETE HISTORY of James Maclean [sic], THE GENTLEMAN HIGHWAYMAN, who was executed at TYBURN on Wednesday, October 3, 1750, for a Robbery on the Highway'*. [1750; Printed for Charles Corbett, London]. Page 52

[2] Anonymous. *'A Genuine Account of the Life and Actions of James Maclean [sic], Highwayman, to the time of his trial and receiving sentence at The Old Bailey, containing his Robberies, Gallantry at Public Places, with other remarkable transactions; together with some account of Plunket his companion'*. [1750; Printed for W. Falstaff, London]. Page 19

[3] Ibid. Page 19

[4] Hare, Augustus John Cuthbert (1834–1903). *'Walks in London' Volume II* [1878; George Routledge and Sons, New York]. Page 369

[5] Anonymous. *'A Genuine Account of the Life and Actions of James Maclean [sic], Highwayman, to the time of his trial and receiving sentence at The Old Bailey, containing his Robberies, Gallantry at Public Places, with other remarkable transactions; together with some account of Plunket his companion'*. [1750; Printed for W. Falstaff, London]. Page 20

6 Ibid. Pages 20 and 21

[7] Ibid. Page 21 and
The London Magazine or Gentleman's Monthly Intelligencers. Volume XIX For The Year MDCCL . August 1750 [1750; Printed for R. Baldwin at the Rose in Pater Noster Row, London]. Page 377

[8] Paget Toynbee, Mrs Helen (–1910). *'The Letters of Horace Walpole' Volume III* [1903–1905; Clarendon Press, Oxford]. Page 7

[9] Pope, Alexander (1668–1744). *'AN ESSAY ON CRITICISM'* [1711; printed for W. Lewis, London] Pages 14, 30 and 36

[10] Kronenberger, Louis (1904–1980). *'Kings and Desperate Men. Life in Eighteenth Century England'* [1942; Alfred A. Knopf, New York].

[11] *The Whitehall Evening Post.* 26–28 July 1750

[12] Anonymous. *'A Genuine Account of the Life and Actions of James Maclean [sic], Highwayman, to the time of his trial and receiving sentence at The Old Bailey, containing his Robberies, Gallantry at Public Places, with other remarkable transactions; together with some account of Plunket his companion'.* [1750; Printed for W. Falstaff, London]. Page 21

[13] Ibid. Page 21

[14] Ibid. Pages 18 and 19

[15] Ibid. Page 22

[16] Ibid. Pages 22 and 23

[17] Cunningham, Peter. *'The Letters of Horace Walpole, Earl of Orford'. Volume II.* 1749–1751. Page 78

[18] Anonymous. *'A Genuine Account of the Life and Actions of James Maclean [sic], Highwayman, to the time of his trial and receiving sentence at The Old Bailey, containing his Robberies, Gallantry at Public Places, with other remarkable transactions; together with some account of Plunket his companion'.* [1750; Printed for W. Falstaff, London]. Page 23

[19] Ibid. Page 23

[20] Ibid. Page 24

[21] Ibid. Page 24

[22] Ibid. Page 25

[23] Paget Toynbee, Mrs Helen (–1910). *'The Letters of Horace Walpole' Volume III* [1903–1905; Clarendon Press, Oxford]. Pages 5 to 7

[24] Sherburn, George Wiley (1884–1962). *'The Correspondence of Alexander Pope'* [1956; Claredon, Oxford]

[25] Taylor, Rev. John. *'THE ORDINARY of NEWGATE'S ACCOUNT of the Behaviour, Confession, and Dying Words, of the TWELVE MALEFACTORS*

Who were executed at TYBURN On Wednesday the 3d of OCTOBER, 1750'.
[1750; Printed for T. Parker and C. Corbett, London] Page 91

[26] Paget Toynbee, Mrs Helen (–1910). *'The Letters of Horace Walpole'*
Volume III [1903–1905; Clarendon Press, Oxford]. Page 13, and
Cunningham, Peter. 'The Letters of Horace Walpole, Earl of Orford'.
Volume II. 1749–1751. Page 87

[27] The London Metropolitan Archives. Hand-written parchment record of
Indictment against Mr James Macklaine [sic]. Manuscript Reference
Number MJ/SR 2946; dated 12 September 1750.

[28] Ibid

[29] THE PROCEEDINGS ON THE King's Commissions of the Peace,
Oyer and Terminer, and Gaol Delivery FOR THE CITY of LONDON;
And also the Gaol Delivery for the County of MIDDLESEX, HELD AT
JUSTICE-HALL in the OLD-BAILEY, On Wednesday the 12th,
Thursday the 13th, Friday the 14th, Saturday the 15th, Monday the 17th,
Tuesday the 18th, and Wednesday the 19th of September. In the 24th Year
of His MAJESTY's Reign. NUMBER VII. for the Year 1749. BEING
THE Third SESSIONS in the MAYORALTY of the Right Hon[oura]ble
John Blachford, Esq; LORD-MAYOR of the CITY of LONDON. [1750;
Printed, and sold by M. COOPER, at the Globe in Pater-noster Row,
LONDON] [Price Four-pence.] Front cover. Page 113

[30] Anonymous. *'the gentleman highwayman; the real james maclaine* (1724–
1750)'. Published in the DVD Booklet of the film, Plunkett & Macleane
[sic], 2000.

[31] Knapp, Andrew and Baldwin, William. *'THE NEW Newgate Calendar*
BEING INTERESTING MEMOIRS OF NOTORIOUS CHARACTERS,
Who have been convicted of Outrage on THE LAWS OF ENGLAND,
DURING THE SEVENTEENTH CENTURY, BROUGHT DOWN TO

THE PRESENT TIME'. Volume II. [1810; Printed for J. and J. Cundee, London]. Page 341

[32] THE PROCEEDINGS ON THE King's Commissions of the Peace, Oyer and Terminer, and Gaol Delivery FOR THE CITY OF LONDON; And also the Gaol Delivery for the County of MIDDLESEX, HELD AT JUSTICE-HALL in the OLD BAILEY, On Wednesday the 12th, Thursday the 13th, Friday the 14th, Saturday the 15th, Monday the 17th, Tuesday the 18th, and Wednesday the 19th of September. In the 24th Year of HIS MAJESTY's Reign. NUMBER VII. For the Year 1749. BEING THE Third SESSIONS in the MAYORALITY of the Right Hon[oura]ble John Blachford, Esq; LORD_MAYOR of the CITY of LONDON. [1750; Printed and sold by M.COOPER, at the Globe in Pater-noster Row, London]. Page 122.

[33] Ibid Page 122

[34] Ibid Pages 122 and 123

[35] Anonymous. '*A Genuine Account of the Life and Actions of James Maclean [sic], Highwayman, to the time of his trial and receiving sentence at The Old Bailey, containing his Robberies, Gallantry at Public Places, with other remarkable transactions; together with some account of Plunket his companion'.* [1750; Printed for W. Falstaff, London]. Pages 26 to 31, and

The Gentleman's Magazine. Volume XX. September 1750. Pages 391 and 392, and

THE PROCEEDINGS ON THE King's Commissions of the Peace, Oyer and Terminer, and Gaol Delivery FOR THE CITY OF LONDON; And also the Gaol Delivery for the County of MIDDLESEX, HELD AT JUSTICE-HALL in the OLD BAILEY, On Wednesday the 12th, Thursday the 13th, Friday the 14th, Saturday the 15th, Monday the 17th, Tuesday the 18th, and Wednesday the 19th of September. In the 24th Year of HIS MAJESTY's Reign. NUMBER VII. For the Year 1749. BEING THE

Third SESSIONS in the MAYORALITY of the Right Hon[oura]ble John Blachford, Esq; LORD_MAYOR of the CITY of LONDON. [1750; Printed and sold by M.COOPER, at the Globe in Pater-noster Row, London]. Pages 123 and 124

³⁶ Anonymous. Engraving: 'James Macleane [sic], *the Gentleman Highwayman at the Bar*'. [29 September 1750]

³⁷ Knapp, Andrew and Baldwin, William. '*THE NEW Newgate Calendar BEING INTERESTING MEMOIRS OF NOTORIOUS CHARACTERS, Who have been convicted of Outrage on THE LAWS OF ENGLAND, DURING THE SEVENTEENTH CENTURY, BROUGHT DOWN TO THE PRESENT TIME*'. Volume II. [1810; Printed for J. and J. Cundee, London]. Page 344

³⁸ The London Metropolitan Archives. Hand-written parchment record of Indictment against Mr James Macklaine [sic]

³⁹ Anderson, Robert MD (1750–1830). '*The Works of The British Poets, with Prefaces, Biographical and Critical' Volume Tenth* [1795; printed for John and Arthur Arch; and for Bell & Bradfute; and J. Mundell & Co., Edinburgh, London]. Page 228

⁴⁰ Anonymous. '*A Genuine Account of the Life and Actions of James Maclean [sic], Highwayman, to the time of his trial and receiving sentence at The Old Bailey, containing his Robberies, Gallantry at Public Places, with other remarkable transactions; together with some account of Plunket his companion*'. [1750; Printed for W. Falstaff, London]. Pages 25 and 26, and Taylor, Rev. John. '*THE ORDINARY of NEWGATE'S ACCOUNT of the Behaviour, Confession, and Dying Words, of the TWELVE MALEFACTORS Who were executed at TYBURN On Wednesday the 3d of OCTOBER, 1750*'. [1750; Printed for T. Parker and C. Corbett, London] Pages 90 and 91

Chapter 5 – Suggested Further Reading

In addition to the above:

The Roots of Evil: A Social History of Crime and Punishment, Hibbert, Christoper (Weidenfield & Nicholson, London, 1963)
Crime in Early Modern England, 1550–1750, Sharpe, J.A. (Longman, London, 1984)
Crimes and the Courts in England, 1660–1800, Beattie, John Maurice (Princeton University Press, New Jersey, 1986)
The Beggar's Opera, Gay, John, Bryan Loughrey and T.O. Treadwell (Harmondsworth, Middlesex, 1986)
Crime and Punishmnet in Eighteenth-century England, McLynn, Francis James (Routledge, London, 1989)
Policing and Punishment in London 1660–1750. Urban Crime and Its Limits of Terror, Beattie, John Maurice. (Oxford University Press, Oxford, 2001)
Criminal London: A Pictorial History from Medieval Times to 1939, Herber, Mark D. (Phillimore & Co., Chichester, 2002)
Crime, Justice, and Discretion in England, 1740–1820, King, Peter. (Oxford University Press, Oxford, 2003)
Tales from the Hanging Court, Hitchcock, Tim and Robert Shoemaker. (Hodder Arnold, London, 2006)

CHAPTER 6

IMPRISONMENT / EXECUTION

Horace Walpole was not slow off the mark in updating his friend Horace Mann on the upshot of Maclaine's trial. He wrote the following letter, the very next day:

> *To Horace Mann,*   *Arlington Street, Sept 20, 1750*
>
> *M'Lean* [sic] *is condemned, and will hang. I am honourably mentioned in a Grub ballad for not having contributed to his sentence. There are as many prints and pamphlets about him as about the earthquake**. His profession grows no joke: I was sitting in my own dining-room on Sunday* [16 September 1750] *night, the clock had not struck eleven, when I heard a loud cry of 'Stop thief!'* a highwayman had attacked the post-chaise in Piccadilly, within fifty yards of this house: the fellow was pursued, rode over the watchman, almost killed him* [Plunket now working alone perhaps?], *and escaped.* [1]

*In the 18th Century anyone hearing the shout (or the "hue and cry") of "Stop thief" was legally obliged to give chase and assist in the apprehension of the criminal.

**The earthquake was very real; in fact in London in 1750 there were two. The first on 8 February 1750, occurred between 12 noon and 1 o'clock in the afternoon, and was small, but caused much anxiety; apparently barristers working in Westminster imagined the halls were falling in around them. The second, exactly one month later, on 8 March 1750, was at half past five in the morning and much stronger; it shook people from their beds who then fled out into the streets. Apparently this second tremor caused church bells to chime and some large stones from the new spire of Westminster Abbey to come crashing down. According to Walpole, *"A person coming into the [White's] Club on the morning of the earthquake, in 1750, and hearing bets laid whether the shock was caused by an earthquake or the blowing up of powder-mills, went away in horror, protesting they* [the gamblers] *were such an impious set that if the last trump were to sound they would bet puppet-show against Judgement."*[2]

Rev. Charles Wesley (1707–1788), brother to Rev. John Wesley (1703–1791) who was the founder of the Methodist Church, who himself was best renowned for being a prolific hymn writer [think, for instance, of 'Hark! The Herald Angels Sing'], delivered a famous sermon on the subject of these earthquakes immediately after their occurrence. It included the following words:

Of all the judgements which righteous God inflicts on sinners here, the most dreadful and destructive is an earthquake. This he has lately brought on our part of the earth, and hereby alarmed our fears, and bid us "prepare to meet our God!"[3]

It nearly led to complete panic on the streets of the City as thousands of people, fearing another occurrence on 8 April 1750, decided to leave the town for the safety of sleeping in open country.

Newgate really was at the time of its construction a "new gate". The original Roman Londinium had only four gated entrances through its walls. Some accounts say Newgate dated right back to 1086 when it was conceived to get over the congestion problems caused by the rebuilding of the old cathedral church of St. Paul, which had then just been destroyed. Re-construction was blocking the great thoroughfare that linked Aldgate in the East to Ludgate in the West. Other accounts assert that Newgate was built in 1120 with a prison function, or Gatehouse, added in 1188 on the orders of King Henry II (1133–1189). Over its history Newgate was modified and re-built several times. It was substantially extended in 1236 and rebuilt in 1422 by the executors (the Worshipful Company of Mercers) of Sir Richard Whittington (1358–1423), Lord Mayor of London in 1397, 1406 and 1419. Added at this time, in the alcoves above the gate itself, were statues representing: 'Peace', 'Plenty', 'Concord', 'Mercy', 'Truth' and 'Liberty' (see Illustration (xiv)).

Captain Alexander Smith, who wrote a great many works on early Highwaymen, left us his enlightened view of Newgate as follows:

Newgate is a dismal prison…a place of calamity… a habitation of misery, a confused chaos…a bottomless pit of violence, a Tower of Babel where all are speakers and no hearers. There is a mingling of the noble with the ignoble, rich with the poor, wise with the ignorant, and the (innocent) with the worst malefactors.

It is a grave of gentility, the banishment of courtesy, the poison of honour, the centre of infamy, the quintessence of disparagement, the confusion of wit. [4]

Illustration (xiv) – Engraving of Newgate Prison frontage circa. 1750–
Unknown

Newgate was completely re-built after the Great Fire of London in 1666. However disease killed on average 30 inmates a year. The prison was completely re-designed after the dreadful outbreaks of typhoid ["Gaol Fever"] and other diseases which, as we have seen earlier (in Chapter 5), were at their worst in 1750. George Dance (1741–1825) 'The Younger', Architect and Surveyor to The Corporation [now City] of London was commissioned for this project. His design included larger cells and ventilation that had previously been sorely lacking. The re-construction took from 1770 until 1778 but within two years it was severely damaged by the Gordon Riots of 1780. These were caused as a result of Lord George Gordon (1752–1793) leading a march of 50,000 anti-Catholics to the House of Commons with a petition demanding the repeal of the Relief Act of 1778, which had itself, repealed previously harsh anti-Catholic legislation from the 17th Century. Chapels, known as Catholic Houses, and public buildings such as prisons were attacked. At Newgate the rioters temporarily released over 300 prisoners, before they torched the place. Again Newgate was re-built within two years, in time for the Tyburn Gallows [see later in this chapter] to be moved to its forecourt where public hangings would continue to take place. It was not until 1902 that the prison was demolished for good to make way for the considerably enlarged Old Bailey that now completely covers the site. Some parts of the older building were retained and can still be seen today such as "Deadman's Walk" where the arches really do get smaller.

Newgate was not only a place for the detention of prisoners awaiting trial at the adjacent Sessions House, it was also a place where convicts were kept whilst awaiting their executions; they were mixed together. Many prisoners did not survive their stay there, having died of any one of the many epidemic diseases that swept through the prison on a regular basis. Newgate was notorious for its cruelty and overcrowding; it was designed, in its 1750 incarnation, to take about 150 inmates, but regularly held 250 or more.

Being sent to Newgate in the middle of the 18th Century was a very expensive business. The prisoners were not provided with any bedding or clothing; these had to be purchased from the Keepers, of whom there were roughly one to every nine inmates. Admission fees were expected on entry and further fees paid if the prisoner wanted any of the day to day comforts or "garnish" of life. We recall at this point the Rev. Archibald Maclaine's letter from Utretch: *"I have given Orders to look towards his Subsistence and what is necessary for it."* Inmates could buy food, drink, tobacco, and access to whores and more comfortable accommodation from the Keepers; rent on a good cell would range between £20–500 per annum. Wives were permitted to stay overnight; prostitutes were able to ply their trade; gambling and dancing were permitted; children and farm animals were able to range freely, even newspapers could be delivered. Every visitor to a convicted criminal had to pay the Keepers for access to their condemned friend. Walpole later wrote that 3,000 people visited Maclaine on the first Sunday [23 September 1750] after his condemnation He had also heard that on that day Maclaine had fainted away twice in the heat of his cell. The Gaolers, in the meantime, must have made a fortune!

Talking of making money out of the prisoners' misery brings us nicely to the role of The Ordinary [the Prison Chaplin] of Newgate. At the time of Maclaine's internment this was one Rev. John Taylor (–1788), he was a great friend of Dr Johnson, whom we first met in the Hebrides in Chapter 1, and who wrote several of his sermons. As well as providing religious comfort and instruction to all the occupants, it was part of The Ordinary's duty to produce a written account of the behaviour, confessions (if he could entice it out of them) and the dying speeches of all the condemned souls from each of the Sessions. These were to be published for sale 'by T. Parker, in Jewin-street, and C. Corbett, over by St. Dunstan's Church, in Fleet Street, the only authorised Printers of the Dying Speeches' with the idea that the profits would be shared out amongst the families of the dying "malefactors". Knowing that their dependants stood to prosper was supposed to get each convict to willingly give up their life stories to The Ordinary.

After the pardons and various other respites and delays for some (see below) there were only twelve men including Maclaine who were awaiting execution from the September 1750 Sessions of whom The Ordinary would include in his Account; these were as follows:

Name	Age	Crime
William Smith	30	Forgery
Richard Wright	25	Theft with violence/ Highway robbery
James Maclean [sic]	26	Ditto
Henry James Saunders	23	Ditto
George Taylor	18	Burglary
George Lloyd	20	Ditto
William a.k.a. Moses Wright	18	Ditto
John Dewick	52	Animal theft [a horse]
William Tyler	41	Ditto [in addition to the theft of the horse for which he was convicted, he also confessed, in detail, to The Ordinary of the theft of a further 45 horses and "Two poor Cows"]
Anthony Whittle	28	Theft with violence/ Highway robbery
John Griffith	20	Ditto
Thomas Shehan	20	Simple grand larceny [stealing a purse and money]

This is what The Ordinary had to say for them as a group: *"These unhappy Persons have most of them constantly attended the Chapel every Day, and, in the general, behaved with great Decency,* and serious *Devotion, as Men ought to be affected with, whose Folly and Vice, have justly rendered them obnoxious to the Punishment due to gross Offenders, against the laws of God, and their Country: Only Dewick, being prevented by great Illness most part of the Time; and Whittle, and Taylor, sometimes by Illness, being obliged to stay away, were visited in their Cells. Shehan being born and bred in the Romish Persuasion, never attended, but was visited by a Roman-Catholic Priest.*"[5]

On writing of Maclaine in particular The Ordinary was kind enough to give us just about the only written description of him that we have: *"James Maclean [sic], aged 26, was in his Person of a middle Size, well Limb'd, a sandy Complexion, a broad open Countenance, pitted with the Small-pox; but though he has been called the Gentleman Highwayman, and in his Dress and Equipage very much affected the fine Gentleman, yet to a Man acquainted with good Breeding, that can distinguish it from Impudence and Affection, there was very little in his Address or Behaviour, that could entitle him to that Character.*"[6] We take it that The Ordinary did not warm to him! At the end of his writings on Maclaine he concluded: *"In the whole of his Department in Newgate, he shewed a very decent Behaviour, a Resignation to the Will of God, a quick Sense of the Wickedness of is past Life, and fortified by the Merit of our blessed Redeemer, looked upon Death as deprived of its Terror, yet could not divest himself of that Horror natural to a Man at the Thoughts of a last and final Dissolution. In short, he was not arrogant enough to brave Death, nor so much wedded to Life, as to dread it like a Coward.*"[7]

Illustration (xiv) — 'JAMES MACLEANE [sic] EXECUTED OCT 3RD 1750 AGED 26 YEARS'. (September 1750) — Louis Philippe Boitard (–1758)

Although it is certain that he met and spent time with him, the Rev. Taylor must have taken the first part of his own description of Maclaine from a pamphlet that was circulating at time purporting to be a 'Genuine Account of the Life and Actions of James Maclean [sic]'. On page 5 of that document Maclaine is described as follows: *"As to his Person, he is about five Foot ten Inches high; his Face is broad, pitted with the Small-Pox; his Nose more of the Flat than Aquiline: of a sandy Complexion, Square-shoulder'd, and well made downwards."*[8] The Rev. Taylor found Maclaine such a rich source of material that he commissioned the writing of a separate "Complete History" of his life. We are again indebted to him for this undertaking as it provided us with the most reliable portrait we have of Maclaine, see Illustration (xv), *"as a Frontispiece, will be press'd, a very neat Picture of Him taken from the Life, while under Sentence, Drawn, and Engrav'd by Mr. Boitard."*[9] Louis Philippe Boitard (fl. 1734–1760) was a very popular artist of the 18th Century; famed for painting the people of London in which he often incorporated "speech bubbles" to animate his work. It is possible that any of Maclaine's private correspondence that he may have had in his possession within his cell, fell into Rev. Taylor's hands as soon as he vacated it; hence the 'Complete History' having such a rich source of letters. The notes beneath the portrait read as follows:

> *Now for these foolish days of wanten pride,*
> *My Soul is justly humbled in the dust,*
> *--------------------------all judging Heav'n,*
> *Who knows my Crimes has seen my sorrow for 'em.*
>
> *Engrav'd from the Original. Drawn from the Life ----*

--------------*while under Sentence; by L.P. Boitard.* [10]

In a quite unusual step for the time Maclaine himself commissioned a separate written account of his behaviour from the day of his condemnation to the day of his execution. This was carried out by The Rev. Dr Fifield Allen (1700–1764), a well-respected Presbyterian Minister; Archdeacon of St. Albans (1738–1741) and Middlesex (1741–1764). When it was published Maclaine's name was at last spelt correctly. The Newgate Calendar quoted heavily from the document starting with the following words:

"The doctor, at his first visit, found his unhappy person under inexpressible agonies of mind, arising from a deep sense of not only of his misery but his guilt. He declared, that altho' most of those, with whom he had lately conversed, ridiculed all religion, yet the truths of Christianity had been so deeply rooted in his mind by a pious education, that he never entertained the least doubt about them, even while he was engaged in courses of the most flagitious wickedness, by which it became his interest to disbelieve them.

He declared also, that neither death, nor the violence and infamy with which, in his case, it would be attended, gave him the least uneasiness; but expressed the most dreadful apprehensions of coming into the presence of the Almighty, whose laws he had known only to violate, and the motions of whose spirit he had felt only to suppress."
11

The Rev. Allen went on to have several meetings with Maclaine and recorded several gems from their conversations. At one point Maclaine declared to him: *"What is Life to me, with my*

Good Name and Character gone? Shunn'd and avoided by the virtuous and sober part of Mankind. What indeed is Life in the gayest Scenes of it? I profess to you, Sir, that I have had more Pleasure in one Hour's Conversation with you, than in all the gay Vanities I have ever engaged in."[12]

Rev. Allen was not slow in pointing out to Maclaine that *"the Defence he made on his Tryal, and the evasive Ways in which he endeavoured to elude the Force of the Confession he had made before Justice L."[13]* was not a token of that sincerity of heart, which he had so solemnly professed. In response, Maclaine admitted:

"That what he had done on that Occasion was by the Advice of a Lawyer ----- That nobody was deceived ----- Nobody less believed that he was guilty, by any thing he there said ----- That he thought it a just Defence in law: and besides, should this Plea have availed for the saving of his Life, the Disgrace that an infamous Death would bring on his Family would have been prevented, and he had determined, by the Help of God, to spend his Life in shewing the Sincerity of his Repentance, and the holy Resolutions he had taken up."[14]

When the Rev. Dr asked him about his father Maclaine apparently burst into tears and expressed how much he regretted violating the principles of which a tender and pious parent had implanted in his mind. He went on to explain that he had often wished that his father had set him for employment that would have made industry necessary as opposed to writing and accounts which was a far too genteel business: *"O, Sir, said he, I have often in my Necessities, before I had broken in upon my Innocence, thought, that had I had a mechanic Trade in my Hands, that would have employed my whole Time, altho' I would have earned by it but Ten Shillings a Week, I had been a happy Man!"[15]*

When Rev. Allen asked Maclaine if he had any hope of a respite he apparently said that he did not, particularly due to the great number of robberies that had lately been committed by persons of a gentile appearance, it was likely he would be made an example of; something that he appeared resigned to: *"Glad I should be, if, as my Life has been vile, my Death might be useful."[16]* Maclaine was probably aware that petitions to spare him from the gallows had been made to the King; then in Hanover (as he often was), who had referred to his Lords of the Regency, and to John Russell (1710–1771), 4th Duke of Bedford; known as Lord Russell and whose first wife was one Lady Diana Spencer (1708–1735)], in his role as Secretary of State. We note also that published in September 1750 was 'A lady's letter to the Honourable Lord P[elham]'; presumably another of Maclaine's lady friends writing directly to the Prime Minister to beg for a reprieve. Whilst Maclaine enjoyed the comfort of his many rich friends in Newgate, he was probably aware that the tide of public opinion was turning against him. The General Advertiser newspaper of Monday 24 September 1750 ran the following article:

We hear that great interest is making for all the 16 male-factors condemned at the last Sessions at the Old Bailey. For some, because they are young, and others because they are old; for some because they are good friends, and others because they are friendless; for some because they are handsome and objects of liking, and for others because they are so ugly that they are the objects of compassion; or some because they have kept good company and are well known, and others because they were never heard of before. At the same time we are informed that the robberies committed within a week last past in and about this Town do at the highest computation amount to scarce 200.

The General Advertiser, 24 September 1750 [17]

There was little doubt as to whom this was aimed at. It may well have been instrumental in all the petitions for Maclaine being refused, as he was shortly to find out. The Ordinary's Account makes note: *On Thursday the 27th of September, Mr Recorder made the Report to the Lords Justices, assembled in Council, of the fifteen Malefactors, when they were pleased to Order   William Smith,   Richard Wright,   James Macklean* [sic], *Henry James Saunders,   John Griffiths,   George Taylor,   John Dewick,   William Tyler,   Anthony Whittle,   Thomas Shehan,   George Lloyd, and   William Wright, for Execution, on Wednesday the 3d* [3 October 1750] *Instant.* [18] From the original 16 malefactors, one (Hugh Burrell, convicted for stealing a cow) was given a free pardon, two (Francis Crocket and William Watson, convicted of highway robbery) were *"respited 'till the Lords Justices pleasure touching them be further known,"* [19] and one (William Riley, convicted for the murder of a Mr. Samuel Sutton in Tothill Fields, Bridewell) *"was not reported; being reserved 'till the Lord Chancellor's Return to London."* [20]

Maclaine was again returned to Newgate; this time to one of the condemned cells, having learned that the intended date for his execution was but a few days ahead. The Rev. Allen at this point noted: *"no additional Dejection or Sadness in his Mind or Countenance, but rather a more visible Composure."* [21] Maclaine asked him if he should receive the sacrament on the morning of the execution with the other criminals, to which Rev. Allen agreed, but at the same time advised "*against considering it as a Charm, or Passport,*"[22] which, the latter feared, was too often done by others in similar circumstances. Maclaine was able to assure him that was not the case and cited the time that he had spent with the other prisoners ordered for execution, helping them with their prayers and their preparations for death. Rev. Allen found Maclaine "*as much shocked at them as myself: and pitied their Souls which were going into Eternity in such a hardened Condition.*"[23]

Some years later the writer James Boswell, whom we met earlier in The Hebrides in Chapter 1, visited the condemned cells at Newgate. He noted in his diary for Tuesday 3 May 1763, having seen the highwayman Paul Lewis, one of the other clergymen's sons, turned bad, that we met in Chapter 2:

Tuesday 3 May
I then thought I should see prisoners of one kind or another, so went to Newgate. I stepped into a sort of court before the cells. They were surely the most dismal places. There were three rows of 'em, four in a row, all above each other. They have double iron windows, and within these, strong iron rails; and in these dark mansions are the unhappy criminals confined. I did not go in, but stood in the court, where were a number of strange blackguard beings with sad countenances, most of them being friends and acquaintances of those under sentence of death.

In the cells were Paul Lewis for robbery and Hannah Diego for theft. I saw them pass by to chapel. The woman was a big unconcerned being. Paul, who had been in the sea-service and was a Captain, was a genteel, spirited young fellow. He was a Macheath [another reference to 'The Beggar's Opera']. *He was dressed in a white coat and blue silk vest and silver, with his hair neatly queued and a silver-laced hat, smartly cocked. An acquaintance asked him how he was. He said, "Very well"; quite resigned Poor fellow! I really took a great concern for him, and wished to relieve him. He walked firmly and with a good air, with his chains rattling upon him, to the chapel.* [24]

On Sunday 30 September 1750 Maclaine and the other malefactors would have been taken to the Chapel in Newgate to hear the Ordinary's Condemned Sermon during which they would be sat in the Condemned Pew, directly in front of the pulpit, with the Rev. Taylor (with a coffin stood behind him), directly in front of them, reading out a burial service. Often wealthy visitors would be able to attend such services and thereby give the Gaolers another opportunity to make money.

The Rev. Allen took Maclaine's behaviour at this time, encouraging the other condemned souls to properly prepare themselves for death, as evidence of his sincerity and recorded it as such in his 'Account'. The day before his execution Tuesday 2 October 1750, in the presence of several gentlemen from Holland, the Rev. Allen gave him a letter from his brother at which, *"he burst into a most violent Agony of Grief: and said, "O, my dear Brother I have broken his Heart!"*[25] James was clearly aware of the earlier letter from Utretch. He continued: *"I have been long educated to Sorrow; and, cutting as this Letter will be to my Heart, I must read it!"*[26] Beginning with first words: *"Unhappy Brother!*, he cried out in great Anguish of Spirit, *Unhappy indeed!"*[27] After composing himself he read the letter, twice through. The letter was also published and thus we are able to include it here:

Hague, Sept. 22, N.S. 1750.
Unhappy Brother!

Y o u have put it out of my Power to write to you without Distraction of Mind: --- Your State and Condition is so deplorable ---- and the Circumstances of it (to which I cannot accustom my Thoughts) so strange – and to me so terrible – that I should have no Repose, did not the Divine Comforts of Religion support me, on the one hand – and my Sorrow and Affliction work upon me sometimes the dismal Effect of Insensibility – on the other.

When I speak of your deplorable State, I do not mean only the Sufferings that load you --- nor the Infamy that, alas! too justly pursues you – and will perhaps unjustly attack those that belong to you: --- These, indeed, are terrible Evils: --- But, in my Esteem, they are nothing in Comparison with the Crimes that have occasioned them --- And would to God you could think so! – I don't mention your Crimes now to express my Indignation at your Conduct, but rather my Compassion for your immortal Soul: My indignation is almost lost in a Sense of your Misery; --- I mention your Crimes chiefly to penetrate your Heart with the deep Contrition ---- that the very Workings of Conscience should produce, if there was not upon Earth one Mortal to be a Witness of your Guilt --- or to pursue it with the Punishment it deserves.

Consider ---- O Consider, in the first place, that All-seeing God ---- whose sacred Laws and Majesty you have trampled upon by such daring, such heinous, such unjustifiable Transgressions: ---- Did not He, in his adorable Goodness, give you the Health and Strength, and those Opportunities --- which many want --- that you might push yourself in the World by honest and virtuous Industry? And have you not often been told, that such Industry, through the Bounty of Providence, would always procure a Provision in Life sufficient for a good Mind ---- a Provision sweetened by those sacred Delights of a peaceful Conscience ---- which the World cannot give ---- and which, amidst all its Changes, it cannot take away? --- Lost to the Sense of God as your Benefactor ---- did you not also lose the View of Him, as your Judge ---- who has in his Hands your everlasting Condition?-- In the same Acts did you not ungratefully despise His Goodness ---- that gave you Life and Being --- and daringly defy that Almighty Justice that can make them both miserable to thee for ever? ---- Have you not sinned against the Ashes of those tender Parents ---- that took care to educate you in the Fear of God ---- and in the Principles of

Virtue? I bless His Name, that He has removed them from this World ------ where, inaccessible to Sorrow and Pain ---- the Sight of your Misery cannot reach them ---- to embitter the Springs of their Happiness ---- as it has done with respect to mine in this Life. The unhappy Companion of your Iniquity ---- will bring down the grey Hairs of his ---- with Sorrow to the Grave ---- tho' they have This for their Comfort ---- that it will be in a good and pious old Age.

I judge also, how far you have been abandon'd ---- when not only the Excellence of Virtue ---- the Horrors of Vice ---- the Presence of the great God ---- and the Prospect of his tremendous Judgments ---- had no Effect upon your Soul ---- to startle it in the Pursuit of such an enormous Course ---- but when you were even lost to a Sense of Self-preservation, a Principle that remains often in the greatest Wretches ---- to hinder them from such Crimes ---- even when every good and worthy Disposition is intirely fled. ---- It is true, indeed, that a Man is not in the least praise-worthy who abstains ---- from such a low Principle as Self-preservation only: ---- But, alas! on the other hand, it is also true --- that Wickedness must be grown to a great Height, when a Principle so strong as Self-preservation ---- will not stop its Course: ---- How few are the Examples of those ---- that have escaped after the Commission of such Crimes, as yours? ---- Has not the Divine Justice seized the most of them here ------ to give them a Fore-taste of what their Crimes may expect hereafter? ---- See, O unhappy Offender! what Fools Vice makes of Men! ---- It shuts their Eyes upon Snares and Precipices ---- that lie as clear before them as the Sun at Noon-day.

When you have entered into all these Considerations, let your Sense of Honour arise ---- If it is not quite extinguished, it will give new Vigour to your Contrition: ---- But still let it be the very last Consideration: ---- Honour is only the Opinion of the World: But it is the World's great Governor and Judge with whom you have had principally to do: ---- The Way to make your Peace with God, will be the way to remove from you the Indignation of the World, if it judges right ---- and if you are to continue in it: But if your Peace is made with Him ---- it is no Matter how the World treats you ---- for He is greater than the World: ---- O that you could feel by Experience ---- that God is greater than the World! ---- But in order to this much is required: -------- You must first know Him: ---- Prostrate yourself before his Mercy, as it is offered in the Gospel to penitent Offenders ---- and perhaps the Consolations of his undeserved Goodness and Grace may yet find an Entrance into your Soul:

---- I implore you, as you regard your Soul's eternal Welfare -- -- not to indulge the Hopes of Life ---- as a Motive to slacken your Repentance ---- for if you have a true Sense of your guilty State -- - you will think nothing of such immediate and indispensable Necessity as to make your Peace with an offended God, whether Life or Death awaits you. ----You may be disappointed in your Hopes of Mercy here below ---- If then in the Expectation of that ---- you neglect all other Considerations ---- Good God! What will become of you? The Mercies of God are sure to those who seek for them sincerely; and they will be the best Preparation for whatever is to be your Lot: ---- You can be no-way instrumental yourself ---- in the Means of escaping the Danger that hangs over you here ---- O turn not then your Thoughts to that Side, ---- but turn them to avert the Danger that hangs over you hereafter; ---- for there you may be successful by your Contrition and Repentance. ---- May God prepare you for whatever is to be your Lot! ---- You have my Prayers and Tears ---- and I hope you will be enabled to pray yourself, and to weep over your Transgressions, as I do. ----I am, with all Sympathy, and in the deepest Affliction,

Yours, &c.

A.M.

I have not heard that you have applied to any Minister to help you to the Consolations of Religion ---- and to renew those sacred Instructions that you have, alas! ---- I fear, intirely defaced In your Heart ---- I own to you, I have dreadful Fears ---- that your Sorrow ---- is rather the Effect of Shame and Fear ---- than a Fruit arising from a Sense of your Guilt ---- O beware of this! [28]

Rev. Archibald Maclaine's letter, as well as re-iterating many of the Presbyterian solas, contains some very profound statements and loving fraternal sentiments, however: *"Only in the last part of the letter does Archibald really come to grips with it. Here no longer the minister writes a sermon, but brother speaks to brother."*[29] A letter to Archibald's best and (eventual) life-long friend Henry Hope (1731–1811) was also published at the same time. Hope was an Amsterdam merchant and banker, whose family at one time owned the deep blue 'Hope Diamond', now housed in the Smithsonian Natural History Museum in Washington D.C. and once described as "the most famous diamond in the world". The second letter was as follows:

My Dear Sir,

IT is truly impossible for me to express the deep and grateful Sense I have of that Friendship, Humanity, and generous Zeal, that you have shewn in the Case of my wretched and unhappy Brother - --- Your discreet and kind Letter to me upon this melancholy Subject gave me the highest Sentiments of your Wisdom, as well as of the amiable Tenderness of your Compassion ---- And shall for ever hinder it from being possible for me to forget how much I owe you.

I always believed myself exposed to Affliction ---- I laid my Accounts for many ---- I had begun to feel some ---- but could never dream of the Possibility of such as have been now sent to cast a Cloud over my Days, and bring down my Head (in all Appearance before it grows grey) with Sorrow to the Grave.

What Anguish must it bring to my Soul ----- to see not only all Sense of Virtue ---- of Providence, and a Judgment to come ---- but also all Sense of Honour and Shame, lost in one ---- whom the Ties of Nature oblige me to call Brother? --- to see him fall, not once only, thro' a sudden Fit of Despair, into such an infamous Crime ---- (which, though inexcusable, would yet have been less heinous) --- but to go on (as I find by Mr D-------'s Letter) for the matter of almost Two Years, in that horrid Course ---- O my Dear H [enry], *this overcomes me ---- this weighs me to the Ground!*

You talk to me of his Penitence ---- God grant it may flow from right Principles! Fear and Shame excite a Sorrow that has often the Mien of Repentance, without the Thing ---- If he repents truly, let him consider the horrible Nature of his Crimes, the Blackness of their Guilt, and the righteous Majesty of Heaven, that is offended by them ---- Let his Heart be melted with Sorrow ---- not so much for the Misery he feels ---- as for the Offences that have been its Cause: ---- Let him not weep over the Consequences of his Crimes ---- but over the Crimes themselves. ---- His outward Misery is little ---- It is but the dark Vision of a Day ---- even when his Life is prolonged to the utmost ---- But the Want of a peaceful Conscience ---- and a Soul loaded with Guilt unrepented of, will poison the Springs of Happiness for ever ---- and make a dismal and miserable Appearance, when the Secrets of all Hearts shall be opened —- My Prayers to Heaven are put up for him Night and Day ---- That God may open his Eyes ---- and make the Adversity his Guilt has involved him in, the Means of his Reformation ----.

Mr., J ----, our common and worthy Friend, will, no doubt, have communicated to you ---- the Orders I have given with respect to his Necessities ---- I have at present a most dismal Head-ach, ---- which, with the Anguish of my Heart ---- prevents my saying any more, than that I am, with all Sincerity and Truth,

Your ever obliged, and most

affectionate humble Servant,

A. Maclaine. [30]

Both these letters served to hold the Rev. Archibald Maclaine in high esteem with the British public and he enjoyed the favour of the editors of The Gentleman's Magazine, who also published them, throughout the remainder of his life.

When Maclaine had finished reading his brother's words, Dr. Allen suggested to those present to unite in a solemn prayer to God for him: *"they consented, and, though strangers to the prisoner, the minister, and each other, there was not a dry eye among them."*[31] That night Maclaine took final leave of Mr. Hope and Dr. Allen; the latter recording: *"He eagerly embraced us both, dropt suddenly on his Knees, and in accents, the Sound of which will never be out of my Ears, he pray'd to God to bless us both for ever; to prosper us and our Families in all our Undertakings; and eternally reward us for all the Compassion and Love we had shewn to such a poor unworthy Creature, as he said he was!"*[32].

Illustration (xvi) — 'Newgate's Lamentation or the Ladies' Last Farewell of Maclean [sic]'. (1750) — Anonymous

About this time an etched print of Maclaine, with visitors in his cell, was published and sold for three pence, see Illustration (xvi). It was entitled: 'Newgate's Lamentation or the Ladies' Last Farewell of Maclaine'. It was almost certainly the print that Walpole was referring to in his letter of 1 September 1750 (see Chapter 5); perhaps he saw an early draft of it? Beneath the picture were the following verses:

> *Farewell my Friends Let not your Hearts Be Fill'd,*
> *my Time is Near & I'll with Calmness Yield.*
> *Fair Ladies Now your Grief I pray forbear,*

Nor wound me with, Each tender Hearted tear.

Mourn Not my fate Your friendships Have been kind,
which I in tears Shall Own till Breaths resign'd.
Oh may the Indulgence of such Friendly Love,
That's Been Bestow'd On me, Be doubled from Above. [33]

We learn that Maclaine, when not receiving visitors or patronising the other prisoners, was busy writing in his cell throughout his time in Newgate. James Sharpe in his 2004 history of 'Dick Turpin; The Myth of the English Highwayman' [2004; Sutton Publishing] informs us that MacLaine [sic], having been dismayed at being incarcerated with a mere footpad [a robber who operated on foot], one Ned Slinker, wrote a pamphlet in which he extolled the virtues of the mounted highwayman over the grubby crimes of lesser thieves such as footpads, house-breakers and pickpockets; see more on this in Chapter 7. Dr Johnson, whom we met earlier in Chapter 1, wrote the following on this very subject to his great friend James Boswell: *"We have more respect for a man who robs boldly on the highway than for a fellow who jumps out of a ditch and knocks you down behind you. Courage is a quality so necessary for maintaining virtue, that it is always respected, even when it is associated with vice."* [34] Apparently Maclaine considered himself a "good thief" as a good highwayman only ever stole from the rich. Clearly Maclaine had studied his trade for he well understood the cult of the profession he had been engaged in. He no doubt knew about many of the more famous highwaymen that had preceded him and he also would have known the fate that had befallen all of them who had been caught.

So it was that we find Maclaine still able to find time, in the small wee hours of the morning of his execution, to write to an otherwise nameless; R_____; possibly the 'Robin', from William Plunket's undated LETTER VII., a very close friend of his. The letter, which clearly shows the calm state of his mind at such a daunting time, is as follows:

Mr Maclaine's Letter to his Friend written the Morning of his Execution

My Cell in Newgate, One o'clock, Wednesday Morning.

*Lest I should be refused the Liberty of bidding my dearest **R**. a last and melancholy Farewel, I have begged a Minute, which to me at this time is worth more than Worlds, to do it in this Manner.*

Oh, my dear, dear Friend! may You live long and happy! But consider, the way to procure that Happiness is by earnestly pursuing a religious virtuous Life ---- Your Youth may naturally prompt you too much to a Fondness for the Gaieties of Life: Oh! In That never let your Inclinations get the better of your Reason; for the indulging of those Appetites produces many bad Consequences; As I am so plain an Example of it, that I need say no more, I hope, to convince You of it. ---- Oh! I wish you could, for one Minute, see the World with my Eyes at this time, and you would not hazard a happy Eternity to be King of it. For God's Sake let me beg of you, if you should find your Desires for the Gaieties of Life, or any vicious Disposition, grow troublesome, think of your unfortunate poor Maclaine, whose Ruin proceeded from such Dispositions not restrained, that I fear you are not a Stranger to. I wish you Happiness, more than I can well express, or would not take up my precious Minutes at this time, to give you an Advice that I hope you will think of.

My dear, dear Mr H. has got two Books, an Inkhorn, therein a Seal, which, with my last Blessing, I beg you'll carry to my good old Landlady at Chelsea. And, my dear Friend, I beg you'll get the little Bible I spoke to you about from Mr S. and after you tear the Leaf out, present it to which of ---- ---- Dr Allen's Family you please, with my affectionate Blessing to them all. ---- My Sleeve-Buttons you are to give to poor N.B. with my last Blessing to her, ---- ----, ---- and ---- ----, &c. My Mother-in-law*; was here this Evening, who begs my Shoe-Buckles, to keep for my poor dear Child; which I think unnecessary; but, as she has no other Token from me, I would indulge her in it. ---- The Stock and Knee-Buckles I desire you'll keep, and wear for my sake; and I would have you convert all my Linen Stock you get from my Washerwoman into Cash, and would have you give my poor Mother-in-law two or three Guineas, to buy some Coals for the Winter, and any little Necessary the poor Child may want. ---- Write to my poor afflicted Sister ---- Direct, To Mrs Anne-Jane Maclaine, at Market-Hill, in the County of Armagh, Ireland.

Have my Life done as soon as you can, to prevent any body else doing it after I am no more. And let it be done in a modest penitent manner. I would desire you, if there are any Profits arising from it, to let my poor Orphan be a Sharer.

I will now commit my poor Body to your Care, which, I hope, you will see decently interred; and take all necessary Precautions to prevent my being a Prey to the Surgeon. (See Chapter 7)

To the Care and Providence of the Almighty I most heartily commit you; and that you may lead such a Life here as will entitle you to Heaven hereafter, is the sincere Wish and Prayer, of

Your loving, affectionate, dying Friend
J. Maclaine.

Oh! Farewel, till we meet in Heaven!

I cannot help telling you, before I finish, the present State of my Mind; and, as I think I am within Eleven Hours of Eternity, will not tell a Lye. ---- My dear R. I never was so happy within myself since I was born: nor ever found my Mind in that Serenity in my Life that I now do; and have got so far above the Fears of Death, that I shall go to Execution without being daunted, but rather with Eagerness, as I begin to long to be with my dear and blessed Redeemer, who, I hope, will be ready to receive my precious Soul, when it departs from its mortal Habitation. ---- You will find Difficulty in reading this; but my Situation will apologize.
Once more, my Dearest, farewel! And remember me for ever. [35]

*Rev. Allen noted the following of Maclaine's Mother-in-law: *"...from the tender leave his Wife's Mother took of him, and what I heard her say to him the Night before his Execution. I remember she took his Hand, with great Tenderness: and, lifting it to her lips, said, Thou wast always the Darling of my Soul."*[36]

This letter was included in the Third Edition of Dr. Allen's 'Account' which, priced at six pence, sold like hotcakes through October 1750. Apparently Dr. Allen passed on all the proceeds to Maclaine's daughter. It is likely the letter was added to the booklet as a substitute for the lack of a dying speech for, as we shall see shortly, Maclaine hardly made much of an effort in that department.

Maclaine's last day, however, had not begun at 1 o'clock with his letter it had actually begun at midnight with the Bellman (or Clerk of the Church) of the adjacent St. Sepulchre Church, the nearest Church to Newgate, ringing a hand-bell outside his 'condemned cell' twelve times and reciting the following traditional verse:

> *All you that in the condemned hole do lie,*
> *Prepare you for tomorrow you shall die;*
> *Watch all and pray: the hour is drawing near,*
> *That you before the Almighty must appear;*
> *Examine well yourselves in time repent,*
> *That you may not to eternal flames be sent.*
> *And when St. Sepulchre's Bell in the morning tolls,*
> *The Lord above have mercy on your soul.* [37]

At about seven o'clock in the morning Maclaine would have been taken in his "fetters"; the handcuffs and leg-irons that we have seen in pictures of him at The Bar (see Illustration (xiii)) and in his cell (see Illustration (xvi)) into the Press Yard which was a place for torture by putting weights on the prisoners' chests to make them confess or make a plead in Court. Here the blacksmith would have removed the fetters and the 'Yeoman of the Halter' would have tied his wrists together in front of him with one cord and wrapped another around his arms and body, just above the elbow. This would effectively still have allowed the prisoner enough movement to be able to pray. The Yeoman would then have placed a noose or 'halter' around Maclaine's neck, wrapping the remaining length of rope around his body. The whole process was known as 'pinioning'. From within the Press Yard the prisoners would clearly hear the bells of St. Sepulchre's Church. Some of the condemned men would take the brief opportunity of being unfettered to change into their best clothes, which might often have been their wedding suits, so as to look their best at the time of their imminent death. It was traditional that these clothes would shortly become the property of the Hangman who would strip the bodies before placing them in their coffins.

The Ordinary, Rev. John Taylor, advises us that: *"On Wednesday the 3d instance, between 8 and 9 o'Clock in the morning, John Griffith, William Tyler, and John Dewick in one cart, Richard Wright, Anthony Whittle, and Thomas Shehan in a second, George Taylor, George Lloyd and William Wright in a third, James Saunders, James Maclean* [sic], *and William Smith in a fourth, were conveyed to the Place of Execution, through a vast Concourse of People, as great as perhaps has at any time been known upon such a melancholy Occasion."*[38] It is understood that the hanging of Maclaine drew a crowd of over 100,000 people; approximately one in five of the population at the time; the largest crowd ever known at such an event. One must stop to think for a moment that 100,000 is larger than the capacities of either the new Wembley Stadium, opened in 2007, or the 2012 Olympic Stadium; a huge turn-out for the time.

Maclaine had originally been expected to travel in a 'morning coach' like "Jenny Diver" had in 1740 so as to be protected from the seething crowds. Her real name was Mary Young (1700–1741) and she was one of the most successful pickpockets ever; who was nicknamed after another character from 'The Beggar's

Opera' (see Chapter 5). Laurence Shirley (1720–1760), 4th Earl Ferrers, also took a morning coach or 'landau' on his last journey. Maclaine, however, insisted on travelling with his fellow condemned in the open, horse-drawn carts, sitting on his coffin in the traditional way. According to Dr. Allen, Maclaine on getting into his cart was heard to exclaim: *"O, my God, I have forsaken thee! But I will trust in thee!"*[39] As the gates to Newgate opened and the Procession pulled out, it would have been led by the City Marshall or Under Sheriff (a court officer responsible for prisoners), the Ordinary, the Hangman and his assistants, who would ride in one of the leading carts so as to arrive early and make preparations, and a troop of javelin men [pike-men mounted on horseback] to keep the crowds away from the carts, for it was not unknown for a last minute rescue to be attempted. The Procession would not have gone far before stopping on the steps of St. Sepulchre's, where the Church bells would be tolled and according to Thomas Pennant (1726–1798); the Welsh naturalist and antiquary who regularly travelled across Great Britain recording his findings, the Clerk would chant: *"You that are condemned to die, repent with lamentable tears; ask mercy of the Lord for the salvation of your souls, through the merits, death and passion of JESUS CHRIST, who now sits at the right hand of God, to make intersession for as many of you as penitently return unto him. LORD have mercy on you, CHRIST have mercy on you."*[40] Friends of the prisoners would grab the chance to pass them colourful nosegays and as the Procession moved off the Minister would tell the crowd: *"All good people, pray heartily unto God, for those poor sinners who are now going to their death, for whom this great bell doth toll."*[41]

I have not yet described where they were heading. It was a place that would strike the fear of God into any condemned man of the time. It was of course Tyburn Gallows; the traditional place for executions in London and Middlesex dating back to at least 1196 when a gallows was first erected on the site. Tyburn was originally a small village in Middlesex that took its name from the Ty Bourne stream; a tributary of The Thames now completely covered over, that ran through it before reaching its end at Vauxhall. It was at the junction of Tyburn Road (now Oxford Street) and Tyburn Lane (now Park Lane). We now know the place where the gallows stood as Marble Arch or, to be more specific, the corner of Edgware Road and Bayswater Road, and there is a plaque there in the pavement that attempts to mark the spot, see Illustration (xvii)

Illustration (xvii) — Photograph of Tyburn Tree plaque; Edgware Road, London. Photographed by N.F.M. 22 September 2011

The first recorded hanging at Tyburn took place in 1196 and was of Dr John Story (–1196), a Catholic agitator who refused to recognise Queen Elizabeth I. It was not until 1571 that the infamous "Tyburn [Gallows] Tree" was erected. This was a simple "three-legged stool" structure, with each leg standing in one of the three adjoining parishes of St. George Hanover Square, St. Marylebone and Paddington. It was made up of three upright wooden columns, approximately 18 feet tall, supporting three horizontal wooden beams that formed a triangle; each beam was 9 feet long and capable of suspending eight criminals at a time. Whilst this structure, also known variously as "the Three-legged Mare", "the Triple Tree" and "the Deadly Never Green", was capable of hanging a total of 24 prisoners at a time, there are only a very few recorded occurrences of it ever being put to its full use. The carts carrying the condemned would be driven under the gallows. The malefactors would be made to stand up towards the back end whilst the Hangman would unwrap the temporarily coiled rope from around their bodies, leaving the noose or "Tyburn Tippet" around their necks, and throwing the loose end up over one of the beams. The ropes would then be tied to leave little or no slack whilst the chaplain would read the funeral sermon. When all was ready, those who wished for it would have a hood put over their heads, and the horses whipped away. As they had not far to fall, the hanged would die of slow strangulation as they danced "the Tyburn Jig".

It was this incarnation of the Tyburn Gallows that saw the end of Maclaine. It stayed as a permanent gallows structure until after 18 June 1759 when it took its last victim, one Catherine Knowland (–1759), a female highwayman. From then until 3

November 1783, when it was used for ending the life of John Austin (–1783); another highwayman, a temporary horse-drawn gallows replaced it. After that it was totally relocated to outside Newgate Prison. Of the estimated 50,000 [3,000 during the 18th Century; proving it was nowhere near as blood-thirsty as one might think, compared with the 16th and 17th Centuries] felons who met their end at Tyburn over the centuries, the following list is just the briefest selection of some of the more noteworthy:

Name	Date	Detail
Robert ("Lucky") Hubert	28 September 1666	"Confessed" to starting the Great Fire of London
Oliver Cromwell*	January 1661	Already dead and buried at the time; King Charles II ordered his body to be hanged
Claude Duval	21 January 1670	French highwayman, (whom we met earlier)
John ("Gentleman Jack") Sheppard	16 November 1724	Notorious thief (whom we met earlier)
Laurence Shirley, 4th Earl of Ferrers**	5 May 1760	Only peer of the realm to be hung for murder (whom we met recently)

* Oliver Cromwell's (1599–1658) remains were exhumed from Westminster Abbey to satisfy the revengeful, restored King.

** Lord Ferrers had petitioned the King to allow him to be beheaded in The Tower of London as was his privilege as a peer of the realm; permission was denied.

Many of the early hangings at Tyburn were much more than just that. In the beginning the felons would be "hung, drawn and quartered" whereby they would be hung until almost dead, taken down and disembowelled, seeing their own guts burned in front of them, before having their arms, legs and head severed from their bodies "to be disposed of at the King's pleasure". As the gallows literally stood in the middle of the roadway, they represented a very menacing deterrent to any would-be thieves of any kind. In addition to the ever-present gallows there were also strategically placed gibbets at other infamous crime spots such as Hounslow Heath, where the slowly rotting, tar-covered, bodies of executed highwaymen would be displayed as a gruesome reminder of the final rewards of such a profession.

The 2½ to 3 mile route from Newgate to Tyburn was westwards, down into the valley of the Fleet River, via Giltspur Street, through Smithfield, along Cow Lane and Crooked Lane past the steps of St. Sepulchre's, then Ozier Lane and down Snow Hill and up Heavy (Holborn) Hill; nowadays one simply crosses Holborn Viaduct over Farringdon Road, below. The "melancholy cavalcade" would leave the City of London at the Holborn Bars, named after the toll-bars on each side of the road at Staple Inn, the Tudor building that can still be seen today on the South side of Holborn near Chancery Lane tube station. The two posts with the City's coat of arms mark the sites of the original bars at the bottom of Gray's Inn Road. The procession continued along Holborn, High Holborn and St. Giles High Street. The reason for the southerly sweep was to avoid a marshy area known as

'Rugmere' that was not developed until 1847 with a road across it called New Oxford Street. It would eventually reach Oxford Road and Tyburn Road. The generally westerly route gave rise to the euphemism that to be hanged at Tyburn would have been to have "Gone West". As a small boy I never stopped to question my grandmother when she said I "had gone West" on the very rare(!) occasions when she found my behaviour not to her liking. Whilst I remember it vividly, you rarely hear it nowadays. There were eight 'Hanging Days' a year in the mid-18th Century; they became known to the people as "the Hanging Match" or "the Tyburn Fare" and were extremely popular days out. The Government of the day positively encouraged attendance by making them public holidays; for seeing the spectacle of these gruesome deaths was another essential part of 'The Bloody Code' (see earlier, Chapter 3). On 3 October 1750, no doubt, the entire route would have been packed with throngs of onlookers, at both street level and crammed into every window of the overseeing buildings; all desperate to catch a glimpse of 'The Gentleman Highwayman' who had so scandalised high society. Whilst the girls would have blown kisses in the traditional way it is likely others would have taken the opportunity to throw rotten food or, even worse, excrement!

The journey for Maclaine would have been particularly poignant, reminding him of better times; as he passed Dean Street and Soho to his left, his in-laws' Inn in the Oxford Road itself, and his old shop in Welbeck Street, off Cavendish Square, just off to his right. He no doubt would have sorely rued all the missed opportunities that he had allowed to pass him by, to put his life back on the right track. Apparently he seldom looked up throughout the entire journey, preferring to read his Bible the whole way.

Stops were usually made at two hostelries along the route where the condemned would be allowed some food and drink. Some would of course take the opportunity to drink to excess ensuring they would be entirely numb by the time of their arrival at the gallows. The first was at 'The Bowl Inn' at St. Giles on the corner of Endell Street and Broad Street, now Shaftsbury Avenue, approximately at the halfway point, and then the chance of a "last gasp" was afforded at 'The Mason's Arms' in Seymour Place. 'The White Hart' in Drury Lane and 'The Three Tuns' in South Portman Mews have also claimed to have been the regular stop-offs. At 'The Mason's Arms' there are still manacles on the walls of the cellars that prove that the City Marshall was taking no chances with his charges. Seymour Place is actually situated a little to the north of Marble Arch so I suspect this stop was chosen to allow the crowds that lined the route time to assemble around the gallows.

So finally the Procession would arrive at Tyburn at about noon, some 3 or 4 hours after setting out from Newgate. Amongst the immense crowds would be various hawkers selling food, drink and souvenirs. Women would often be found selling pamphlets, or 'chapbooks', of the life histories of the condemned, some purporting to include their confessions and "last dying speeches", despite the fact that they would not have delivered them yet! There were galleries full of people who had paid to get a good seat and view of the proceedings. For those with a real sense for the macabre the best seats were in 'Mother Proctor's Pews', which could be secured for 2 shillings, from where you would be close enough to hear the prisoners' last words and their cries and screams as they "croaked". On one occasion the stand collapsed, reportedly killing and injuring hundreds of people.

A nearby house, with iron railings across its balconies, provided the vantage point for the City Marshall and Sheriffs of the City of London and the Under Sheriff of Middlesex, together with their guests.

William Hogarth, whom we met earlier at Vauxhall Gardens (see Chapter 3), captured the awful assembly of a typical day at Tyburn Fair with one of his plates from his series of four, entitled 'Industry and Idleness', which he painted in 1747. Through these engravings *"Hogarth shows the progression in the lives of two apprentices, one who is dedicated to hard working, the other idle that leads to crime and his execution. This shows the work ethic of Protestant England, where those who work hard get rewarded, such as the industrious apprentice* [Frances Goodchild] *who becomes Sheriff (plate 8), Alderman (plate 10), and finally Lord Mayor of London in the last plate in the series. The idle apprentice* [Tom Idle], *who begins with being "at play in the church yard" (plate 3), ends up "in a Garrett with a Common Prostitute" (plate 7) and "executed at Tyburn" (plate 11)* (see Illustration (xviii)). *The idle apprentice is sent to the gallows by the industrious apprentice himself."*[42] Personally I never tire of looking at this, or indeed any other of Hogarth's paintings; I always find something new in them each time I look.

Illustration (xviii) — 'Industry and Idleness, Plate II: The IDLE 'PRENTICE Executed at Tyburn'. (30th September 1747) — William Hogarth (1697–1764)

The verse beneath the picture is a quotation from The Bible as follows:

Proverbs CHAP I. Verſs 27, 28.

When fear cometh as desolation, and their destruction cometh as a Whirlwind; when distress cometh upon them, they shall call upon God, but he will not answer.

These "Hanging Matches" were so popular that they were by far the number one form of entertainment for the mass population of London at the time. The victims were expected to go to their deaths with bravery and put on a good show for the crowds, who would appreciate a "good dying", where the criminal would make a defiant last speech or behave with particular bravado, but would jeer a "bad death" where the victim showed any sign of weakness or gave poor value for money by making no spectacle at all. Maclaine's death would probably have been considered "bad" on account of the latter.

The courage that some felons showed at their final curtain would amaze visitors from abroad. 'The Foreigner's Guide to London' of 1740 written by Joseph Pote (1704–1787) provided the following detail in relation to Hanging Days: *"The rope being put around his neck, he is fastened to the fatal tree when a proper time being allowed for prayer and singing a hymn, the cart is withdrawn and the penitent criminal is turned* ["turned off"] *with a cap over his eyes and left hanging for half an hour."*[43] Maclaine apparently declined the cap or 'hood'. The Guide went on to warn: *"These executions are always well attended with so great mobbing and Impertinences that you ought to be on your guard when curiosity leads you there."*[44] Certainly pick-pocketing was said to be rife at these gatherings which seems a little odd considering to be caught at it would result in a re-appearance for the perpetrator at the same venue as soon as twelve weeks later!

The day after James Boswell went to Newgate and saw Paul Lewis's final preparations for death, see earlier, he followed it up by going to Tyburn to see the *"spirited young fellow"* turned off. The record he made in his diary for Wednesday 4 May 1763 was as follows:

Wednesday 4 May
My curiosity to see the melancholy spectacle of the executions was so strong that I could not resist it, although I was sensible that I would suffer much from it. In my younger years I had read in the Lives of the Convicts [perhaps he had even read about

Maclaine?] *so much about Tyburn that I had a sort of horrid eagerness to be there. I also wished to see the last behaviour of Paul Lewis, the handsome fellow whom I had seen the day before. Accordingly I took captain Temple with me, and he and I got upon a scaffold very near the fatal tree, so that we could clearly see all the dismal scene. There was a most prodigious crowd of spectators. I was most terribly shocked, and thrown into a very deep melancholy.* [45]

The Hangman; or 'Lord of the Manor of Tyburn' as he might have been called, on Wednesday 3 October 1750 was one John Thrift (–1752), who had held the position since 1735. He was apparently *"prone to nerves, susceptible to the drama of the moment, he was unsure of the rope, inexpert with the axe and inaccurate with the cleaver"* [46] Not only that, but Thrift had a very bad reputation with the people of London, particularly in 1746 when he dealt very poorly and unprofessionally with the job of hanging, drawing and quartering the Jacobite leaders and conspirators that had taken part in the '45 Rebellion in support of "Bonnie Prince Charlie" (see Chapter 1). Of particular note were his botched attempts at despatching William Boyd (1709–1746), 4th Earl of Kilmarnock, and Arthur Elphinstone (1688–1746), 6th Lord Balmerino; the latter having sufficient ligaments still intact to twist his neck around and look Thrift in the eye after the first and second blows of the latter's axe had failed to fully decapitate him! Thrift was later responsible for beheading Simon Fraser (1667–1747), 11th Lord Fraser, Chief of Clan Fraser, who had the dubious distinction of being the last man to be beheaded by axe in Britain. As the Hangmen were watched so frequently they became as famous as the best known actors of the time and the spectators looked for any signs of drunkenness, clumsiness or incompetence to criticise. Other Jacobites such as Colonel Francis Townley (1709–1746) and Captain George Fletcher (– 1746) of the Manchester Regiment were so incompetently butchered as they were despatched at the hands of Thrift that their suffering was greatly enhanced, if that were possible! Their heads were afterwards displayed on poles on Temple Bar, which at the time straddled Fleet Street at the junction between the City of London and Westminster. The Temple Bar was one of the Sir Christopher Wren (1632–1723) designed gateways to the City which has only recently been relocated back to the City of London (in 2004) and is now situated at the recently redeveloped Paternoster Square after a holiday in the country (at Theobalds Park in Hertfordshire) of some 126 years.

Thrift had only just narrowly escaped the noose himself earlier in the year after being accused and found guilty of murder at the Old Bailey on 25 April 1750, in which case he also escaped the "gaol fever" outbreak as well. He lived at Coal Yard, the reputed birthplace of Nell Gwynn (1650–1687), the most famous of King Charles II's mistresses, nowadays known as Stukeley Street. On 11 March 1750 Thrift took offence at some passers-by who had made reference to him as "Jack Ketch" i.e. John 'Jack' Ketch (– 1686); England's most notorious Hangman ever, who had an even worse reputation for botching his executions, such that every Hangman after him had to suffer being called by his name; even the Hangman in the Punch and Judy shows. Thrift went after his tormentors, chasing them across Drury Lane and into an archway in Shorts Gardens where he slashed one of them, a David Faris, with a cutlass several times over. Faris later died of his wounds on 19 March 1750 which is probably not surprising as we have learnt that Thrift had no reputation for getting the job done swiftly!

Whilst Thrift was sentenced to death at his trial, this was later reprised and then commuted to transportation for fourteen years, before he finally received a full pardon. The Gentleman's Magazine of September 1750 remarked: *that having become obnoxious to the Jacobites, for his celebrated operations on Tower Hill, and Kennington Common, he was pardoned in Terrorem, and to mortify them.*[47]

Six days after his death on 5 May 1752, John Thrift's body was taken to St. Paul's Church in Covent Garden for burial. The funeral was watched by a large, hostile crowd and the attendants, including Thrift's successor, Thomas Turlis, had to carry the coffin into the church to avoid trouble. They waited a very long time for the crowds to disperse before they ventured back outside to complete the task.

The Gentleman's Magazine in October 1750 commented on the executions from the beginning of the month and advised that when Maclaine came into sight of the gallows he looked up and sighed: *"Oh Jesus!"*[48] *"He took no notice of the populace, but was attentive to his devotions, and spoke not at all but to the constable who first took him, and who desired to shake his hand, and hoped he would forgive him, which he said he did."*[49] John Taylor, The Ordinary, concluded his Account in the following manner: *"When they came there, they were all put into one Cart, severally lamenting their Case, and praying fervently, while the Executioner was tying them up. Little otherwise remarkable happened among them, only Maclean* [sic], *when he got out of the Cart he was brought, into that from whence he was to be turned off, in a very devout Manner, with uplifted Hands and Eyes expressed himself, saying, "O God, forgive my Enemies, bless my Friends, and receive my Soul." Smith* [who was also the son of a Presbyterian Minister from Ireland] *did not, as was expected make any Speech to the spectators, being better advised. And after some time spent in Prayer, the Cart drew away under them, every Thing having been conducted with great Decency.*"[50] Another anonymous writer who wrote and distributed a pamphlet entitled 'Execution of Maclean [sic]; commonly known by the name The Gentleman Highwayman', as late as 1795, recorded the following of Maclaine's last few words, *"A gentleman who saw him executed, says, That just before the cart, in which he stood, was drawn from under him, as it was a very fine day, and the sun shone bright, he looked all around him with great composure, and then said, "I must never more behold this beauteous sun!—do thou, O Sun of righteousness! Shine on my departing soul!"*"[51]

When the carts did pull away it was customary for the Hangman and his assistants, or the friends of those being hanged, to rush up and hang onto the legs of the "sufferers" as they were known. In this way the weight of the "hangers-on"; an expression still in use day with an altered meaning, would speed up the strangulation process, putting the victim out of their misery quickly. Some sources say that as his cart pulled away James Maclaine kicked off his shoes and jumped in the air with his knees close to his chest in order to speed his process. It was otherwise quite possible that the dancing of the "Tyburn Jig" could take as long as three quarters of an hour. It was a telltale sign of death when urine ran down the leg; the Hangman could at this point be fairly sure that his job was done and he could cut the corpse(s) down, although he could never be certain, and there were always grisly stories of the odd body being revived, in agony as the blood's circulation returned. Writing in 1725 on his first hand experiences of witnessing such hangings, the Dutch philosopher and satirist, Bernard de Mandeville (1670–1733) wrote a pamphlet in which he noted: *"There is nothing in being hang'd but a wry Neck, and a wet pair of Breeches."*[52] As well as having the clothes from the corpses it was the Hangman's good fortune to be able to sell the rope, particularly that which was used on a notorious criminal, by the inch, to souvenir hunters, giving rise to the saying "money for old rope." A thrifty [forgive the pun] Hangman might also charge on-lookers a fee for allowing them to touch the hands of the lifeless bodies for in the 18th Century there was still a belief that a dead man's hand held healing powers. Carrier pigeons were at this time set free to fly back to Newgate to inform the Gaolers that the criminals had been successfully dispatched.

César de Saussure, the Swiss traveller whom we met in Chapter 3, commenting on both Coffee Houses and Highway Robbery, left us an excellent summary of hanging at Tyburn, in yet another of his letters home:

Criminals are not executed immediately after their trial, as they are abroad, but are given several days to prepare for death. During that time they may ask for anything that they require either for the soul or for the body. The chaplain of the prison (for there is one) does not leave them, and offers every consolation in his power. The day before the execution those who desire it may receive the sacrament, provided the chaplain thinks that they have sincerely repented and are worthy of it. On the day of execution the condemned prisoners, wearing a sort of white linen shirt over their clothes and a cap on their heads, are tied two together and placed on carts with their backs to the horses' tails. These carts are guarded and surrounded by constables and other police officers on horseback, each armed with a sort of pike. In this way part of the town is crossed and Tyburn, which is a good half-mile from the last suburb, is reached, and here stands the gibbet. One often sees criminals going to their deaths perfectly unconcerned, others so impenitent that they fill themselves full of liquor and mock at those who are repentant. When all the prisoners arrive at their destination they are made to mount on a very wide cart made expressly for the purpose, a cord is passed round their necks and the end fastened to the gibbet, which is not very high. The chaplain who accompanies the condemned men is also on the cart; he makes them pray and sing a few verses of the Psalms. The relatives are permitted to mount the cart and take farewell. When the time is up – that is to say about a quarter of an hour – the chaplain and relations get off the cart, the executioner covers the eyes and faces of the prisoners with their caps, lashes the horses that drew the cart, which slips from under the condemned men's feet, and in this way they remain all hanging together.

You often see friends and relations tugging at the hanging men's feet so that they should die quicker and not suffer. The bodies and clothes of the dead belong to the executioner; relatives must, if they wish for them, buy them from him, and unclaimed bodies are sold to surgeons to be dissected. You see most amusing scenes between people who do not like the bodies to be cut up and the messengers the surgeons have sent for the bodies; blows are given and returned before they can be got away, and sometimes the populace often come to blows as to who will carry the bought corpses to the parents who are waiting… [53]

Maclaine's body was apparently collected by his friends, put in his coffin and taken by hearse to the house of a Mr. Harrison, an undertaker in Clare Market, off The Strand. It was later decently interred in St. Margaret's Churchyard in Uxbridge. Dr Allen closed his Account of Maclaine with the following words: *"and I hope* [that he] *has found that Mercy with God which he so earnestly sought."*[54]

Perhaps it is fitting that this Chapter should both open and now close with a letter from Maclaine's "friend" Mr. Walpole:

To Horace Mann,   *Arlington Street, Oct. 18, 1750*

Robbing is the only thing that goes on with any vivacity, though my friend Mr M'Lean [sic] *is hanged. The first Sunday after his condemnation, three thousand people went to see him; he fainted away twice with the heat of his cell. You can't conceive the ridiculous rage there is of going to Newgate; and the prints that are published of the malefactors, and the memoirs of their lives and deaths set forth with as much parade as – as – Marshal Turenne's* – we have no generals worth making a parallel.*

Horace Walpole [55]

*Marshal Turenne was Henri de La Tour d'Auvergne (1611–1675), Viccomte de Turenne, a very famous and successful French General. Emperor Napoleon Bonaparte (1769–1821) later described him as one of history's "seven greatest captains"; he was the only Frenchman on his list. Bonaparte had Turenne's remains exhumed from their grave in Saint-Denis and transferred to a new tomb in the Invalides Church in Paris in 1808.

Maclaine may have been gone in body at this point but he was *"still the fashion"* for quite some time…

Chapter 6 – References

[1] Paget Toynbee, Mrs Helen (–1910). *'The Letters of Horace Walpole'* *Volume III* [1903–1905; Clarendon Press, Oxford]. Page 18, and Cunningham, Peter. 'The Letters of Horace Walpole, Earl of Orford'. Volume II. 1749–1751. Page 90

[2] Steinmetz Esq'., Andrew (1816–1877). *'The Gaming Table; Its Votaries and Victims'. Volume II.* [1870; J. Tinsley Brothers, London]. Page 68

[3] Wesley, Charles (1707–1788). *'The Cause and Cure of Earthquakes'*

[4] Smith, Captain Alexander and Hayward, Arthur Lawrence. *'A Complete History of the Lives and Robberies of the most notorious Highwaymen, Footpads, Shoplifts and Cheats of Both Sexes'* [1926; George Routledge & Sons, London]. Page 153

[5] Taylor, Rev. John. *'THE ORDINARY of NEWGATE'S ACCOUNT of the Behaviour, Confession, and Dying Words, of the TWELVE MALEFACTORS Who were executed at TYBURN On Wednesday the 3d of OCTOBER, 1750'.* [1750; Printed for T. Parker and C. Corbett, London] Page 83

[6] Ibid. Pages 84 and 85

[7] Ibid. Page 91

[8] Anonymous. *'A Genuine Account of the Life and Actions of James Maclean [sic], Highwayman, to the time of his trial and receiving sentence at The Old Bailey, containing his Robberies, Gallantry at Public Places, with other remarkable transactions; together with some account of Plunket his companion'.* [1750; Printed for W. Falstaff, London]. Page 5

[9] Taylor, Rev. John. *'THE ORDINARY of NEWGATE'S ACCOUNT of the Behaviour, Confession, and Dying Words, of the TWELVE MALEFACTORS Who were executed at TYBURN On Wednesday the 3d of OCTOBER, 1750'.* [1750; Printed for T. Parker and C. Corbett, London] Page 91

[10] Anonymous. 'A COMPLETE HISTORY of James Maclean [sic], *THE GENTLEMAN HIGHWAYMAN, who was executed at TYBURN on Wednesday, October 3, 1750, for a Robbery on the Highway'*. [1750; Printed for Charles Corbett, London]. Front cover

[11] Knapp, Andrew and Baldwin, William. *'THE NEW Newgate Calendar BEING INTERESTING MEMOIRS OF NOTORIOUS CHARACTERS, Who have been convicted of Outrage on THE LAWS OF ENGLAND, DURING THE SEVENTEENTH CENTURY, BROUGHT DOWN TO THE PRESENT TIME'*. Volume II. [1810; Printed for J. and J. Cundee, London]. Page 344

[12] Allen, Rev. Fifield (1700–1764). *'AN ACCOUNT Of the BEHAVIOUR of Mr James Maclaine, From the TIME of his CONDEMNATION To the DAY of his EXECUTION, OCTOBER 3. 1750. By the REVEREND Dr. ALLEN, Who attended him all that time, to assist him in his PREPARATIONS for ETERNITY. Drawn up and published at the earnest Desire of Mr MACLAINE himself. The THIRD EDITION, With the Addition of a LETTER written by Mr Maclaine to a Friend, the Morning of his Execution. Which did not come to hand time enough to be inserted before'* [1750; Printed for J. NOON, in Cheapside: and A. MILLAR in the Strand, LONDON] [Price 6d]. Page 9

[13] Ibid. Pages 9 and 10

[14] Ibid. Page 15

[15] Ibid. Page 15

[16] Ibid. Page 15

[17] The General Advertiser, 24 September 1750

[18] Taylor, Rev. John. *'THE ORDINARY of NEWGATE'S ACCOUNT of the Behaviour, Confession, and Dying Words, of the TWELVE MALEFACTORS Who were executed at TYBURN On Wednesday the 3d of OCTOBER, 1750'*. [1750; Printed for T. Parker and C. Corbett, London] Page 83

[19] Ibid. Page 84

[20] Ibid. Page 84

[21] Allen, Rev. Fifield (1700–1764). *'AN ACCOUNT Of the BEHAVIOUR of Mr James Maclaine, From the TIME of his CONDEMNATION To the DAY of his EXECUTION, OCTOBER 3. 1750.* By the REVEREND Dr. ALLEN, Who attended him all that time, to assist him in his PREPARATIONS for ETERNITY. Drawn up and published at the earnest Desire of Mr MACLAINE himself. The THIRD EDITION, With the Addition of a LETTER written by Mr Maclaine to a Friend, the Morning of his Execution. Which did not come to hand time enough to be inserted before' [1750; Printed for J. NOON, in Cheapside: and A. MILLAR in the Strand, LONDON] [Price 6d]. Page 16

[22] Ibid. Page 17

[23] Ibid. Pages 17 and 18

[24] Pottle, Frederick Albert (1897–1987). *'Boswell's London Journal 1762–1763'* [1950, London], and

Boswell, James. *'London Journal: A Visit to Tyburn and Newgate (1762–3), A True and Perfect Relation of the Tryall, Condemning of the 24 prisoners. at Tyburn'* [1763; Thomasson Collection, British Museum, London}

[25] Allen, Rev. Fifield (1700–1764). *'AN ACCOUNT Of the BEHAVIOUR of Mr James Maclaine, From the TIME of his CONDEMNATION To the DAY of his EXECUTION, OCTOBER 3. 1750.* By the REVEREND Dr. ALLEN, Who attended him all that time, to assist him in his PREPARATIONS for ETERNITY. Drawn up and published at the earnest Desire of Mr MACLAINE himself. The THIRD EDITION, With the Addition of a LETTER written by Mr Maclaine to a Friend, the Morning of his Execution. Which did not come to hand time enough to be inserted before' [1750; Printed for J. NOON, in Cheapside: and A. MILLAR in the Strand, LONDON] [Price 6d]. Page 19

[26] Ibid. Page 19

[27] Ibid. Page 19

[28] Ibid. Pages 20 to 25

[29] Harmens, Dr A. '*A Complete History of James Maclean, the gentleman highwayman. Anonymous. Commentary by A. Harmens*' [23 April 1987; Bowdon, Cheshire. Unpublished]. Page 7

[30] Allen, Rev. Fifield (1700–1764). '*AN ACCOUNT Of the BEHAVIOUR of Mr James Maclaine, From the TIME of his CONDEMNATION To the DAY of his EXECUTION, OCTOBER 3. 1750.* By the REVEREND Dr. ALLEN, Who attended him all that time, to assist him in his PREPARATIONS for ETERNITY. Drawn up and published at the earnest Desire of Mr MACLAINE himself. The THIRD EDITION, With the Addition of a LETTER written by Mr Maclaine to a Friend, the Morning of his Execution. Which did not come to hand time enough to be inserted before' [1750; Printed for J. NOON, in Cheapside: and A. MILLAR in the Strand, LONDON] [Price 6d]. Page 31 and 32

[31] Knapp, Andrew and Baldwin, William. '*THE NEW Newgate Calendar BEING INTERESTING MEMOIRS OF NOTORIOUS CHARACTERS, Who have been convicted of Outrage on THE LAWS OF ENGLAND, DURING THE SEVENTEENTH CENTURY, BROUGHT DOWN TO THE PRESENT TIME'. Volume II.* [1810; Printed for J. and J. Cundee, London]. Page 347

[32] Allen, Rev. Fifield (1700–1764). '*AN ACCOUNT Of the BEHAVIOUR of Mr James Maclaine, From the TIME of his CONDEMNATION To the DAY of his EXECUTION, OCTOBER 3. 1750.* By the REVEREND Dr. ALLEN, Who attended him all that time, to assist him in his PREPARATIONS for ETERNITY. Drawn up and published at the earnest Desire of Mr MACLAINE himself. The THIRD EDITION, With the Addition of a LETTER written by Mr Maclaine to a Friend, the Morning of his Execution. Which did not come to hand time enough to be

inserted before' [1750; Printed for J. NOON, in Cheapside: and A. MILLAR in the Strand, LONDON] [Price 6d]. Page 26

[33] Anonymous. 'Newgate's Lamentation or the Ladies' Last Farewell of Maclean [sic]'. (1750) –

[34] Boswell, James Esq. (1740–1795). *The Life of Dr Johnson*, LL.D. Comprehending an account of his studies and numerous works, in chronological order; A series of of his Epistolary correspondence and conversations with many eminent persons and various original pieces of his composition, The whole exhibiting a view of literature and literary men in Great Britain; for near half a century during which he flourished' [1830; printed for John Sharp, Piccadilly: and William Jackson, New York, London] Page 573

[35] Allen, Rev. Fifield (1700–1764). *'AN ACCOUNT Of the BEHAVIOUR of Mr James Maclaine, From the TIME of his CONDEMNATION To the DAY of his EXECUTION, OCTOBER 3. 1750.* By the REVEREND Dr. ALLEN, Who attended him all that time, to assist him in his PREPARATIONS for ETERNITY. Drawn up and published at the earnest Desire of Mr MACLAINE himself. The THIRD EDITION, With the Addition of a LETTER written by Mr Maclaine to a Friend, the Morning of his Execution. Which did not come to hand time enough to be inserted before' [1750; Printed for J. NOON, in Cheapside: and A. MILLAR in the Strand, LONDON] [Price 6d]. Pages 33 to 36, and

Anonymous. *'A COMPLETE HISTORY of James Maclean [sic], THE GENTLEMAN HIGHWAYMAN, who was executed at TYBURN on Wednesday, October 3, 1750, for a Robbery on the Highway'.* [1750; Printed for Charles Corbett, London]. Pages 62 to 64

[36] Ibid. Pages 10 and 11

[37] *Executions at Tyburn. 'The Fatal Bellman'.* Retrieved 18/10/11

[38] Taylor, Rev. John. *'THE ORDINARY of NEWGATE'S ACCOUNT of the Behaviour, Confession, and Dying Words, of the TWELVE MALEFACTORS Who were executed at TYBURN On Wednesday the 3d of OCTOBER, 1750'.* [1750; Printed for T. Parker and C. Corbett, London] Page 106

[39] Allen, Rev. Fifield (1700–1764). *'AN ACCOUNT Of the BEHAVIOUR of Mr James Maclaine, From the TIME of his CONDEMNATION To the DAY of his EXECUTION, OCTOBER 3. 1750.* By the REVEREND Dr. ALLEN, Who attended him all that time, to assist him in his PREPARATIONS for ETERNITY. Drawn up and published at the earnest Desire of Mr MACLAINE himself. The THIRD EDITION, With the Addition of a LETTER written by Mr Maclaine to a Friend, the Morning of his Execution. Which did not come to hand time enough to be inserted before' [1750; Printed for J. NOON, in Cheapside: and A. MILLAR in the Strand, LONDON] [Price 6d]. Page 26

[40] Pennant, Thomas (1726–1798). *'Of London'* [1790; Printed for ROBT FAULDER, London]. Page 221

[41] Smith, Captain Alexander and Hayward, Arthur Lawrence. '*A Complete History of the Lives and Robberies of the most notorious Highwaymen, Footpads, Shoplifts and Cheats of Both Sexes'* [1926; George Routledge & Sons, London]. Page xvii

[42] Wikipedia entry on William Hogarth's *'Industry and Idleness'*. Retrieved 18/10/11

[43] Pote, Joseph (1704–1787). *'The Foreigner's guide: or, a necessary and instructive companion both for the foreigner and native, in their tour through the cities of London and Westminster'* [1740; J. Joliffe, London]

[44] Ibid

[45] Pottle, Frederick Albert (1897–1987). *'Boswell's London Journal 1762–1763'* [1950, London]

[46] Stockman, Rocky. 'The Hangman's Diary: A Calendar of judicial Hangings' [1993; Headline Book Publishing, London]

[47] *The Gentleman's Magazine*; September 1750. Page 425

[48] *The Gentleman's Magazine.* October 1750. Page 473

[49] Ibid. Page 473

[50] Taylor, Rev. John. *'THE ORDINARY of NEWGATE'S ACCOUNT of the Behaviour, Confession, and Dying Words, of the TWELVE MALEFACTORS Who were executed at TYBURN On Wednesday the 3d of OCTOBER, 1750'.* [1750; Printed for T. Parker and C. Corbett, London] Page 106

[51] Anonymous. *'Execution of Maclean Commonly known by the name of The Gentleman Highwayman'* [1795; (Sold by J. Marshall, Printer to the Cheap Repository fo [sic] Moral and Religious Tracks) No.17, Queen's Street, Cheap side, and No. 4, Aldermary Church Yard, and R.WHITE, Piccadilly, London] By S. Hazard (Printer to the Cheap Repository) at Bath; and by all Booksellers, Newsmen, and Hawkers, in Town and Country.... Great Allowance will be made to Shopkeeper and Hawker. PRICE 1d. each or 4s, 6d. per 100,.....2s, 6d. per 50,.....25 for 1s, 6d. Page 20

[52] de Mandeville, Bernard (1670–1733). *'An Enquiry Into the Cause of the Frequent Executions at Tyburn* (1725)'. Published in Series of letters to The British Journal.

[53] Van Muyden, Madame. *'A FOREIGN VIEW OF ENGLAND IN THE REIGNS OF GEORGE I. & GEORGE II.* The Letters of Monsieur César de Saussure to his Family' [1902; John Murray, London].

[54] Allen, Rev. Fifield (1700–1764). *'AN ACCOUNT Of the BEHAVIOUR of Mr James Maclaine, From the TIME of his CONDEMNATION To the DAY of his EXECUTION, OCTOBER 3. 1750.* By the REVEREND Dr. ALLEN, Who attended him all that time, to assist him in his PREPARATIONS for ETERNITY. Drawn up and published at the

earnest Desire of Mr MACLAINE himself. The THIRD EDITION, With the Addition of a LETTER written by Mr Maclaine to a Friend, the Morning of his Execution. Which did not come to hand time enough to be inserted before' [1750; Printed for J. NOON, in Cheapside: and A. MILLAR in the Strand, LONDON] [Price 6d]. Page 27

[55] Paget Toynbee, Mrs Helen (–1910). *'The Letters of Horace Walpole' Volume III* [1903–1905; Clarendon Press, Oxford]. Pages 20 and 21, and Wright, John and Ellis, George Agar (1797–1833), 1st Baron Dover. 'THE LETTERS of HORACE WALPOLE, EARL OF ORFORD'. Volume I. (1735–1745) [1840; Printed by Richard Bentley, London]. Pages 359 and 360

Chapter 6 – Suggested Further Reading

In addition to the above:

The Annals of Newgate or The Malefactors Register. Containing a Particular and Circumstantial Account of the Lives, Transactions and Trials of the Most Notorious Malefactors, Villette, Rev. John (Printed for J. Wenman, London, 1776)

Facts Relating to the Punishment of Death in the Metropolis, Wakefield, Edward Gibbon (J. Ridgway, London, 1832)

Chronicles of Newgate, Griffiths Arthur (Chapman & Hall, London, 1884)

The Old Bailey and Newgate, Gordon, C. [Pseudonym for Ashton, John] (T. Fisher Unwin, London, 1902)

Tyburn Tree: Its History and Annals, Marks, Alfred. (Brown, Langham & Co., London, 1908)

Hangmen of England, Bleakley, Horace (Chapman and Hall, London, 1929)

Hue and Cry: The Birth of the British Police, Pringle, Patrick (Museum Press Limited, London, 1955)

The Road to Tyburn: Jack Sheppard and the Eighteenth century Underworld, Hibbert, Christoper [1957; Longmans, London]

The Triple Tree. Newgate, Tyburn and Old Bailey, Rumbelow, Donald (Harrap, London, 1982)

The Common Hangman. English and Scottish Hangmen before the abolition of Public Executions, Bland, James (Ian Henry Publications, Romford, 1984)

The Spectacle of Suffering: Executions and the Evolution of Repression, from a Pre-industrial Metropolis to the European

Experience, Spierenburg, Petrus Cornelis (Cambridge University Press, Cambridge, 1984)

Hangmen of England. A History of Execution from Jack Ketch to Albert Pierrepont, Bailey, Brian (W.H. Allen, London, 1989)

Lords of the Scaffold: A History of the Executioner, Abbott, Geoffrey (Robert Hale, London, 1991)

Lord High Executioner: An Unashamed Look at Hangmen, Headsmen and Their Kind, Engel, Howard (Robson Books, London, 1997)

The Hanging Tree. Execution and the English People 1770–1846, Gatrell, Vic A. C. (Oxford University Press, Oxford, 2000)

The London Hanged, Limebaugh, Peter (Verso Books, London, 2003)

Tyburn: London's Fatal Tree, Brooke, Alan and David Brandon. (Sutton Publishing Limited, Gloucestershire, 2004)

London: The Executioner's City, Brandon, David and Alan Brooke (Sutton Publishing Limited, Gloucestershire, 2006)

The Gaol: The Story of Newgate, London's Most Notorious Prison, Grovier, Kelly (John Murray Publishers, London, 2009)

CHAPTER 7

AFTERMATH

Maclaine's notoriety persisted long after his execution and there are a few more things worthy of note in concluding his story.

William Hogarth, whom we met at Vauxhall Gardens in Chapter 3 and at Tyburn in the previous Chapter, continued to turn out his satirical and moralistic engravings. In 1751 he completed and published four more plates entitled 'The Four Stages of Cruelty'. The first plate shows one Tom Nero and others indulging in cruel acts against dogs, cats and an array of other animals. The second shows him as a coach driver beating his horse although it is already apparent the poor animal has broken its leg on the cobbled streets of Westminster. The third casts Tom as a murderer with the woman, whose throat he has slit with a knife, laying before him as he forcibly restrained by those who witnessed his latest brutal act. The fourth plate entitled 'The Reward of Cruelty', see Illustration (xix) is the one of significance to our story. The scene is of one of the lecture rooms of Surgeon's Hall which has recently identified as the Cutlerian Theatre of the Royal College of Physicians in Warwick Lane, off Newgate Street, which was used by the Surgeons' Company from 1745 to 1751 after splitting from the old Barber-Surgeons' Company. Tom's body lies on a table in the middle, being dissected by a group of medical students, under the direction of

John Keane (1688–1755), a famous surgeon and benefactor of St. Bartholomew's Hospital. A dog in the foreground is pictured chewing on Tom's heart.

In the background of this picture on the right hand side is hanging a skeleton that Hogarth has clearly labelled 'Macleane' [sic]. On the left hand side hangs that of James Field (–1749), an eminent pugilist [fist-fighter] of the time. Field's name above this skeleton had replaced that of Henry [a.k.a. 'Gentleman Harry'] Simms (–1747), another young highwayman with the "Gentleman tag", who was executed on 16 November 1747. We have no idea if Maclaine's body really was exhumed and dissected or whether Hogarth just added his name to the print to add "weight" to his picture. It is most likely that it was for the latter reason. However we will recall that Maclaine, in his last letter on the morning of his execution, made a clear plea to his friend to *take all necessary Precautions to prevent my being a Prey to the Surgeon."*[1]

Illustration (xix) — 'THE REWARD OF CRUELTY' [Plate IV of IV from series 'The Four Stages of Cruelty']. (1st February 1751) —William Hogarth (1697–1764)

The practice of utilising corpses, particularly of hanged criminals, in the interest of advancing medical science, was widely practised at the time, but not in fact legitimised until an Act of Parliament was passed in 1752 ['The Murder Act 1751'] that provided for that part of a death sentence to include a direction that after a hanging a murderer's corpse should be delivered to Surgeons' Hall for anatomical study [or "anatomization"] and preferment of medical knowledge. Up until then the surgeons were allowed only a total of ten bodies per year. Despite it becoming legitimate the Hanging Tree could not bare enough fruit for the insatiable appetite of the surgeon's knife. Grave robbers and body snatchers therefore flourished well into the 19th Century. We all recall the infamous William Burke (−1829) and William Hare (−1859); the two Irish labourers who went to Edinburgh to work on the Union Canal, whose surnames became synonymous with the trade. They ran into trouble when they got tired of digging, and waiting for bodies to be buried. Instead they started murdering their victims with a strangulation method they had perfected that would leave no trace. No one knows for sure but it is thought they murdered anywhere between 16 and 30 people, just to sell their bodies to the local surgeon, Dr Robert Knox (1791–1862). Hare turned King's Evidence against his partner in crime and Burke was convicted and sentenced to hang on 28 January 1829. His body was naturally passed over to the surgeons for *"useful dissection"*[2] Some students apparently took off some of his skin and had it tanned to cover their books. His skeleton still hangs in Edinburgh University's Medical School. Burke was said to have died a penniless pauper in London in 1859. Grave robbing was rife at times in London and in 1776 more than 100 bodies were discovered in a shed in Tottenham Court Road on their way to the Surgeon's Table.

London had its on famous bodysnatchers or "resurrectionists" who were said to have modelled their exploits on Burks and Hare and came to prominence in Bethnel Green at the end of the 1820s the number of hangings in London had reduced significantly by that time and only produced about fifty cadavers a year whilst demand existed for ten times as many. The most notorious gang became known as The London Burkers and they may have been responsible for retrieving up to one thousand freshly buried bodies before being captured and hanged at Newgate on 5 December 1831.

The case of The London Burkers led to the Anatomy Act of 1832 that finally provided for an adequate and legitimate supply of corpses for the medical schools.

At Tyburn it was not unknown for riots to break out beneath the gallows as friends and family fought off the anatomists as they believed that only an entire body at burial would lead to resurrection and life after death. On the other hand some of the poorest families would sell the bodies of their loved ones, as they could not afford a burial, let alone a coffin.

Not long after Maclaine's death the English poet, author and Member of Parliament, Soame Jenyns (1704–1787), appended to the end of his poem 'The Modern Fine Lady' the note:

She weeps if but a handsome thief is hung,

Some of the brightest eyes were at this time in tears for one M'Lean [sic], *condemned for a robbery on the highway.* [3]

Some years later Soame Jenyns was to lock literary quills with the Rev. Archibald Maclaine, James Maclaine's brother, and come away worse off. Having had his previous attempt at a serious essay, 'A Free Inquiry into the Nature and Origin of Evil' (1756), brutally but eloquently, rubbished by Dr Samuel Johnson whom we met earlier in the Hebrides in Chapter 1 and at the Westminster Gatehouse in Chapter 5. Not deterred by this humiliation Jenyns went on to publish a further essay entitled 'A View of the Internal Evidence of the Christian Religion' (1776). The Rev. Maclaine took a particular dislike to what he considered to be the shallowness of Jenyns' attempt at writing on such a deep theological subject that he wrote a series of letters to him that were themselves later published. These letters proved so popular with the public that they went on to a Second Edition in 1778.

Writing about this exchange of correspondence at the time of Rev. Archibald's funeral in 1804, Rev. John [Sylvester John] Gardiner D.D. (1765–1830), the Welsh-born, eminent Rector of Trinity Church, Boston, Massachusetts for nearly forty years, reported: *"I am far from classing Soame Jenyns among the insidious enemies of the Christian faith --- on the contrary, his production in support of it appears, to be the genuine result of a sincere and upright zeal. But we all know that a good cause may be injured by a bad defence in he hands even of a zealous advocate; especially when this advocate has acquired reputation in another walk of literature, and when the defence itself contains many useful and pertinent remarks, expressed in popular and captivating form. This observation may be illustrated by Mr. Jenyns' 'View of the Internal Evidence of Christianity.' Such a favourite was this little book with the publick, that it run through four editions before it reached Dr. Maclaine. He was well acquainted with the celebrity of the author, and perceived at once the evil consequences of his work --- he anticipated with anxiety the occasional triumph which artful unbelievers would gain from s crude and feeble vindication of the Faith --- he was convinced that it abounded with inferences adverse to the cause which it was meant to support; and his conviction gave birth to a beautiful specimen, an admirable model of liberal, of sound and lively criticism. The style of Dr. Maclaine's 'Letters to Soame Jenyns, Esq.' is animated, pure, and nervous --- and he exposes in them with vivacity and moderation, with perspicuity and vigour, the many vague affections, loose reasonings, and untenable positions into which the precipitate judgement of that author has unhappily led him. In saying this, however, let me not be thought to censure with exaggeration, or to disparce beyond reason, Mr. Jenyns's work. Let it be consulted with Dr. Maclaine's judicious structures, and it may contribute both to the pleasure and advantage of the reader.*[4] Soame Jenyns's reputation as a serious prose writer never did recover.

"The Gentleman Highwayman" was still a strong story in the mid-1760s. By example The Public Advertiser in 1764 published more detail of James Maclaine's written exchange with his cellmate Ned Slinker, the footpad, written from his condemned cell at Newgate (see Chapter 6). Maclaine started by boasting:

From: James Maclaine, Esquire and Highwayman
To: Ned Slinker, Footpad, Pick-pocket and House-breaker

I cannot reproach myself with doing any Thing unbecoming a Gentleman. When the scanty Allowance of five Hundred a year that I had from that Old Gripe my Father was gone, having always entertain'd a just Contempt for the Pedantry of study, and being above any mechanic Employment, I embraced the only Scheme left for a man of Spirit, and commenced a Gentleman of the Shade; in which Occupation I have acquitted myself with equal Courage, Honour and Genius.

My irregularities were always conducted more with the Spirit of a Gentleman. There has not been for some years an Instance in the Papers of Generosity, Complaisance to Ladies, or Dexterity of Contrivance, that I cannot justly claim the Honour of. I was the person who obliged a couple of sneaking footpads to refund the week's wages they had taken from a poor labourer.

The Public Advertiser, 29 February 1764 [5]

Slinker's response was robust:

There is no great difference between us, either in point of honour, courage or genius. I confess I do not see the difference whether a man robs on horseback, or on foot: with a pistol, or a dash of his pen. If you avoid robbing the poor, I cannot but fancy, if your motives were examined, 'tis not so much from principle of generosity, as that you have not the spirit to venture your neck for sixpence. And as to dexterity, everyone must allow, that 'tis much easier to escape on horseback than on foot.

The Public Advertiser, 1 March 1764 [6]

The Public Advertiser was originally known as the 'London Daily Post and General Advertiser' and then the 'General Advertiser', before being re-launched and overall by its printer, Henry Sampson Woodfall (1739–1805). The Public Advertiser published between 21 January 1769 and 21 January 1772 the famous letters of the anonymous writer 'Junius' from Chapter 2.

We have already heard what a stir Maclaine's arrest, court appearance and execution caused in the high society of London of 1750. His notoriety went on to help bring about change to the way London was policed at the time, which itself hastened the end of highway robbery. There was much debate in the public newspapers and journals about the extent of criminal activity in the lead up to Maclaine's execution and in the months thereafter. By way of example, one anonymous writer, using the pseudonym 'Brittannicus Esq.' [anonymous letter writing was a popular way of expressing political views throughout the 18th Century (see also 'Junius' from Chapter 2)] had his 'Letter to the Honourable House of Commons, relating to the present situation of Affairs, to which is added an address to all generous and humane minds, occasioned by the execution of Mr. James Maclaine, etc., recommended to the serious perusal of all those who have any reward left for their Country'. This was published and sold by E. Withers at the Seven Steps, next the Inner-Temple-Gate in Fleet Street. MDCCL. Price sixpence. Some extracts of the letter relating to Maclaine are as follows:

> *For God's sake Gentlemen, take these things into consideration, let not the dying breath of an unfortunate convict [Mr. Maclaine], lately executed be spent in vain, nor hear sermons delivered at the gallows without regard this Unhappy Gentleman is a melancholy instance of the general fate of those whose being elated with the hopes of acquiring a plentiful fortune are tempted to throw away what little money they have in expectation of grandeur and affluence, til*

they turned stripped of all, forsaken by their associates, and then turn out to shift for themselves.

What heart that is lest affected with tenderness and humanity, but must bleed at so shocking a spectacle? What eye can refrain from tears, to behold youth, strength, and genius, make so untimely an exit?

As the writer of Mr. Maclaine's life very justly observes, hanging is now a pastime and sport, and the Triumph of the King of Terrors, in the mockery of the unthinking multitude, one would be apt to imagine so shocking a scene would strike every breast with awe, so melancholy an appearance fill every mind with gloom and horror.

No sooner are they masters of their own fortunes, but they give the world an early specimen of what they may justly expect from them in future life, by spending their money in whoring, drinking and gambling and all other bad and vicious courses, which custom has authorised with the popular. Where these things in general end, it is no hard matter to determine, when by their profuseness and extravagancy they have wasted their subsistence, and then turned robbers, or else by their irregular manner of living, bring upon themselves the sharpest disorders and pains. In short, nothing has a greater tendency to hasten on destruction than the false notions we imbile in education, and parents should be very careful, that the ruin of their children may never be justly charged upon their overfondness, or bad example.

Self-conscious of our crimes, remorse will sharply sting us, and one continual gloom reside in our breasts. Fear will perpetually molest and disturb us, and terror and distress be our constant companions. The vicious man who makes inroads upon the public stock, is, when free from intoxication, continually afraid of falling

into the hands of Justice. This was the case of Mr. Maclaine, who
always, skulking from one place to another, without finding that
quiet situation of mind he so earnestly sought after. When necessity
called upon him to return to his former method of supply, conscience
spread a terror through all his limbs, and the blush of guilt reddened
his countenance, his courage failed him, and his dread struck him
almost examinate.[7]

Henry Fielding (1707–1754) [the playwright, novelist, barrister and political writer who used the pseudonym "Captain Hercules Vinegar" and was for over thirty years a contributor to the Gentleman's Magazine, a regular columnist to 'The Rambler' and, from 1739, Editor of 'The Champion'. His best known novel was 'Tom Jones' (1749)] became Justice of the Peace for Middlesex and Westminster on 25 October 1748, having owed his appointment to John Russell (1710–1771), the 4th Duke of Bedford, in his capacity as the Secretary of State. On 9 December 1749 he took over the Magistrates Court set up by Sir Thomas de Veil (1684–1746), the previous Justice and renowned Jacobite hater, at 4 Bow Street in 1740 as a "Rotation Office", where the public could be assured of gaining access to a Magistrate between fixed hours; just by the Covent Garden Playhouse, at the South end of Drury Lane. Fielding realised the limitations of the policing system that Brittannicus and every other writer was complaining about. He well knew that the locally appointed constables did not have their hearts in their work and that they would all too readily sub-contract it if they could afford to; and that the Night Watchmen, known as "Charleys" since their introduction by King Charles II, were often so frightened that they stayed cowering in their boxes or happily took pay from the robbers to do so. He was also painfully aware that the professional thief-takers, who started to flourish in the early 1700s and acted more like receivers of stolen goods and gangland bosses than law enforcers, were almost totally corrupt as proven by Jonathan Wild (see Chapter 3).

Maclaine's high profile case and the proliferation of written opinion on the inadequacies of the system for capturing criminals at the time drove Fielding to write and publish a pamphlet in 1751 entitled 'An Inquiry into the Causes of the Late Increase in Robbers etc'. He clearly realised that that The Bloody Code and the execution of criminals was not succeeding in its intent of deterring others and he constantly looked for the causes that made people turn to crime in the first place. His conclusions were:

- *Too many people coming to London expecting an easy life* [Maclaine being a prime and well publicised example].
- *Corruption in the Government, setting a bad example.*
- *People were choosing crime rather than hard work* [We recall Plunket's work ethic: *"while the dull, plodding knaves, etc...."*].
- *The constables were mostly useless; only 6 out of 80 from his district* [St. Giles and the Drury Hundred] *were worth keeping on**... [8]

*But keep them on he did. He took these six best men whom he could trust to do their duty in a thorough and diligent manner; supplemented their numbers by a further two, and set them up as a team (not to carry out patrols but) to pursue known criminals, and to go to the scene of any reported crime to gather evidence and give chase to the perpetrators. They were quickly successful in apprehending many robbers and as their reputation grew as a force to be reckoned with, they became known as the "Bow Street Runners". Initially they worked for reward money, like any other thief-takers, but were later given a guinea a week plus a bonus for each successful prosecution.

When Henry Fielding retired due to his deteriorating health [he long suffered from gout] in 1754, his position was taken over by his younger, half-brother, John Fielding (1721–1780) [later, in 1761, Sir John Fielding]. John Fielding had been blind since the age of 19 and had been assisting his brother at Bow Court for four years. He continued to build on the successes of the Bow Street Runners and within two more years had dramatically reduced street robberies in the capital. He then introduced the Bow Street Horse Patrol; a mounted version of the Runners, with men equipped with truncheons, cutlasses and pistols, whose job it was to patrol London in a six mile radius of Charing Cross. He also set up a system for rapid communication of crimes and published details of crimes, stolen goods and descriptions of wanted criminals in the 'Covent Garden Journal'. He became known as the 'Blind Beak of Bow Street' and was said to be able to recognise over 3,000 criminals, just by hearing their voices.

It was really the Runners that put pay to the scourge of the highwaymen. The profession died out fairly rapidly, with the last highwayman in the London area being executed in 1802. This was James (a.k.a. Robert) Snooks (1741–1802) and he was hanged on Boxmoor Common, near Hemel Hempstead, as close as possible to the scene of his crimes. John Fielding lobbied tirelessly throughout his life for a national police force, but was always knocked back on the strength of arguments over the loss of civil liberties and the financial burden of its upkeep, see earlier in Chapter 3. It was not until 1829 that the Prime Minister at the time, Sir Robert Peel (1788–1850) finally brought in his "Bobbies" (or "Peelers" as they were also known) as the first truly professional London Metropolitan Police force.

I would not wish to complete the story of James Maclaine without leaving a "sting in the tail" and he, very kindly, left us a real beauty. Before I divulge it, it is first necessary to remind ourselves of the very sincere and penitent way Maclaine behaved in his last days in Newgate and on his final journey to the gallows. Perhaps we should ask ourselves what would have become of him if indeed the King had allowed the petition to spare his life; would he have changed his ways and would he *spend his Life in shewing the Sincerity of his Repentance, and the holy Resolutions he had taken up*"? (see Chapter 6). We would certainly not be the only ones to ask that question. In 1818 one Sir James Stonehouse, Baronet, M.D., had published a book entitled 'Every Man's Assistant and the Sick Man's Friend' in which he speculated:

This unhappy man shewed great signs of penitence; but none can presume to form a judgement of his salvation; or whether his repentance was genuine, or not. That must be left to the great day, when the secrets of all men's hearts shall be revealed. Archbishop Tillotson* has observed that "it is difficult for any man to be assured of the truth and reality of his repentance when there is no sufficient opportunity to make a trial of the sincerity of it".

There is, I think, no doubt of the sincerity of this condemned malefactor at the time Dr Allen attended: but the question is, What would his temper and conduct have been had his life been spared for a number of years? He might have been a true penitent, and (through merits of Christ) have been accepted as such: but, as he did not live to "bring forth fruits meet for repentance," (which the Gospel requires,) it is beyond the knowledge of man to determine his future state. 9

*Archbishop Tillotson would have been John Tillotson (1630–1694), Archbishop of Canterbury.

Sir James Stonehouse and Archbishop Tillotson were right to be sceptical on the matters as not long after Maclaine's death, before the end of the year of 1750, there was published a "secret" letter that Maclaine had written from his condemned cell in Newgate to his *"Dear Countrymen and Brother Adventurers"* in 'The Honourable Society of Hibernians' together with their resulting response. Hibernia was the Roman name for Ireland. Many secret societies, of various religious persuasions, were set up by the Irish to look-out for the interests of their fellow countrymen no matter where they were in the world. One of Maclaine's biographers referred to The Honourable Society of Hibernians in the following way: *"a Group of Irish Rapperies, Gamesters, Fortune-Hunters, or Brothers in Equity, with interest in the Court End of Town."[10]*

This letter and its various attachments were published under the following title: 'M__cL__n's [sic] CABINET broke open; OR, His private List of the DUCHESS DOWAGERS, COUNTESSES, WIDOW LADIES, WIDOWS and MISSES of Honour, Virtue and large Fortunes in England TOGETHER With their several Places of Abodes, AND ALSO His Charge and Advice to the Honourable Society Of Hibernians: With their Orders and Resolutions' (Printed for

Patrick McLaughter, near St Pauls). A small extract of Maclaine's ten-page letter is as follows:

My Dear Countrymen and Brother Adventurers,

As untimely Fate has ordained my Stay here among you to be but very short, I thought it incumbant on me, for the Preservation of that beloved Honour, which we have so justly acquired, and for the Pleasure and Happiness of the true Lovers of it, to lay before you the following weighty Affairs, worthy of your Consideration... [11]

What followed were ten pages of prose advising of the need to send more young Irishmen to England to make use of his painstakingly gathered intelligence, relating to the names and whereabouts of England's richest ladies, so that they might have the good fortune to marry into their money. The list attached to the letter is nothing short of remarkable; it contains the names, and in many cases the addresses, for no less than 9 Duchesses [wives or widows of a Duke], 2 Marchionesses [wives or widows of a Marquis; a.k.a. a Marquise], 10 Countess Dowagers [wives or widows of a an Earl; a 'dowager' would be a wife or widow who holds a title or property derived from her deceased husband], 58 Widow Ladies, 21 Maiden Ladies, 130 Widows and 333 Misses. With a total of 563 names, this was not something Maclaine could possibly have done from memory; although perhaps many of the ladies might have been of his "personal acquaintance". He must have had access to the private papers from within the trunk from his lodgings. This fits in well with our suspicion that upon his exit from Newgate, all of Maclaine's correspondence will naturally have fallen into the hands of the Ordinary, Rev. John

Taylor, who would have quickly passed it on to his pet hacks in Fleet Street.

The reaction of the recipients of Maclaine's letter and enclosures was recorded in the following 'Orders and Resolutions of the Brave and Heroic Society of Hibernian Adventurers, for Incorporating and Manufacturing of British Commodities':

Veneris Nov 1750

Resolved nem, con. [nemine contradicente = unanimously]

That the Honourable Society being truly sensible of the Good Advice given to us by our Dear Deceased Brother, do with Souls full of Joy implore the Blessing of Our Saint upon him for his Wisdom and Goodness to Us, and that a petition be prepared and sent to the Head Governor of the Society at Dublin, for a draught to be immediately embarked for England.

Ordered,

That our Dear Deceased Brother's glorious advice with his list annexed, be forthwith printed and that copies be given only to ourselves and that no Soul do presume to show it to any body else, but those of Our Nation.

M. FitzPatrick, Secretary [12]

It is not clear if this secret publication got into the hands of the general public at the time of its printing in late 1750, nor what they would have made of it if it had, or if it only came to light some years after Maclaine was long forgotten. Certainly we now definately know that Maclaine would not have reformed his character and would no doubt have soon slipped back into his old ways.

So we find that Maclaine was not only a thief, an extortioner, a compulsive gambler, a womaniser, a rake, a cad and a coward, but also a complete scoundrel, through and through. He was happy to "pull the wool" [black wool from a very Black Sheep!] over the eyes of the Ordinary of Newgate, the Rev. Dr Allen, his mother-in-law, his brother's friends and anyone else he conversed with during the time of his condemnation, outwardly behaving with deepest penitence and sincerity, whilst all the while secretly plotting to leave his mark on the whole country, from beyond the grave!

With Maclaine's story now fully told there is just the small matter of what happened to William Plunket, necessary to complete this tale…

Chapter 7 – References

[1] Allen, Rev. Fifield (1700–1764). '*AN ACCOUNT Of the BEHAVIOUR of Mr James Maclaine, From the TIME of his CONDEMNATION To the DAY of his EXECUTION, OCTOBER 3. 1750*. By the REVEREND Dr. ALLEN, Who attended him all that time, to assist him in his PREPARATIONS for ETERNITY. Drawn up and published at the earnest Desire of Mr MACLAINE himself. The THIRD EDITION, With the Addition of a LETTER written by Mr Maclaine to a Friend, the Morning of his Execution. Which did not come to hand time enough to be inserted before' [1750; Printed for J. NOON, in Cheapside: and A. MILLAR in the Strand, LONDON] [Price 6d]. Pages 33 to 36, and Anonymous. 'A COMPLETE HISTORY of James Maclean [sic], THE GENTLEMAN HIGHWAYMAN, who was executed at TYBURN on Wednesday, October 3, 1750, for a Robbery on the Highway'. [1750; Printed for Charles Corbett, London]. Pages 62 to 64

[2] Scottish History Online. William Burke & William Hare, '*The Resurrectionists*'. Retrieved 12/10/11

[3] Anderson, Robert M.D (1750–1830). '*A complete edition of the Poets of GREAT BRITAIN*'. *Volume the Eleventh.* [1795; Printed for John & Arthur Arch, London]. Page 1000

[4] *THE GENTLEMANS MAGAZINE* For MARCH, 1805. Page 243

[5] *The Public Advertiser*, 29 February 1764, and Beattie, John Maurice. 'Crime and the Courts in England, 1660–1800' [1986; Princeton University Press, New Jersey]

[6] *The Public Advertiser*, 1 March 1764

[7] Brittannicus, Esq,. '*A Letter to the Honourable House of Commons, relating to the present situation of affairs. To which is added, an address to all generous and*

humane minds, occasioned by the execution of Mr James Maclaine, etc' [1750; Sold by E. Withers, London]

[8] Fielding, Henry (1707–1754). *An inquiry into the causes of the Late Increase of Robbers, etc. With some Proposals for Remedying this Growing Evil. In which the Present Reigning Vices are impartially exposed; and the Laws that relate to the Provision for the Poor, and to the Punishment of Felons are largely and freely examined*. [1751; London]

[9] Stonehouse, Sir J., Baronet, M.D. *'Every Man's Assistant and the Sick Man's Friend'* Ninth Edition. [1818; printed by W. Baxter; Oxford]. Page 142

[10] Anonymous. *'A Genuine Account of the Life and Actions of James Maclean [sic], Highwayman, to the time of his trial and receiving sentence at The Old Bailey, containing his Robberies, Gallantry at Public Places, with other remarkable transactions; together with some account of Plunket his companion'*. [1750; Printed for W. Falstaff, London].

[11] *'M__cL__n's [sic] CABINET broke open; OR, His private List of the DUCHESS DOWAGERS, COUNTESSES, WIDOW LADIES, WIDOWS and MISSES of Honour, Virtue and large Fortunes in England TOGETHER With their several Places of Abodes, AND ALSO His Charge and Advice to the Honourable Society Of Hibernians: With their Orders and Resolutions'* [1750; Printed for Patrick McLaughter near St. Pauls, London]. Page 5

[12] Ibid. Page 42

Chapter 7 – Suggested Further Reading

In addition to the above:

An Equiry Into The Causes Of The Late Increase In Robbers With Some Proposals For Remedying This Growing Evil, Fielding, Henry (printed for A. Miller, London, 1751)

A Plan For Preventing Robberies Within Twenty Miles Of London. With An Account of the Rise and Establishment of Real Thieftakers. To which is added, Advice to Pawnbrokers, Stable-keepers and Publicans, Fielding, John (printed for A. Miller, London, 1755)

The History of the Bow Street Runners, 1729–1829, Armitage, Gilbert (Wishart & Co., London, 1932)

The Life and Works of Sir John Fielding, Leslie-Melville, Ronald (Lincoln Williams Limited, London, 1934)

The Thief-Takers, Pringle, Patrick (Museum Press, University of Michigan, 1958)

Hogarth to Cruikshank: Social Change in Graphic Satire, George, Mary Dorothy (Walker, New York, 1967)

A House on Bow Street: Crime and the Magistracy, London 1740–1881, Babington, Anthony (MacDonald & Co., London, 1969)

Engravings by Hogarth, Shesgreen, Sean. (Dover publishing Inc., New York, 1973)

England in the Age of Hogarth, Jarrett, Derek (Yale University Press, 1986)

Policing and Prosecution in Britain, 1750–1850, Hay, Douglas and Francis G. Snyder (Claredon Press, Oxford, 1989)

The Resurrection Men: A history of the Trade in Corpses, Bailey, Brian J. (MacDonald, 1991)

The English Police: a Political and Social History, Emsley, Clive (Longman, London, 1996)

British Artists. William Hogarth, Crask, Matthew. (Princetown University Press, 2001)

Crime and Society in England 1750–1900, Emsley, Clive. (Pearson Education, London, 2005)

The Knife Man. Blood, Body-Snatching and the Birth of Modern Surgery, Moore, Wendy (Bantam Press, London, 2005)

Hogarth, Clayton, Tim (British Museum Press, London, 2007)

CHAPTER 8

PLUNKETT / PLUNKET

This Chapter has been included for those readers who may be curious to know as to what may have been the true fate of William Plunket, James Maclaine's "partner in crime". In Chapter 5 it was stated that after Maclaine's arrest William Plunket quickly disappeared without trace and that "he was never heard of again". Certainly this is what all the newspapers and pamphlets of the time naturally recorded. However it seems you cannot keep a good *"evil Genius"* down for too long and so it was that Plunket duly returned to some prominence again in the mid–1770s; this time ironically on the right side of the Law, as a Colonial County Justice and Colonel in the American Colonial Wars.

There are really only two ways to spell Plunket(t). William Plunket (1725–1791), the Highwayman, definitely came from a family line that spelt their surname with just the one 't'. One of Plunket's later-life biographers reinforced this point in the following words: *"From his autograph, now in the possession of the writer, he signed his name with one t, but custom and the courts have long since been in the habit of spelling it with two tt's."[1]*

Just like James Maclaine it transpires that William Plunket came from a quite well-to-do and religious family. His father, Reverend Patrick Plunket (1684–1760), was another Presbyterian Minister, who married one Isabella Baxter (c.1693–   ) in approximately 1720. She is said to have been a descendant of Sir William Welles (1409–1463); Lord Chancellor of Ireland. William's elder brother, (Doctor) Robert Plunket, was born in 1721. He had three other younger siblings: James Plunket (1727–), Margaret Plunket (1729–   ) and (Reverend) Thomas Plunket (1731–1778), more of whom later. The family resided in the village of Glennan within the Parish of Donagh in County Monaghan, Ireland, where all the children were born. A Family Tree of the Plunkets is below (see Illustration (xx) – Family Tree of Another Highwayman):

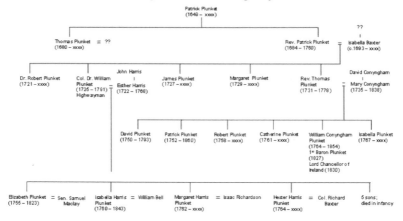

Illustration (xx) – Family Tree of Another Highwayman.
(2011) – N.F.M.

324

It appears that Plunket at some point, either from London or from somewhere back in Ireland, had managed to escape the authorities by stowing away on board a ship bound for North America. Another of Plunket's later biographers noted of him: *"... he became involved in an assault upon an English Officer, in which the latter sustained severe bodily injuries; although disguised, Plunket was recognized by his stature, and, in imminent danger of arrest, was smuggled on board a vessel in a barrel or hogshead. Thus he came to America, and located at Carlisle, Cumberland County, Pennsylvania, then the western limit of civilization,"[2]* and *"In personal appearance he is described as a man of large stature, great muscular development, and powerful strength, while an imperious disposition was among his distinguishing mental traits."[3]* By way of example of the latter the same biographer also records the following tale: *"On one occasion, with several boon companions, he was engaged in some hilarious proceedings at an Irish inn; the adjoining room was occupied by an English nobleman, who had a curious and valuable watch, which he sent to Plunket with a wager that he could not tell the time by it; that gentleman coolly put it in his pocket, and sent a message to the Englishman to the effect that he should call upon him in person if he wished to know the time. This he never did, evidently out of respect to Plunket's well known physical prowess, and the latter, it is said, retained the watch to the end of his life."[4]*

Plunket seems to have arrived in North America just before the war between Great Britain and France which raged from 1754 to 1763. He was able to settle into the Carlisle community as their first resident doctor. He married Esther Harris (1722–1768) daughter of John Harris of Harris' Ferry who had died, before Plunket's arrival, in 1748 and had been buried at the site where he had almost lost his life some time before: *"Near it are the remains of the mulberry to which he was tied by the Indians, to be burned. I will only add to the story, that it was his negro slave, Hercules, who crossed the river, and brought the neighboring Indians to his rescue, while the drunken Indians were about applying fire to him. For this he gave Hercules his freedom, and directed his burial on the same spot."*[5] It was Esther's elder brother, another John Harris, who went on to become the founder of Harrisburg, built on the site of Harris' Ferry, which was named the Pennsylvanian state capital in October 1812, and has remained so since.

William and Esther went on to have five sons, all of whom tragically died in infancy; however by contrast their four daughters all survived into adulthood and made good marriages. The eldest daughter, Elizabeth Plunket (1755–1823) married on 10 November 1773 (Senator) Samuel Maclay (1741–1811); Isabella Harris Plunket (1760–1843) married William Bell of Elizabethtown, New Jersey; Margaret Harris Plunkett (1762–   ) married Isaac Richardson of New York State, and lastly Hester Harris Plunket (1764–   ) married her cousin Richard [or Robert] Baxter, a Colonel in the British Army. Sadly for the latter couple Hester died within a year of their marriage. According to the Annals of Buffalo Valley: *"The* [other] *three sisters, Mrs Maclay, Mrs Bell, and Mrs Richardson survived to a good old age, and resided together, in Mifflin county. Mrs Maclay was a Presbyterian, Mrs Bell an Episcopalian, and Mrs Richardson a Quaker. They were all three remarkable ladies. Mrs Bell was a very handsome and highly polished woman. She had a boarding school at Albany, New York, where Mrs Catharine* [Maria] *Sedgwick* [(1789–1867), the American novelist, greatly admired by Edgar Allan Poe (1809–1849), the better known American author and poet] *and many of the celebrated ladies of the time, received their education.*[6] As each of these ladies and also Hester Baxter's daughter all went on to have large families, and judging by the numerous Public Member Trees currently on the Ancestry.com website that include their progeny, there is no doubt that a number of American families can trace themselves back to a once notorious highwayman; if only they knew!

When war broke out with the French, Plunket was commissioned with the help of his new community and relations on 12 June 1756 as a lieutenant and surgeon in Captain John Hambright's company within Colonel William Clapham's 3rd Battalion of the Pennsylvania Provincials. Putting his apothecarial skills to immediate use he gained quite a reputation for being able to successfully dress the wounds and treat the heads of his comrades who had suffered the misfortune to have been scalped by the Indians. However it was Plunket's obvious leadership and organisation skills; no doubt honed on the High Tobies of the Home Counties of England and in the woods of Hyde Park in London, that saw him rise steadily through the ranks.

In 1769 Captain Plunket was rewarded for his services to the Province during the Pontiac Wars which were a series of battles and sieges lead by Chief Pontiac (1720–1769) of the Ottawa tribe at the head of a confederacy of a number of others disaffected by British rule immediately following the British victory in the French and Indian War. He was granted some 600 acres of land in Buffalo Valley, above Chillisquaque Creek, a tributary branch of the Susquehanna River. The latter River was spelt "Sasquesahanough" on the 1612 map of Captain John Smith (1580–1631), the famous soldier and explorer, whose life was saved by Pocahontas (1595–1617), daughter of Chief Powhatan of Virginia. She was later known as Rebecca Rolfe and died in Gravesend, Kent, where a life-size bronze sculpture at St. George's Church commemorates her life. Plunket named his estate 'The Soldier's Retreat' and started residing there almost immediately.

Whilst Esther Plunket, nee Harris, had unfortunately died in 1768, and although William Plunket never remarried, it seems he and his daughters were not always without wider family visitors. According to one biographer: *"A brother of Doctor Plunket came to this country, bringing with him a daughter, Margaret, who married Samuel Simmons, of Pine creek. His name was Robert. Another brother* [I suspect actually a nephew], *David Plunket, settled at Baltimore and was lost at sea on a voyage to the West Indies."*[7]

On 24 March 1772 Plunket was commissioned a Justice of the Peace for the newly erected Northumberland County and as he was the only one of twelve judges with a familiarity with English Court procedures he officiated as the Presiding Justice throughout the colonial period. So not only was it ironic that he was now keeping on the right side of the Law, he was the Law. In January 1775 he was a Representative from Northumberland County in the Provincial Convention in Philadelphia which resolved to make the North American Colonies increasingly independent of Great Britain. Throughout the remainder of 1775 all the other colonies agreed *"to stop importing and using British tea; to stop importing all goods from England (except medicine) beginning on November 1; and to cease exporting all goods to Great Britain after August 10."*[8]

Whilst the greater theatre of war, being the American Revolutionary War 1775–1783, was looming large William

Plunket, now commissioned Colonel William Plunket, still had some colonial issues to attend to as part of some of the ongoing hostilities of the 'Pennamite-Yankee' Wars. A mistake by King Charles II of England seems to have led to the troubles. In 1662 he granted land along the northern branch of the Susquehanna River in the Wyoming Valley to the colony of Connecticut. However on 4 March 1681 he unfortunately included the same parcel of land in his grant to William Penn (1644–1718). Penn was a Quaker from the age of 22; he was an early champion of democracy and religious freedom and founder of Pennsylvania. He wrote an amendable constitution for the settlement to support his aim of it becoming a political utopia where a free and fair trial by jury would be available to anyone accused of committing a crime. James Maclaine would have liked to have lived in Pennsylvania as the only crimes punishable by death were treason and murder however he would not have approved of some of Penn's other ideals: *"The laws of behaviour he laid out were rather Puritanical: swearing, lying and drunkenness were forbidden as well as "idle amusements" such as stage plays, gambling, revels, masques, cock-fighting and bear-baiting."*[9] In relation to Pennsylvania's tolerance to religious freedoms, Voltaire, who was introduced to us by Horace Walpole in Chapter 4, praised William Penn for creating the only government in the world responsible to the people and respectful of minority rights. In the King's lifetime and for many years beyond this was not an issue as the Susquehannock Indians were putting up fierce resistance to any settlement whatsoever. The problem really came to light in 1769 when 200 settlers from Connecticut came to set up their townships and found the lands already occupied by families from the Colony of Pennsylvania. King George [William Frederick]

III (1738–1820); King of Great Britain and King of Ireland from 25 October 1760 until the Act of Union on 1 August 1800 after which he became King of the United Kingdom of Great Britain and Ireland, confirmed Connecticut's claim in 1771 however the Pennsylvanians simply refused to leave.

Colonel Plunket initially had some success when on 28 September 1775 he led 700 Pennsylvania 'Pennamites' against 100 Connecticut 'Yankees' and managed to clear them all from their settlements of Judea and Charleston along the west banks of the Susquehanna River. One Yankee was killed, eight wounded and the Pennamites took all their possessions and livestock to auction. All those Yankees who had been captured were taken to the prison at Sunbury and later released and fled back to Wyoming City. Following the weakness of the response to the Yankee's complaints by the Continental Congress on 4 November 1775, the Pennamites became further emboldened thinking they should extend their strikes to include those Yankees on the east side of the River. John Penn (1729–1795), the last Governor of colonial Pennsylvania before it became an independent Commonwealth during the American Revolution, sent the following instructions to his Colonel and Justices:

November 25, 1775 – Gov. Penn's letter to Wm. Plunket and his associate Justices of the Peace, for the county of Northumberland

I have just now received a message from the Assembly, founded on a letter addressed to them from the county of Northumberland respecting the Connecticut settlers at Wyoming, etc, requesting me to give orders for a due execution of the laws of this Province in the counties of Northampton and Northumberland.

In consequence thereof I do most cheerfully order you, to use your utmost diligence and activity in putting the laws of this Province in execution throughout the county of Northumberland; and you may depend on the faith of the House, and my concurrence with them, that every proper and necessary expense that may be incurred on the occasion will be defrayed.

John Penn [10]

Colonel Plunket immediately set about raising and equipping a force of some 650 men in four companies at Fort Augusta [named after Princess Augusta of Saxe-Gotha (1719–1772), mother of King George III], the largest of the Provincial forts, in readiness for his next expedition which would be the one for which he will be most remembered in American history. The aim was to once and for all evict the Yankees and bring the Valley under Pennsylvanian authority. He set off with his militia which also had two artillery pieces in a snowstorm on 15 December and by 20 December 1775 had reached Nescopeck Creek some 20 or so miles from Nanticoke Falls where he perceived he might engage resistance, if it were coming.

In response the Yankees, under the command of Colonel Zebulon Butler (1731–1795) [later (1 January 1777) Lieutenant Colonel of the 3rd Connecticut Regiment of the Continental Army and commander of the garrison at Fort Forty at the time of the infamous Wyoming Massacre on 3 July 1778], raised a force of some 400 Connecticut men, and headed south along the Susquehanna reaching a point at Harvey's Creek, opposite the Nanticoke Falls by 23 December. On Christmas Eve 1775 the two sides came together. Unknown to Colonel Plunket the Yankees had split their forces to allow smaller teams of up to 30 men to lay in wait to undertake a series of ambush attacks; the bulk of their force had retreated to a place called 'Rampart Rocks'. In the middle of a heavy snowstorm the Pennamite forces moved into a storm of musket fire from their assailants; four men were instantly killed and the Pennamites retreated to re-think their next move.

Believing that the Yankees were amassed at Rampart Rocks Colonel Plunket decided to cross the River, going around them and attack the hub of all Yankee activity in the Valley i.e. the township of Wilkes-Barre which he anticipated would be unguarded. Under cover of darkness and more snow they set out across the River above the Falls. Unfortunately for the Pennamites the Yankees had another ambush team under the command of Captain Lazarus Stewart (1734–1778) [the leader of the notorious Paxton Boys, a vigilante group who, as well as massacring a number of peaceful dwelling Susquehannock/ Conestogas Indians during the Pontiac Wars, also, on 27 December 1763, broke in on the last remaining fourteen Conestogas living under Governor John Penn's protective custody and killed and mutilated them all] and *"Once again even in the dark the Yankee balls were finding targets and panic set in among the men in boats who hurried back across the river to where they started. Some of them giving in to panic rode their boats straight over the falls."*[11]

On Christmas Day 1775 Colonel Plunket led his men back to the scene of the first ambush at Nanticoke. Splitting them into two forces he left the first to make a frontal assault on the Yankees, pinning them into position, whilst the second climbed the cliff face to the left of the Yankees with the intention of out-flanking them. *"The fighting raged most of the day. The Pennsylvanians were making little headway against the well entrenched Yankees, losses were quickly mounting with Yankee casualties amounting to three killed and ten wounded and the attackers suffering 50–60 total killed or wounded."*[12] *"Unable to dislodge or go around the yankees and suffering from an erosion of morale the Pennamites broke contact and fell back to Fort Augusta."*[13] Thus it was that Colonel William Plunket's last military action for which he would remembered was actually a defeat or as better described at the time *"[an] inglorious retreat."*[14]

The various protagonists in the Pennamite-Yankee Wars, from both sides, then joined together under their respective colonial Regiments, fighting for their independence from Britain which they achieved in 1783. Land disputes and colonial battles in the Wyoming Valley continued throughout the War and for many years after it until eventually the Continental Congress awarded the Wyoming Valley to Pennsylvania with the compromise that the existing Yankee settlers became Pennsylvanians with legal claims to their lands.

There are conflicting reports as to the part played by Colonel William Plunket in the American Revolutionary War, such as: *"At the beginning of the war for independence he entered heartedly into the contest and was commissioned Colonel of the Second battalion of Northumberland county associators in* [on 13] *March 1776, but for some cause or another, possibly at the instigation of his Wyoming enemies, he was arrested as being inimical to the principles of the revolution. He was afterwards released as nothing treasonable could be proved against him,"*[15]; also *"All of his friends and family connections were ardent for independence and he would have entered heartedly into the struggle, but with the other officers of the French and Indian war, they found themselves supplanted by inexperienced men as officers, and this, rankled in their bosoms and they stood aloof. At this distance from that era it is difficult to inquire into the causes as to why old and well-tried officers were totally ignored in the organization of the Pennsylvania Line, and the chief places given to men who knew not the "art of war." Plunket and his fellow officers of the Provincial war, at the outset of the revolution, hurriedly organized the militia of the counties, but when the continental Line was formed they were left out of the organization. And so the old hero quietly retired to domestic life, only annoyed by repeated charges of disloyalty to the cause of liberty,"[16] and, "During the struggle for American independence he remained neutral (through fear of forfeiting his title to Irish estates, it is said) and does not thereafter appear in the public affairs of the county."[17]*

There may be some truth behind the last remark as, back home in Ireland, Colonel Plunket's younger brother, Reverend Thomas Plunket, had made a good marriage and was gradually climbing the social and political ladder and the Colonel would not have wished to cause any hardship to his brother or any other of his relatives in their endeavours to better themselves. Whilst it would have been unknown to Colonel Plunket at the time his nephew, Reverend Thomas Plunket's son, William Conyngham Plunket (1764–1854) was destined for altogether greater things including becoming a Member of the King's Counsel in 1795, a Member of the Irish Parliament in 1798, Solicitor General for Ireland in 1803 and Attorney General in 1805 (a post he held again between 1822 and 1827). In 1827 William Conyngham Plunket was ennobled in the Peerage of the United Kingdom as Baron Plunket of Newton, County Cork and lastly held the office of Lord Chancellor of Ireland from 1830 to 1841. Captain Robin Rathmore Plunket is the current 8th Baron Plunket and he lives in London in easy reach of his seat in the House of Lords.

Meanwhile on 14 November 1776 Colonel Plunket was once again rewarded for his services to the Province with a further grant of six tracts of land, this time amounting to 1,978 acres. These lands were surrounding a tributary of Loyalsock Creek in the Chesapeake Bay drainage basin. There is no evidence that Colonel Plunket ever took up any residence on his new lands which were simply named 'Plunkett's Creek', rather he preferred to remain close to Fort Augusta in the newly formed township of Sunbury, staying in the house of his Maclay in-laws. *"He became totally blind in the later years of his life, when a rope was stretched from his residence to his office so that he could still go back and forth without aid. As shown by his will, which is dated, January 3, 1791, and proved, May 25, 1791, he died in the spring of that year, and is buried in an unmarked grave in the Sunbury cemetery."*[18]

In 1836 the inhabitants within the nearest adjacent townships petitioned for a new town at Plunkett's Creek itself. The original proposal was to call the new town 'Plunkett Township' but this was not without controversy and the surveyors had to negotiate with the local inhabitants to settle on a compromise: *"When they had finished their* [surveying] *work Mr* [William] *Wilson proposed to call the new township Plunkett, but* [John] *Barbour objected to the name, saying that "Plunkett was an old tory." During the Revolution he had remained passive and was more than once suspected of disloyalty.* [William] *Packer then proposed to add the word "creek," to which Wilson consented and Barbour did not object. Hence it was so named, and became a township by decree of court in 1838."*[19] Plunketts Creek Township is nowadays in what is called

Lycoming County and has approximately 800 residents. In its heyday, in the mid to late 19th Century, Plunketts Creek was a centre for large scale logging and tanning industries.

There is perhaps one more story worth recounting from Doctor Plunket's *"quiet retirement"* relating to an Indian attack in 1778 that was part of what was termed "The Big Runaway" when the Susquehanna settlements were attacked by Loyalists and Native Americans during the American Revolutionary War: *'In the fall of '78, as a company of settlers were leaving the country on account of the Indians, they were fired at and Mrs Durham's infant was killed in her arms, she fell with it, and they came and tomahawked and scalped her, and when the men went to count the dead, she raised up and asked for a drink of water. Elias Williams, one of the men, ran to the river and brought his hat full of water and gave her a drink, they put her in a canoe and took her to Northumberland, where Dr Plunket dressed her head, she recovered and lived about fifty years.'*[20] The Mrs Durham that was treated by Doctor Plunkett was Margaret Durham (nee McClintock) (1755–1829) and the attack took place near Fort Freeland; she has many descendents still living in the area.

Charles Miner (1780–1865) when writing his 'History of Wyoming In a Series of Letters from Charles Miner to his Son, William Penn Miner, Esq.' [1845: J. Crissy, Philadelphia] was the first to confirm the link between the "old hero" Colonel/ Doctor William Plunket and his criminal past. A "literary friend" had sent him the details from a manuscript note contained within a copy of the Gentleman's Magazine of September 1750 from the collection of the Library of the Athenaeum Club in Pall Mall, London, which stated: *"Plunket, the companion of Maclean* [sic]*, escaped, emigrated to America, reformed and became a very respectable* character. He was for many years on of the Associate Judges of the Court of Common Pleas, of Northumberland county, Pa., and died."[21]; "In 1750 it is affirmed that he was concerned in several robberies in England. By his own admission he was concerned with Maclean [sic] in the attack upon Lord Eglintoun [sic] on Hounslow Heath."[22]; "Plunket was recognized in America by a person who had known him in England, and who kept his secret,"[23] and, "He regretted this action, as one of his youthful crimes, and afterwards became a very useful member of society."[24] Another of Plunket's biographers drew our attention to a particular book which was one of his treasured possessions, discovered upon his death, that provides us with further evidence linking him to a certain place and time: 'Synopsis of Medicines, or a Summary View of the Whole Practice of Physick' by John Allen MD, FIS, printed in London, 1749. Plunket no doubt picked up his copy of John Allen's book when it was brand new whilst he was in London engaged in a treble-life of doctoring, playing the Squire's footman and highway robbery.

We have now reached the limit of our knowledge of what happened to William Plunket and have therefore come to the final end of the true stories of 'Plunkett & Macleane' [sic]. For those that have seen the film and have now read the book I would like to pose the question: Is it true that "fact is often stranger than fiction"? With regard to the factual and fictional stories of Plunket and Maclaine, I will let the Reader ponder than one. In the meantime...

FINIS

Chapter 8– References

[1] Meginess, John Franklin (1827–1899). *'History of Lycoming County Pennsylvania'*. [1892; Brown, Runk and Co., Chicago]. Page 625

[2] Milliken, Charles, F. *'The History of Ontario County, New York and Its People'*. Volume II. [1911; Lewis Historical Publishing Co., New York].

[3] Ibid.

[4] Ibid.

[5] Linn, John Blair (1831–1899). 'Annals of Buffalo Valley, Pennsylvania, 1755 – 1855'. [1877; Harrisburg, Pennsylvania.]. Page 271

[6] Ibid. Pages 272 and 273

[7] Ibid. Page 272

[8] North Carolina History Project; Provincal Convention (1775)

[9] Dobrée, Bonamy (1881–1974). *'William Penn: Quaker and Pioneer'*. [1932; Houghton Mifflin Co., New York]. Page 149

[10] Miner, Charles (1780–1865). *'History of Wyoming, In a Series of Letters, from Charles Miner, to his Son, William Penn Miner, Esq'*. [1845; J. Crissy, Philadelphia]. Page 170

[11] Penguins JmA Articles; Yankee-Pennamite Wars. 12 February 2006.

[12] Ibid.

[13] Ibid.

[14] Hollister, Gideon Hiram (1817–1881). *'The History of Connecticut, From the First Settlement of the Colony to the Adoption of the Present Constitution'*. Volume II. [1857; Case, Tiffany and Company, Hartford, Connecticut]. Page 339

[15] Linn, John Blair (1831–1899). *'Annals of Buffalo Valley, Pennsylvania, 1755 – 1855'*. [1877; Harrisburg, Pennsylvania.]. Pages 87 and 88

[16] Milliken, Charles, F. *'The History of Ontario County, New York and Its People'*. Volume II. [1911; Lewis Historical Publishing Co., New York].

[17] Ibid.

[18] Ibid

[19] Meginess, John Franklin (1827–1899). *'History of Lycoming County Pennsylvania'*. [1892; Brown, Runk and Co., Chicago]. Page 625

[20] Linn, John Blair (1831–1899). *'Annals of Buffalo Valley, Pennsylvania, 1755 – 1855'*. [1877; Harrisburg, Pennsylvania.]. Page 352

[21] Miner, Charles. 1845. *'History of Wyoming, In a Series of Letters, from Charles Miner, to his son William Penn Miner, Esq'*. 1892. Page 180

[22] Ibid. Page 180

[23] Ibid. Page 180

[24] Ibid. Page 180

Chapter 8 – Suggested Further Reading

In addition to the above:

Biographical Sketches of Loyalists of the American Revolution with an Historical Essay. Volumes I and II, Sabine, Lorenzo (Little, Brown and Company, Boston, 1864)

History of Northumberland County, Pennsylvania, Bell, Herbert C. (Brown, Runk and Co., Chicago, 1891)

TIMELINE TO DESTRUCTION

Date/Approximate Timing	Event / Activity
Early 1748	Wife dies
Mid-1748	*"a Flaming Beau"* returns. Fortune hunting in London, Bath and Tunbridge Wells
Mid-Late 1748	First robberies; Hounslow Heath, St. Albans and the Portsmouth Road
February 1749	"The Big One"… East India Company "stock" on Shooter's Hill
March-April 1749	Lying low in the low countries; living it up in The Hague whilst scheming with Plunket, all the while
26 April 1749	Back in time for the Jubilee Masquerade
May-October 1749	Summer of Love and back on the Road for *"a further Recruit"*; the Chester Road and a "load of Cock and Bull"

8 November 1749	Robbing Horace Walpole in Hyde Park; a defining moment
December 1749–January 1750	*"the Season of Cocking"* excursion
February–June 1750	More robberies: Sir Thomas Robinson, Mrs Talbot and others
26 June 1750	A "double-whammy"...Robbing the Salisbury Stage Coach and Lord Eglinton on Hounslow Heath
Late-July 1750	A rash moment... selling distinctive stolen lace and clothes
29 July 1750	Arrest; Westminster Gatehouse
1 August 1750	Thomas Lediard's Examination
12 September 1750	Trial at The Old Bailey "a social occasion"
12–29 September 1750	Newgate Prison, at His Majesty's Pleasure
29 September 1750	Sentencing
3 October 1750	*"a last and melancholy Farewel"*. Execution at the Tyburn Fair; the final "drop-fell"

INDEX OF NAMES, PLACES AND EVENTS